GENTLEMEN'S GARMENT CUTTING AND TAILORING

-THE DRESSMAKER'S GUIDE-

BY

VARIOUS

British Library Cataloguing-in-Publication Data
A catalogue record for this book is available from the
British Library

Contents

Dressmaking And Tailoring 1

Trouser Cutting 7

Corpulent Draft. Diagram 2 14

Style Details And Top Finishes 20

Riding Breeches 33

Coat Cutting 58

Cutting Of Overgarments 102

Cutting For Corpulent Figures 134

Variations From The Normal Draft 156

Motor Liveries 161

How To Make Trousers 172

How To Make A Lounge Jacket 194

Cutting And Making Canvas 205

How To Make A Waistcoat 227

Garments For Men And Boys 237

Men's House Coats And Robes 273

Dressmaking and Tailoring

Dressmaking and Tailoring broadly refers to those who make, repair or alter clothing for a profession. A dressmaker will traditionally make custom clothing for women, ranging from dresses and blouses to full evening gowns (also historically called a mantua-maker or a modiste). Whereas a tailor will do the same, but usually for men's clothing - especially suits. The terms essentially refer to a specific set of hand and machine sewing skills, as well as pressing techniques that are unique to the construction of traditional clothing. This is separate to 'made to measure', which uses a set of pre-existing patterns. Usually, a bespoke tailored suit or dress will be completely original and unique to the customer, and hence such items have been highly desirable since the trade first appeared in the thirteenth century. The Oxford English Dictionary states that the word 'tailor' first came into usage around the 1290s, and undoubtedly by this point, tailoring guilds, as well as those of cloth merchants and weavers were well established across Europe.

As the tailoring profession has evolved, so too have the methods of tailoring. There are a number of distinctive business models which modern tailors may practice, such as 'local tailoring' where the tailor is met locally, and the garment is produced locally too, 'distance tailoring', where a garment is ordered from an out-of-town tailor, enabling cheaper labour to be used - which, in practice can now be done on a global scale via e-commerce websites, and a 'travelling tailor', where the man or woman will travel between cities, usually stationing in a luxury hotel to provide the client the same tailoring services they would provide in their local store. These processes are the same for both women's and men's garment making.

Pattern making is a very important part of this profession; the construction of a paper or cardboard template from which the parts of a garment are traced onto fabric before cutting our and assembling. A custom dressmaker (or tailor) frequently employs one of three pattern creation methods; a 'flat-pattern method' which begins with the creation of a sloper or block (a basic pattern for a garment, made to the wearer's measurements), which can then be used to create patterns for many styles of garments, with varying necklines, sleeves, dart placements and so on. Although it is also used for womenswear, the 'drafting method' is more commonly employed in menswear and involves drafting a pattern directly onto pattern paper using a variety of straightedges and curves. Since menswear rarely involves draping, pattern-making is the primary preparation for creating a cut-and-sew woven garment. The third method, the 'pattern draping method' is used when the patternmaker's skill is not matched with the difficulty of the design. It involves creating a muslin mock-up pattern, by pinning fabric directly on a dress form, then transferring the muslin outline and markings onto a paper pattern or using the muslin as the pattern itself.

Dressmaking and tailoring has become a very well respected profession; dressmakers such as Pierre Balmain, Christian Dior, Cristóbal Balenciaga and Coco Chanel have gone on to achieve international acclaim and fashion notoriety. Balmain, known for sophistication and elegance, once said that 'dressmaking is the architecture of movement.' Whilst tailors, due to the nature of their profession - catering to men's fashions, have not garnered such levels of individual fame, areas such as 'Savile Row' in the United Kingdom are today seen as the heart of the trade.

GEORGE DUNCAN, WEARING HIS SPECIALLY SELECTED DESIGN IN "SPORTEX."

BY COURTESY OF DORMEUIL FRÈRES.

HAWKES & CO., LTD., SAVILE ROW, LONDON, W.I.
CUTTING HALL.

ABE MITCHELL, WEARING HIS SPECIALLY SELECTED DESIGN IN "SPORTEX."
BY COURTESY OF DORMEUIL FRÈRES.

TROUSER CUTTING

NORMAL DRAFT. Diagram 1

FEATURES:—*Medium width at knee and bottom. Plain bottoms.*

MEASURES:—30″ *waist;* 36″ *seat;* 41″ *side seam;* 29″ *inside leg;* 20″ *knee width;* 16″ *bottom.*

INSTRUCTIONS FOR DRAFTING

FOR drafting purposes and to make the working out of the fractional quantities a little less formidable, the seat and waist measures are halved as follows:—Seat 18⊠; waist 15⊠. Line 0-0 in section A of the diagram can either represent the primal construction line when making a pattern or the selvedge when drafting straight on to the cloth.

If there is no distinct stripe in the material, and it is necessary to be strictly economical, point 18 section A may be brought nearer to the selvedge when the pattern is being marked round.

1/4⊠seams are provided through the draft.

THE TOPSIDES. SECTION A

Draw the construction line 0–0;

1 from 0 = the inside leg length (29⊠);

2 from 0 = the side seam/length (41⊠), plus making up allowance, say 1/2⊠;

Square out from the above points.

3 from 1 = one-third seat (6⊠);

4 from 3 = one-sixth seat (3⊠);

5 from 4 = one-sixth seat plus 1/4⊠ (3 1/4⊠);

Square down from point 3 and up from point 4.

6 is located where the line from 3 intersect the base line from 0;

7 is located where the line from 4 intersects the line from 2.

8 from 7 = 2⊠: square out;

9 from 8 = half waist plus 1/2⊠ for two seams;

10 is obtained by springing out from 9;

Strike a line midway across the angle at fork outlined by points 5, 4, and 7;

11 from 4 = half 4 to 5 plus 1/4⊠;

Shape the fork curve from 12, which is one-sixth seat up from 4;

13 from 4 = one-sixth seat (3⊠);

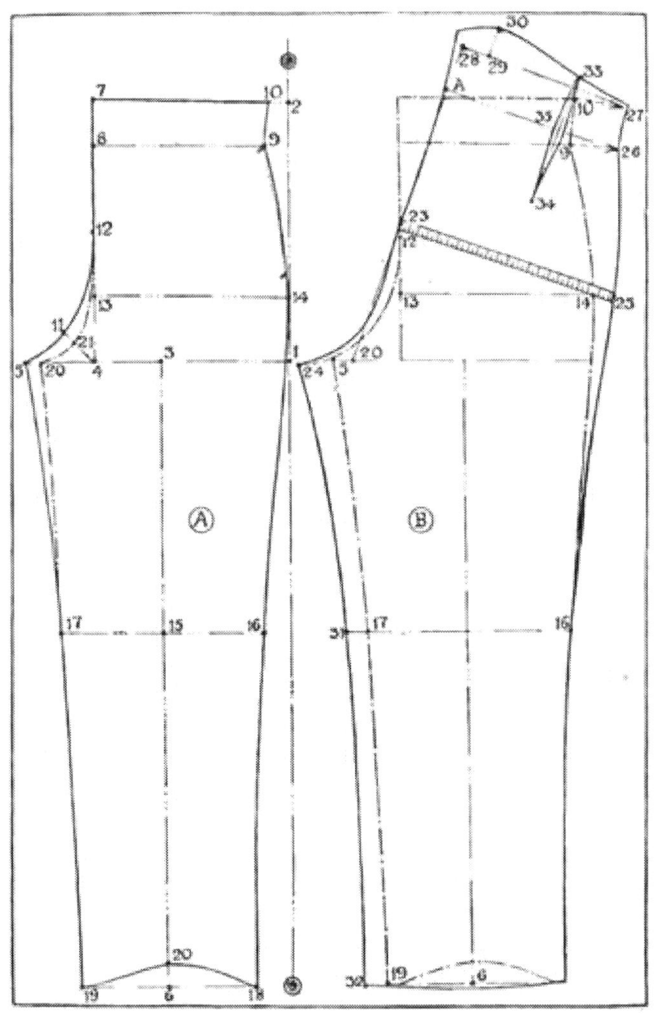

DIAGRAM 1.

14 is located by squaring out from 13;

15 from 3 = half leg length less 2⊠ (12 1/2) for knee line; 16 from 15 = one-fourth knee (5⊠);

17 from 15 is the same.

18 from 6 = one-fourth bottom (4⊠);

19 from 6 in the same.

Having joined 9 and 10, continue down through 14 to 16 and 18 (ignoring point 1);

From 5 curve to 17 and continue to 19;

20 from 6 in this instance is 3/4⊠, but the quantity will vary with the type of bottom required.

For instance, if the bottom is required wider than the measure given, then this distance can be decreased to allow the fronts to fall more on to the boot. The reverse would apply in the case of a narrower bottom.

DRESS

This is a sartorial term used in defining the quantity by which one side of the fork is reduced to accommodate the requirements of the figure.

A man usually "dresses" on the left side—this is readily ascertained at the time of measuring—we therefore reduce the right topside fork as follows:

20 from 5 = 3/4⊠;

21 from 11 is also 3/4⊠;

Curve from 12 through 21 to 20 and down towards 17.

THE UNDERSIDES. SECTION B

In preparation for the drafting of the undersides it is necessary, of course, to cut out the constructed topside.

Having laid this in a convenient position proceed as follows:

23 from 12 = 1/2☒;

Draw the seat line from 20 through 23 and forward towards 28;

Using 17 as a pivot, sweep out from 5 to 24;

24 from 5 = 1 1/2☒;

25 from 23 = the seat measure plus 2☒ (20) less the distance across the topsides from 13 to 14. The 2☒ addition represents the allowance for seams and ease.

Using 16 as a pivot, sweep from 9 and 10 as shown;

Fix point A (on the seat line) 1/2☒ above the topside;

26 from A = half waist plus 1 1/2☒ (9☒);

Spring out from 26 on to top sweep at 27.

Using the seat line 20 to A square from 28 to 27;

29 from 28 = 1 1/2☒;

30 from 29 = 1 1/2☒;

Shape the top as shown, springing out 1/2☒ at 28;

Hollow the fork 1/4☒ inside the seat line from 23 to 24;

31 from 17 and 32 from 19 are each 1☒;

Curve the bottom of the underside 1/4☒ below 6;

For the back dart or "fish" mark 2 1/2⊠ from 27 to 33;

Square down 6⊠ from 33 to 34.

The deepest part of the dart lies at point 35 on the line A to 26, where 1/2⊠ is taken out.

NOTES ON THE DRAFT

The crease in the finished trouser should come down the centre line 3 to 20.

When a more roomy seat is required to go with a wider knee and bottom, point 14 can be brought outside the construction line and the quantity added over the seat measure from 23 to 25 increased.

Although it is detrimental to the fit at the back, some cutters prefer to omit the dart at 33, thus reducing the cost of making. When this is required, the quantity from A to 26 should read: Half waist plus 1/2⊠.

CORPULENT DRAFT. DIAGRAM 2

FEATURES:—*Fly fronts. Plain bottoms. Side pockets. Moderate width at knee and bottom.*

MEASURES:—48" *waist;* 45" *seat;* 42" *side seam;* 28" *inside leg;* 23"; 19" *bottom.*

DISPROPORTION

THROUGHOUT the Trade the accepted proportionate or ideal waist is determined by deducting 6⊠ from the measured seat. Therefore where a comparison of the seat and waist shows a difference of more or less than this standardised quantity, the figure is said to be disproportionate. For the purposes of this draft we will further add that as the difference becomes gradually less, so is the figure progressing towards the corpulent state. Opinions vary respecting the stage at which a man becomes corpulent, but this need not worry the student, as the system laid down automatically adjusts the draft to meet all degrees of disproportion.

FORMULA

In order to allocate correctly the waist increment in the draft, it is necessary to know the correct amount of disproportion. This is found as follows:—Seat 45⊠ less 6⊠ gives the proportionate waist 39⊠. Compare the measured waist (48⊠) with this and we have the amount of disproportion, viz. 9⊠.

INSTRUCTIONS FOR DRAFTING

All points below the fork line (1) are found as in the previous draft.

To accommodate the straightness of the back waist and the erectness of carriage, which is typical of such a figure, a little variation is made to run of the seat line 20 and 22.

In measuring up the waist of the undersides there is no necessity for the 1⊠ allowance for the back fish or dart, as this is omitted for figures of such proportions.

The half-seat 22 1/2⊠ and half-waist 24⊠ are the quantities referred to in the instructions below.

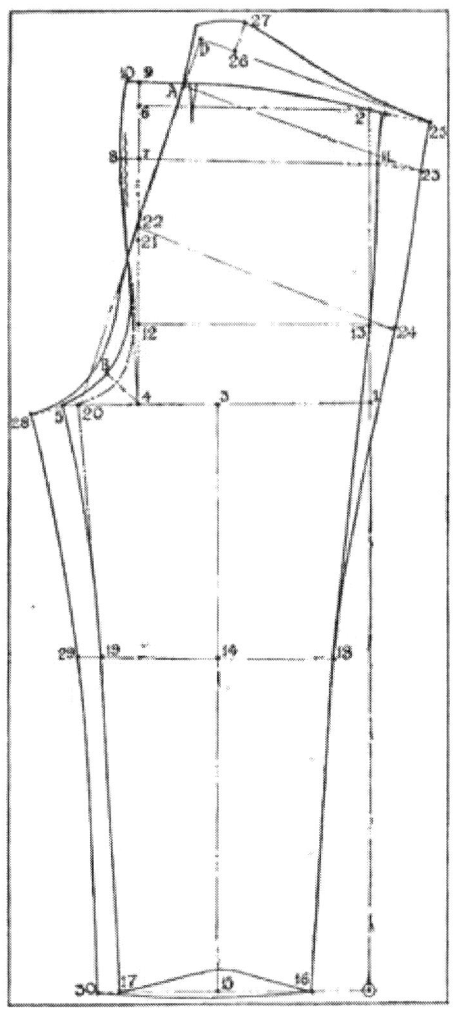

DIAGRAM 2.

THE TOPSIDES

Square lines from 0;

1 from 0 = the leg length 28⊠;

2 from 0 = the side length 42⊠ plus allowance for making-up;

Square out from these points.

3 from 1 = one-third seat (7 1/2⊠);

4 from 3 = one-sixth seat (3 3/4⊠);

5 from 4 = one-sixth seat; no addition is made as in the previous draft.

Square down from 3 and up from 4;

6 is located where line from 4 intersects the line from 2;

7 from 6 = 2 1/2⊠;

8 from 7 = one-eighth disproportion (1 1/8⊠);

9 from 6 = 7 to 8;

10 from 9 is 1/4⊠ less than 7 to 8;

11 from 8 = half waist plus 1/2⊠;

12 from 4 = one-sixth seat (3 3/4⊠);

13 is found by squaring across from 12;

14 is half leg less 2⊠ from 3 for knee-line;

Square out on either side of 14;

16 from 15 = one-fourth bottom 4 3/4⊠;

17 from 15 is the same;

18 from 14 = one-fourth knee 5 3/4⊠;

19 from 14 is the same.

To complete the topsides, draw from 11 through 13, straight down to 18 and 16.

B from 4 = half 4 to 5 plus 1/4⊠;

Join 8 to 4 and use this line as a guide when shaping fork.

20 for the dress side is 3/4⊠ from 5;

Mark in the same quantity at B and follow the run of dot and dash line.

Hollow bottom above 15.

THE UNDERSIDES

21 from 4 = one-third seat plus 1/2⊠;

22 from 21 = 1/2⊠;

Draw through 22 from 20 and continue up towards D;

Using point 18 as a pivot, sweep 11 and 13;

23 from A = half waist plus 1/2⊠;

24 from 22 is the seat measure plus 2⊠ (24 1/2) less 12 to 13;

Shape the side seam from 23 through 24 to knee and spring out to 25 on top line.

Square D–25 by line 20–22;

26 is 2⊠ from D and 27 is 1 1/2⊠ above 26;

28 is 1 1/2⊠ from 5;

29 and 30 are each 1⊠ from the topsides.

NOTES ON THE DRAFT

In order to distribute the round more evenly over the front, a small dart is taken out in the topside (near A). This dart is also influential in keeping the top edge nice and snug to the figure.

The quantity from 21 to 22 must vary with the degree of disproportion as follows:—Where the amount recorded is 6⊠, 21 to 22 should read 1/4⊠ and in extreme cases, such as a 12⊠ disproportion, this distance should be made 3/4⊠, and so on.

Some fat men stand and walk with their feet well apart. This should be carefully noted at the time of measuring, and draft adjusted by moving line 3–15 (1/2⊠ to 1⊠) nearer the side line 1–0. Normal cut trousers on such figures would swing away from the inner side of boot.

STYLE DETAILS AND TOP FINISHES

DIAGRAM 3 has been devoted to a display of various styles of finish that the trouser cutter may be called upon to produce. No apology is offered for the inclusion of such backdated top finishes as Whole Falls, French Bearers, etc. These are still being asked for in some of the Provincial trades, and there are many cutters whose careers do not date back to the period when such styles were in universal use.

PLEATED TOPS. SECTION A

This is a modern top finish, introduced to distribute the extra hip size that present fashion demands.

The pleats are inserted in the top side, the allowance being made at side-seam. In some instances one pleat only is introduced, but the allowance made is the same as for the two.

1 is the waist-line, 1 1/2⊠ below the ordinary top or 1 1/2⊠ less than the body-rise from 0.

2 from 1 = half waist plus 1/2⊠;

3 from 2 = 2⊠ for the pleats;

5 from 4 = one-third 2 to 3;

When measuring up the seat to point 6, add 2 1/2⊠ to 3⊠ over the measure.

7 for the first pleat is situated on the centre line;

8 is midway between 8 and 3;

10 is half waist plus 1 1/2⊠ as usual, but the top is kept straight and the vee is made without the convex curve.

TOP BAND

This is cut 2⊠ wide and the length from 11 to 12 = half waist plus 1/2⊠.

The dash line extension shows the addition necessary when the right side is required to go across the fly.

Curve the band 1/2⊠ below 12.

SIDE POCKET. SECTION B

The opening for this commences at the waist at (1) and extends 6⊠ to 6 1/2⊠ down the side seam of topside to 2. The facing shown at 3 may be left grown-on or cut separately. The outline of the pockets is shown by dash lines.

FLY AND FRENCH BEARER. SECTION B

Both the right and left fly are cut together, the left or dress side being used for the shaping as shown at 4. The width is about 2 1/2⊠.

French Bearers are adjuncts frequently ordered by stout men. The bearer, which is lined and interlined, is an extension of the button fly (see 5) and carries the two holes for fastening. These fasten on to a short strap inserted in the left side seam and shown at 6.

P.T.U.'S. SECTION C

This particular bottom finish requires a shorter leg length than the ordinary plain style, the amount being 1/2″ to 1″ according to the width of bottom.

1 to 2 is the actual length required.

1 to 7 and 7 to 5 represent the width of turnings.

3 and 4 represent the position of the top of the turn-up.

Square down from 3 and 4 to locate 5 and 6;

From 1 and 2 shape to 7 and 8 going 1/8″ outside the line from 4.

Add 1/2″ to 3/4″ below 5 to 6 for turning.

WHOLE OR FULL FALLS. SECTION D

In this finish flys are dispensed with, the front seam being sewn up.

As in the case of pleated top, the part above the waist line is cut away, as shown at 1 and 2. A bearer is then cut to make up the deficiency, as shown by dotted lines at 3 and 4.

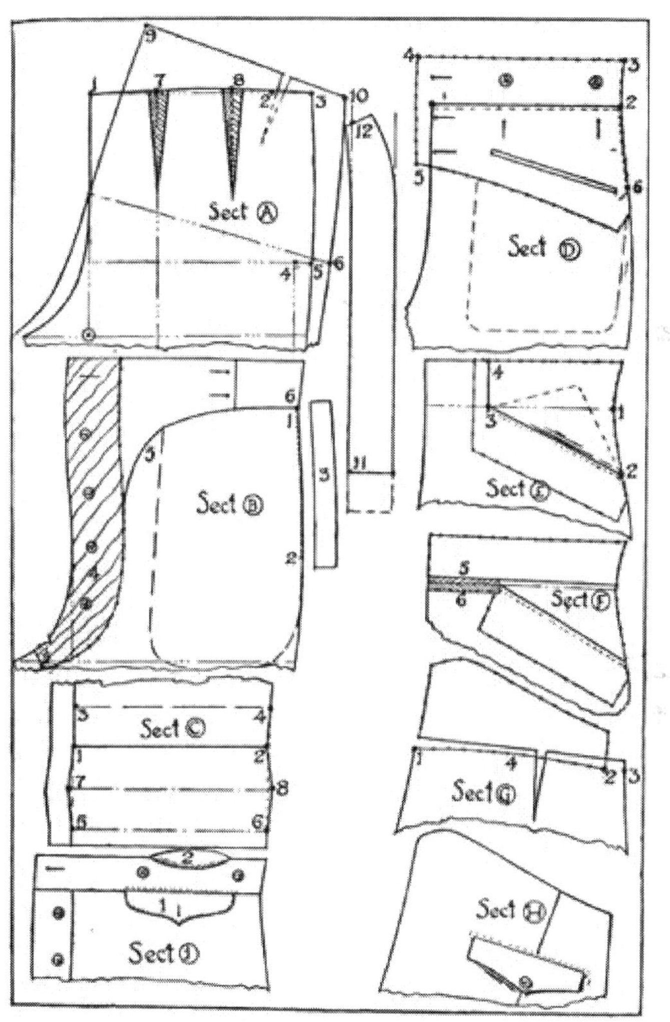

DIAGRAM 3.

The front of the bearer projects 1/2⊠ beyond the front and is made 4⊠ deep.

6 is 3 1/2⊠ down from 2 for the slit at the side, the bearer extending below this.

Jetted pockets are placed in the bearer, 1/2⊠ from the tack at 6, and extending 6⊠ in an upward incline.

The bearer, 3 to 6, is sewn to the undersides.

The topsides, 1 to 2, are faced deeply and have holes inserted to fasten to corresponding buttons on the bearer.

Dress can be taken out in the usual way, but in heavy materials both sides are left the same.

CROSS POCKETS. SECTIONS E AND F

For this particular finish the back tack is placed at 3 1/2⊠ down from the waist (1 to 2); 3 from 2 (on waist line) is 6⊠;

The tops are slit down from 4 to 3 and the right-hand portion is cut away to form the facing, as illustrated by dash lines.

The bearer (dotted line) is then cut to fill in the vacancy, 1/2⊠ being allowed beyond points 3 and 4 for seams.

Section F demonstrates how the bearer would be cut where there is a top welt.

The topsides in this case are cut away a seam's width above the waist line (5).

The bearer is shown in dotted lines, a seam being allowed below the waist at 6.

SEAT PIECE. SECTION G

Where short lengths or "long" customers are the rule, it may be necessary to piece out the undersides. The dotted lines here illustrate how this should be carried out, when there is a dart in the waist.

1 and 2 are 1/2⊠ down from the body part for seam allowance.

2 from 3 = 1⊠ the amount taken up by the dart.

Shape from 1 to 2, hollowing a little at 4 to give spring to the tops.

HIP POCKET. SECTION H

The position of the hip or "pistol" pocket is situated 1⊠ from the side-seam at 1 and 3⊠ to 3 1/2⊠ from the top at the fore end. The flap, which covers the mouth, is 5⊠ wide, and the back end 4 1/2⊠ from the top.

CASH AND FOB POCKET.

SECTION I

The cash pocket (1) is 5⊠ long and is placed on the waist line with the rear end 1⊠ out from the side seam.

The fob pocket (2) is placed between the two front buttons, the tops being hollowed out and a deep facing sewn on to the rear of the pocket to fill in the vacancy and to give easy access.

PLUS FOURS

Diagram 4

FEATURES:—*The modern style of this garment is represented with a medium "fall over" and moderate width in the legs; pleated tops and waistband; strap and buckle at the small for fastening.*

MEASURES:—32″ *waist;* 38″ *seat;* 42″ *side;* 30″ *leg;* 12″ *round small of leg;* 13″ *round calf.*

The leg and side measures are taken in exactly the same fashion as for trousers.

INSTRUCTIONS FOR DRAFTING

THE full side measure not being used, we have dispensed with the side line in this draft.

The process of producing the pattern is the same as in previous drafts, the topside being cut out and the underhalf drafted by it.

There is a decided change in the run of the seat line in this draft from what was shown for trousers. It has a much straighter or upright run and is well hollowed in the fork. This change has been introduced to give a clean hanging underhalf below the brow of the seat.

The half-seat (19☒) and waist (16☒) measures are referred to in the details below.

THE DRAFT. SECTION A

Draw a line from 0.

1 from 0 = one-third seat (6 3/8☒);

2 from 1 = one-sixth seat plus 1/2☒ (3 3/4☒);

3 from 2 = one-sixth seat less 1/2☒ (2 5/8☒);

Square up from 2 to 4.

The difference between the leg and side measures is 12☒.

4 from 2 = the above difference less 1 1/2☒ (10 1/2☒).

Square out from 4.

5 from 2 = half 2 to 3 plus 1/4⊠;

6 from 2 = 1/6 seat;

Square out to locate point 7.

8 from 7 = 1 1/4⊠, but this quantity can be varied to accord with the amount of bagginess required.

9 from 4 = half waist plus 1/2⊠ for seams and 2⊠ for pleats (10 1/2⊠);

Give a little round from 4 to 9.

10 from 1 = half leg length;

Square out on either side.

11 from 10 = 7 3/4⊠ for a medium "fall over."

12 from 11 = one-fourth small measure plus 1⊠ for gathering or pleats.

13 from 11 = 11 to 12;

14 from 10 = 1 1/2⊠ more than 11 to 13;

15 from 10 = 2 1/2⊠ more than 11 to 12;

Both the above quantities can be varied for style purposes.

16 from 12 = 1/2⊠;

Shape side and leg seams as shown in diagram.

The first pleat is situated on the centre line and the rear one midway between the side seam and the front pleat.

Join 16 and 13 dropping 1/4⊠ for seam and giving a little round.

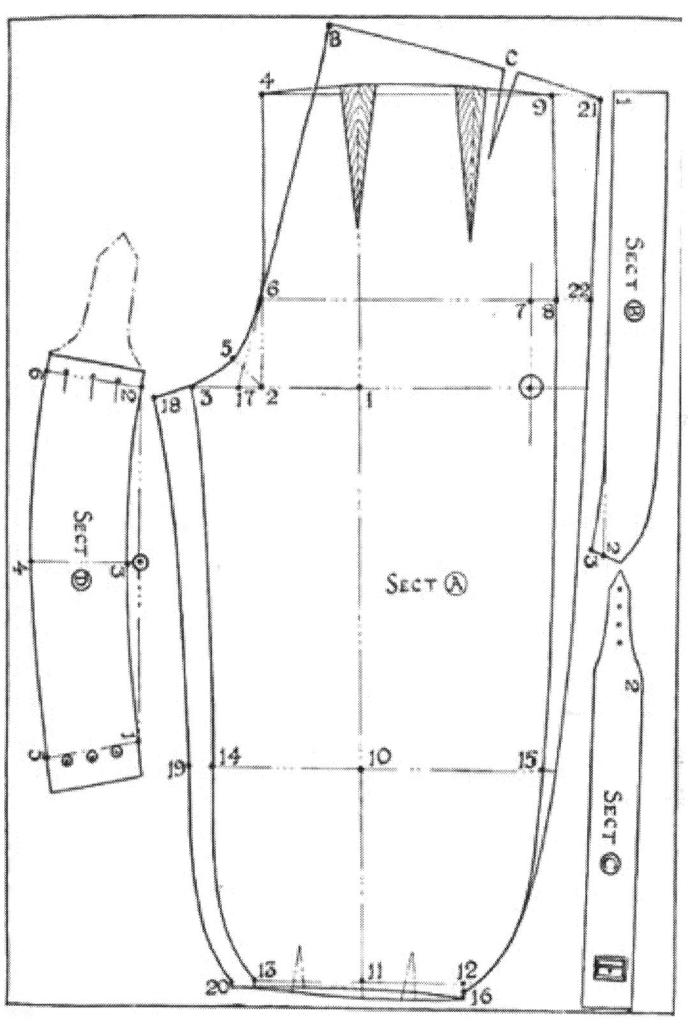
SECT Ⓐ
SECT Ⓑ
SECT Ⓒ
SECT Ⓓ
B
C
4
9
21
6
22
7
8
5
18
3
17
2
1
14
10
15
19
13
11
12
20
16

DIAGRAM 4.

UNDERSIDE

17 from 3 = half the distance 3 to 2 plus 3/8⊠;

Draw through 6 from 17 for seat line;

18 from 3 = 1 1/2⊠;

Curve run from 6 as shown.

19 from 14 = 1⊠;

20 from 13 = 1⊠;

Shape leg seam through 19 from 18.

21 from seat line in region of B = half waist plus 1 1/2⊠.

B is definitely located by squaring from the seat line (17–6) to 21.

Take 1/2⊠ vee out at C as shown.

22 from 8 = 1 1/4⊠;

Shape side seam from 21 through 22 and down to 16.

TOP BAND. SECTION B

The width of the band is 2⊠.

2 from 1 = the waist measure 16⊠ plus 1/2⊠ for seam.

3 from 2 = 1/2⊠

Shape from 1 curving down to 3.

STRAP. SECTION C

This is the strap that is sewn round the base of the legs of the knickers. It carries eyelet holes which connect with a buckle sewn about 1 1/2⊠ from the opposite end. This is the most popular method of finishing the bottoms.

The width is about 2⊠ with seams and the length from 1 to 2 equals the size of the small. The extension for fastening end is about 3⊠ in length.

AN ALTERNATIVE FINISH.
SECTION D

The broad band is a relic of the cycling knickerbocker days, but it is still asked for by quite a number of people.

1 from 0 = half small plus 1/4⊠;

2 from 0 is the same.

3 from 0 = half the difference between the calf and small measures (1/2).

4 from 3 = 3 1/2⊠;

Curve the base parallel with the top.

5 and 6 are each half the calf measure plus 1/4⊠, from 4.

Add 1 1/4⊠ for button stand at 1 to 5 and 1/2⊠ for the hole side at 2 and 6.

Three buttons and holes comprise the fastening as a rule, but some favour an extension (similar to that given on the narrow strap) for fastening to a buckle in place of the buttons and holes.

NOTES ON THE DRAFT

For corpulent figures the disproportion will be applied in the same manner as for trousers, point 4 being advanced and the tops raised above the squared line.

Pleats are not recommended, however, for such figures.

Darts or pleats can be utilised as a means of bringing the bottoms to fit in the strap. An alternative method is to gather or draw-in the bottom with a thread.

Where a distinct check is embodied in the design of the material, care will have to be exercised when laying the pattern out on the material.

RIDING BREECHES

Diagram 5

FEATURES:—*Fly front; moderate side pouch; centre front knee fastening; cross pockets.*

MEASURES:—32" *waist;* 38" *seat;* 14" *length to knee;* 16 1/2" *length to small or hollow;* 19 1/2" *length to calf;* 13 1/2" *knee width;* 12" *small width*; 13 1/2" *calf width; inside leg length* 32"; *outside leg* 44".

INSTRUCTIONS FOR DRAFTING

COMPARED with ordinary trousers riding breeches require a little different treatment in the trunk section of the draft, to provide the necessary ease for mounting and for the astride position when in the saddle.

The position of the fastening on the leg is affected by the situation of line E in the topsides. If the fastening is required more to the side of the leg, the distance 12 to E must be increased.

Half seat (19⊠) and half waist (32⊠) are the measures referred to in the instructions below.

THE DRAFT

Draw lines from 0.

1 from 0 = one-third of seat (6 3/8);

2 from 1 = one-sixth of seat (3 1/8);

3 from 2 = one-sixth of seat plus 3/4☒;

Square up from 2.

4 from 2 = the body rise (12☒) found by deducting the inside leg 32 from the outside 44;

Add making-up allowance, say 1/2☒;

5 from 4 = 2☒;

6 from 5 = half waist plus 1/2☒;

7 is located by springing out to top-line from 6.

8 from 2 = half the distance 2 to 3 plus 1/4☒;

9 from 2 = one-third seat (6 3/8) minus 1/2☒;

Shape fork curve as shown.

10 from 1 = 3/4☒;

Square down;

11 from 10 = 1 1/2☒ for ease;

12 from 11 = length to knee 14☒;

13 from 11 = length to small 16 1/2☒

14 from 11 = length to calf 19 1/2☒;

The average distances of 2 1/2☒ from 12 to 13 and 3☒ from 13 to 14 can be used where the inside trouser leg is the only length measure available.

A from 12 = 1/4 knee width 3 3/8;

B and C are located by squaring down from A;

15 from A = half knee (6 3/4⊠);

16 from B = half small (6⊠);

17 from C = half calf (6 3/4⊠);

Shape inseam through 15, 16 and 17, commencing at 3;

E is 1/2⊠ out from 12;

Square down to H;

18 from 0 = 1 1/2⊠;

Join to E;

19 is midway between 18 and E;

20 from 19 = 2 1/2⊠ to 3⊠;

Shape side seam from 18 to 7 and down from 18 to E;

Drop the fronts 3/4⊠ at 4.

UNDERSIDE

21 from 3 = 3/4⊠;

Draw from 21 through 9 for seat line;

22 from 3 = 1 1/2⊠;

Sweep out from 3 pivoting at 15;

Square 23 to 24 by seat line.

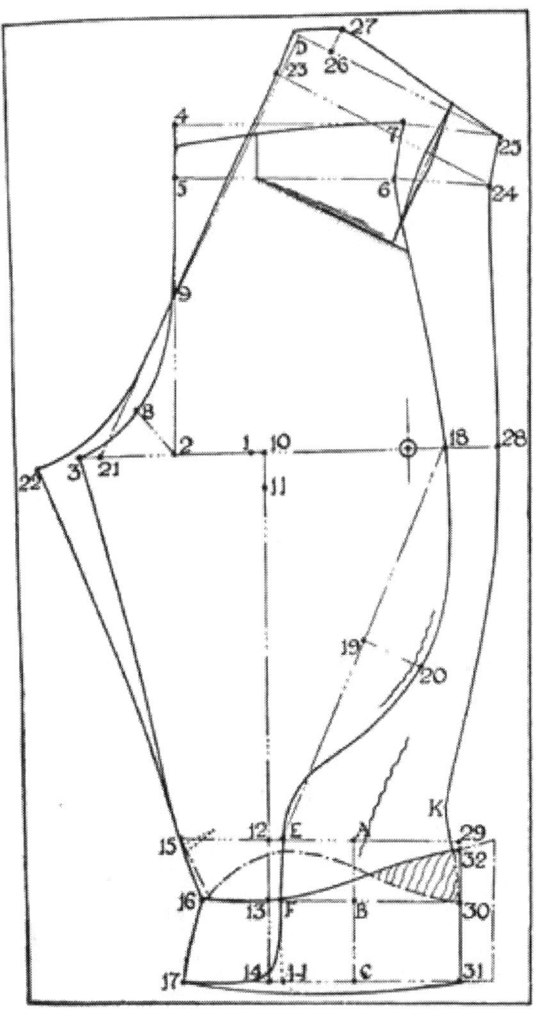

DIAGRAM 5.

24 from 23 = half waist plus 1 1/2☒ (9 1/2).

Spring out from 24 to 25.

D is located by squaring to 25 by the seat line.

26 from D = 2⊠;

27 from 26 = 1 1/2⊠;

Shape top as shown.

Take out a cut of 1/2⊠ in the waist;

Apply the knee width plus 1⊠ (14 1/2⊠) from E to 15 and from 15 out to 29;

Apply the small width plus 1⊠ (13⊠) from F to 16 and from 16 to 30;

Apply the calf width plus 1⊠ (13 1/2⊠) from H to 17 and from 17 to 31.

28 from 18 = 2 1/2⊠;

32 from 29 = 3/4⊠;

Shape to 13 and 16;

Measure from 18 round the curve of side seam to E;

Apply the amount registered plus 3/4⊠ from 28 to locate upper seam of cut at 30;

Curve upper half of cut as shown, taking 2⊠ out above 13;

Hook the leg seam in at 16 (dot and dash lines), to make the length of the upper part of the seam agree with the lower half.

When shaping side-seam curve in at K to compare with the outline of topside above E.

NOTES ON THE DRAFT

Provision for corpulency will only be affected at 5 and 4 as in trousers.

No provision for fulling at knee is made in this draft, and unless the fastening is arranged at the side of the leg, none is required.

The small knee cut below 15 in the topsides is only possible where strappings are to be worn.

Before joining the side-seams, the undersides must be shrunk to a nice hollow in the region of A (see wavy line).

TOP AND KNEE FINISHES. Diagram 6

THIS diagram has been devoted to illustrations of various top and knee finishes which are frequently asked for in Breeches Trades. With the diagrams and details given below the student should not experience any difficulty when it becomes necessary to infuse any of these style details into the full draft, already given in the last section.

SPLIT FALLS. SECTION A

This little sketch depicts the upper section of a pair of breeches finished with Split Falls. If referred to when the various parts have been cut out, it will help those unacquainted with the style in the checking up of the parts and show how they are assembled.

In the sketch the "fall" is shown detached from the buttons and laid over, exposing the inside finish.

SECTION B

This illustrates the preliminary trimming of the tops and the construction of the slit-bearer. The dash lines 1 and 2 represent the waist line.

The top of the "fall" runs 1/2⊠ above this line and extends 21/4⊠ from 3 to 4.

The top side is slit down to a depth of 6⊠ from 4 to 5 for the "fall."

Point 5 is situated 3 1/4⊠ from the fly or front line.

The remaining section of the top-side is cut away 1/4⊠ above the waist line as from 6 to 7.

8 from 2 is 3⊠ for the depth of the pocket.

9 from 8 = 6⊠ for the pocket mouth.

The front bearer is shown by dot and dash lines extending from 6 out to 10.

10 from 1 = 1⊠;

11 from 10 = 2 1/2⊠;

Curve the bearer from 11 down to 5 as shown.

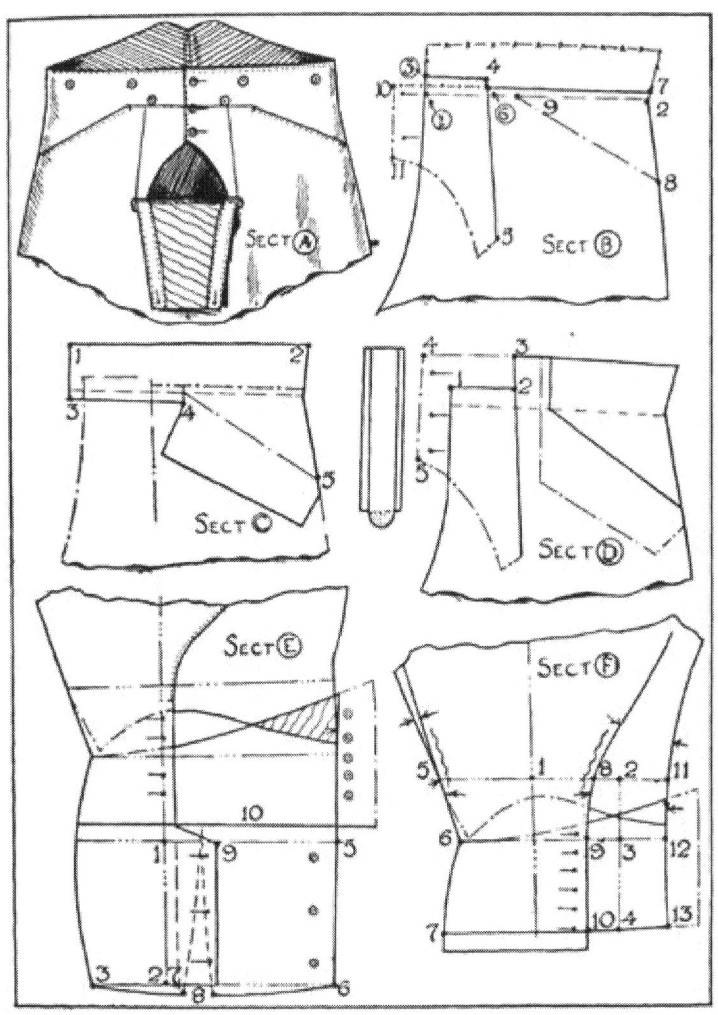

DIAGRAM 6.

SECTION C

This illustrates the cutting of the top and pocket bearer. Dot and dash lines show the outline of trimmed topside. This bearer, which is carried up to complete the height of the tops at 1 and 2, is extended 1/2⊠ beyond the front line.

A seam is allowed below the waist line from 3 to 4 and the pocket extension made below 4 and 5 as shown by solid line.

A welt cut to finish 3/4⊠ to 1⊠ wide is constructed to be sewn down the side of the fall.

SECTION D

This depicts an alternative method of constructing Split Falls. Here the ordinary cross pocket is given, the facing and bearer being cut in accordance with the details laid down in the trousers section.

The front part of the topside is trimmed so that the "fall" 1 to 2 lies 1/2⊠ above the waist line.

The bearer is then cut to come right to the top as shown by dot and dash lines at 3, 4, and 5.

CONTINUATIONS. SECTION E

This forms an extension of the breeches down below the calf, to a distance which is generally arranged to accord with the wishes of the customer.

The upper section at knee, small and calf is constructed as described in the full draft given previously.

2 from 1 is the extra length.

3 from 2 = 1/4 the bottom measure.

NOTE.—The length of the continuation must be taken into account when measuring.

6 is squared down from 5.

Apply the full bottom measure plus 1⊠ from 7 to 3 and from 3 out towards 6. Any surplus is taken out in a dart as shown at 8 (dash lines).

In order to prevent pressure of the buttons on the shin bone, the top-sides are carried over to the side as shown at 9.

The continuations may be left on with the upper part, or they may be cut away on Hne 10 and made up in linen.

FASTENING AT SIDE OF KNEE.
SECTION F

This diagram shows the altered outline of the breeches when the fastening has been arranged at the side of the knee.

2 from 1 = 1/4 knee width;

3 and 4 are squared down from 2;

5 from 2 = half knee;

6 from 3 = half small;

7 from 4 = half calf;

8, 9, and 10 are placed 2⊠ out from the centre line at 1;

Apply knee measure plus 1⊠ from 8 to 5 and from 5 to 11;

Apply small plus 1⊠ from 9 to 6 and 6 to 12;

Apply calf plus 1⊠ from 10 to 7 and 7 to 13.

The overlap for the cut is found as before. With the seam coming down the side of the leg, it is necessary to infuse a little fullness on either side of topside knee to provide for the kneebone. This is accomplished by extending the topside 1/2⊠ below 7 and 10, and the placing of balance marks 3⊠ apart on the underside and 3 1/2⊠ on the topside as shown by arrows.

VEST CUTTING

S.B. AND D.B. STYLES. BY A PROPORTIONATE SYSTEM.
Diagram 7

FEATURES.—*Single breasted. No collar. Medium points and opening.*

MEASURES.—36″ *breast;* 32″ *waist;* 16 1/2″ *waist length;* 12″ *opening;* 25 1/2″ *full length.*

INSTRUCTIONS FOR DRAFTING

IN this draft all the points are found by taking fractional quantities of a scale, which is derived from the circumference of breast measure.

The scale in this instance is 18⊠ and is found by taking one-third the breast measure and adding 6⊠. This formula obtains in all sizes from 36 upwards; but below 36 half breast gives the scale—i.e.—36 B = 18 scale; 42 B = 20 scale; 32 B = 16 scale—and so on.

No special provision is made for irregular figures in the working of the system, all deviations being made from the standard outline when marking out on the material.

S.B. VEST. SECTION A

Square lines from 0.

1 from 0 = half scale (9⊠);

2 from 0 = waist length (16 1/2⊠);

3 from 2 = 1⊠; join to 0;

4 from 3 = 1/2⊠;

Curve centre seam from 0 to 5 and down through 4;

6 from 0 = one-sixth scale plus 1/4⊠;

7 from 6 = 3/4⊠;

Draw back neck to 0;

8 from 0 is one-fourth the distance 0 to 1 (2 1/4⊠);

Square out;

9 from 8 = one-third scale plus 1 3/4⊠ (7 3/4⊠);

10 is located by squaring down from 9;

11 from 5 = one-fourth full breast size, plus 1⊠ (10);

12 from 5 = half breast plus 1 1/2⊠;

13 from 11 = one-twelfth scale plus 1/2⊠: square up;

14 from 13 = one-sixth scale (3): square up;

15 from 14 = half scale (9);

Join 15 to 9;

16 from 15 is 3/8⊠ less than the back shoulder seam from 7 to 9.

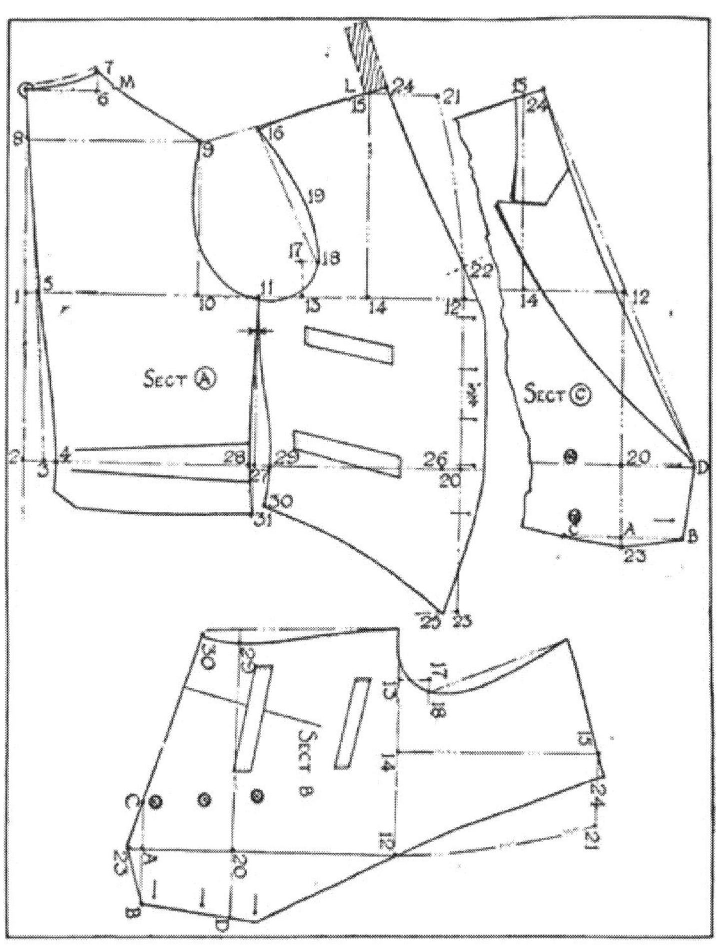

DIAGRAM 7

Drop 1/4″ below the line;

17 from 13 = 1 1/2″;

18 from 17 = 3/4″: join to 16;

Shape scye hollowing 1/2⊠ at 19, dropping 1/4⊠ below breast line and hollowing 1/4⊠ behind line from 10.

20 is found by squaring down from 12 in all instances where there is a difference of not less than 3⊠ between the breast and waist.

21 from 15 = one-sixth scale;

Curve line to 12;

22 from 15 (by sweep) is the opening measure plus 1/2⊠ and less back neck 0 to 6;

23 from 15 (direct) = full length measure plus 1⊠ and less the distance 0 to 6;

24 is a continuation of the shoulder and is 3/4⊠ out from 15;

25 is 1⊠ from 23. This distance will vary to accord with the shape of the points desired.

Shape from point 24 through 22 and down to 25 extending 3/4⊠ beyond centre line for button stand.

26 from 4 = half waist plus 1 3/4⊠;

27 is squared down from 11;

28 from 27 = 1/4⊠;

29 from 28 = the waist surplus shown at 26 to 20.

Shape side seams as shown, making 30, 2⊠ to 2 1/2⊠ below the waist line and the back at 31, 1/2⊠ lower.

The back neck piece, which is usually cut on the crease edge of the material, is sewn on at 24.

The exact run of this is shown by the shaded portion between dot and dash lines.

The lower pocket is 5⊠ to 5 1/2⊠ in length, and its position 1⊠ away from the side seam, 3 1/2⊠ from the bottom at the rear end and 5⊠ at the front.

The top pockets are placed 5⊠ above the lower ones and made 3 1/2⊠ to 4 1/2⊠ wide.

D.B. NO-COLLAR VEST.
SECTION B

This diagram depicts the full length double-breasted shape with a no-collar finish.

The back section remains the same and the numbers, which correspond to those given in the previous draft, are found as described for that vest.

23 is the full length to measure.

A is 1/2⊠ up from 23;

Square out on either side;

B from A = 2 1/2⊠: C from A is the same.

D from 20 = 3 to 3 1/2⊠;

Draw from B through D and curve bottom run through C;

The opening is continued from 24 through 12 (or opening point) until it cuts the line up from D;

The lapel section in front of line 12–23 may be cut off and sewn on separately.

The distance between the line of buttons and the centre line is made 3/4⊠ less than the overlap given beyond 20 and A.

D.B. COLLAR VEST.
SECTION C

This diagram displays the new shape of the D.B. variety with a short and straight bottom run.

23 is 3 1/4⊠ from 20;

A is 3/8⊠ above 23;

B from A = 2 3/4⊠: C from A is the same;

D from 20 = 3 3/4⊠;

Join D to 24 and hollow slightly as shown.

The collar, which is made up separately and sewn on, is shaped with a bold curve.

The position of the step should be located slightly lower than the midway point between the neck 15 and the breast line 14.

To give a better effect and to facilitate the making up, the upper section can be cut separately and joined on, thus forming a natural "break seam" similar to a coat.

NOTES ON THE DRAFT

The indifferent manner in which vests are often put together is chiefly the cause of the badly wrinkled shoulders of which customers so frequently complain.

Balance marks should therefore be placed at the shoulders L and M, and also in the side seams, for the guidance of the work-hand.

When chalking round the back on the Italian, a small turning-up allowance should be left at back neck, as outlined by dot and dash lines.

When sewing the back centre seam, the stitching should come 1/4" inside the pattern line. Facings are frequently left on down the opening edge (12 to 24), when cutting from the cloth. When this is done, the work-hand must be instructed to turn the edge so that the thread marks lie 1/4" inside and not on the line of edge, as is so frequently done.

DRESS VEST BY DIRECT MEASURES.
Diagram 8

FEATURES:—*Single-breasted. Roll collar. Semi-vee opening. Three buttons.*

MEASURES:—36" *breast;* 32" *waist;* 9" *scye depth*; 16 1/2" *waist length*; 12 3/4" *front shoulder;* 17 3/4" *over shoulder; full length and opening to style.*

NOTE.—The front shoulder has been made 1/4⊠ and the across chest 1/2⊠ less than the measures taken over the lounge jacket.

INSTRUCTIONS FOR DRAFTING

IN this draft the application of the short direct measures is shown. The great virtue of this system lies in the complete manner in which it provides for irregular figures direct on the draft, without the use of judgment.

The construction of the draft for dress vests is practically the same as for the ordinary no-collar type, the only variation being at the front.

There are many varieties of front finish, but the selection given here has been confined to the more standard shapes.

The working scale 18 is found as explained in the previous draft.

ROLL COLLAR VEST. SECTION A

Square lines from 0.

1 from 0 = scye depth 9⊠;

2 from 0 = waist length 16 1/2⊠;

3 from 2 = 1⊠: join to 0;

4 from 3 = 1/2⊠;

Shape back seam from A;

5 from 1 = one-third the over-shoulder measure plus 3/4⊠;

Square out;

6 from 5 = one-third scale plus 1 3/4⊠ (7 3/4⊠);

7 from 0 = one-sixth scale plus 1/4⊠ (3 1/4⊠);

8 from 7 = 3/4⊠;

Shape to 0 and join to 6.

9 is squared down from 6;

10 from A = one-fourth breast plus 1⊠;

11 from A = half breast plus 1 1/2⊠;

12 from 11 = across chest measure 7 1/2⊠;

13 from 12 = one-sixth scale;

Square up;

Deduct the width of back neck 0 to 7 from the front shoulder measure and sweep the remainder from 12 through line 13 as shown by 14.

Deduct 1/2⊠ from the over-shoulder measure and apply the remainder from A to B (centre of shoulder) and from 12 to 15 by a sweep.

15 from 14 = 8 to 6 less 3/8⊠;

16 from 12 = 1 1/2⊠;

17 from 16 = 3/4⊠;

Join to 15;

Shape the armhole hollowing 3/4⊠ at 18; dropping 1/4⊠ below 10 and up 1/4⊠ behind line 9 to 6;

19 is squared down from 11 for all sizes where the waist is 3⊠ or more less than the breast.

20 from 19 is the length desired, in this instance 5 1/2⊠.

21 from 20 = 1⊠;

Add 3/4⊠ beyond centre line 19 for button stand and fix the opening 1 1/2⊠ to 2⊠ up from the waist at 22.

C is 3/4⊠ out from 14;

Connect to 22 and hollow the neck 1⊠;

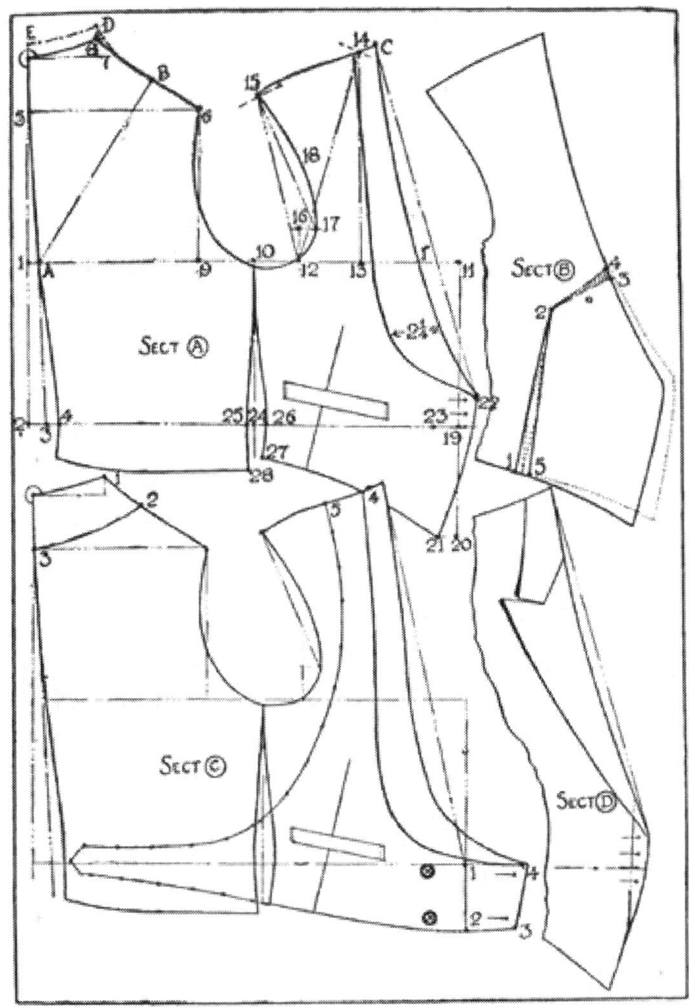

DIAGRAM 8.

23 from 4 = half waist plus 1 1/2☒;

24 is squared down from 10;

25 is 1/4☒ from 24;

26 from 25 = the waist surplus shown from 23 to 19.

27 from 26 = 1 1/2⊠;

28 is 1/2⊠ lower than 27;

Shape side seam as shown giving a little spring at the bottom.

MANIPULATION OF THE FRONT. SECTION B

The manipulation of the pattern shown in this diagram has the twofold effect of giving an elegant-shaped waist for normal figures and providing a close sit at the opening. Both these features are essential to a good-fitting vest.

Cut the pattern upon the dart line from 1 to 2 as shown.

Pleat the front over 1/4⊠ to 1/2⊠ at 3 and 4 and the forepart will swing forward as shown by dotted line. The dart is also opened from 1 to 5.

Shape the waist dart, filling in to a point midway between 1 and 5.

When chalking out on the cloth follow the dotted line at the front.

D.B. BACKLESS VEST. SECTION C

For this modern type of finish the draft is produced in ordinary manner as described above.

The back part is cut away to a narrow neck band as outlined by dotted lines at 1, 2, and 3.

The front shoulder is then shortened to meet the alteration in the back, 4 to 5 being the same distance as 2 to 3.

From 5 curve down the shoulder, well clear of the scye front, and on to the side waist. Here the forepart is extended to form an adjusting strap at back waist.

The front shown is the very popular D.B. buttoning two with a straight bottom run.

2 from 1 = 3⊠;

3 from 2 = 2 3/4⊠;

4 from 1 = 3 1/2⊠

Join front to the neck and hollow 1⊠ as shown.

VEE-SHAPED POINTED LAPEL. SECTION D

This is another popular front finish with the opening carried straight to the first buttonhole. The collar shown is the ordinary pointed step.

NOTES ON THE DRAFT

In order to dispense with the carrying of the collar round to the back neck, the lining of the back can be extended right through to the top. The alteration necessary for this is shown by dot and dash lines at E and D, these two points being located 5/8⊠ above 0 and 8.

From D run gradually out into the shoulder seam as shown.

Provision for increased waist size will be shown in a later draft.

COAT CUTTING

S.B. LOUNGE. BY A PROPORTIONATE SYSTEM. Diagram 9

FEATURES:—*Single-breasted; step collar; button three; seam back; moderately high and shaped waist.*

MEASURES:—36" *breast;* 32" *waist*; 38" *seat;* 7" *back width;* 16 1/2" *waist length;* 29" *full length. Scale* 18".

INSTRUCTIONS FOR DRAFTING

THE formula for finding the scale (18") is the same as explained for the vest. The draft can be worked out direct on the cloth by first of all constructing the back section, then cutting it out and laying it in a convenient position.

The back has a seam (1/4") allowed down the centre, so where an inlay is allowed, special instructions should be given to the work-hand to sew a quarter-inch inside the chalk line.

The shape of the front in this draft is not standard and can be varied to button two or only one by lowering the crease line of the lapel.

The breast cut at 32 is optional, but should be included when a close-fitting waist is desired. This particular dart should be sewn in the chalk lines; that at 31, 1/4⊠ inside the line.

SECTION A

Square lines from 0.

1 from 0 = half scale (9⊠);

2 from 0 = waist length, 16 1/2⊠, less the amount the waist is required above the natural.

3 from 2 = 1 to 2 plus 1 1/2⊠;

4 from 0 = full length;

5 from 2 = 3/4⊠: join to 0;

6 from 5 = 3/4⊠;

Curve gradually into 0 5 line;

7 from 4 = 1 1/4⊠;

8 from 0 = one-fourth the distance 0 to 1; square out;

9 from 8 = 2 3/4⊠ in sizes 36 and above;

Below 36 breast 9 is made one-fourth scale plus 1/4⊠ from 0;

10 from the inside line at 9 = back width plus 1/2⊠ for two seams.

11 and 12 are located by squaring from 10 by 9;

13 from 12 = 1/2⊠;

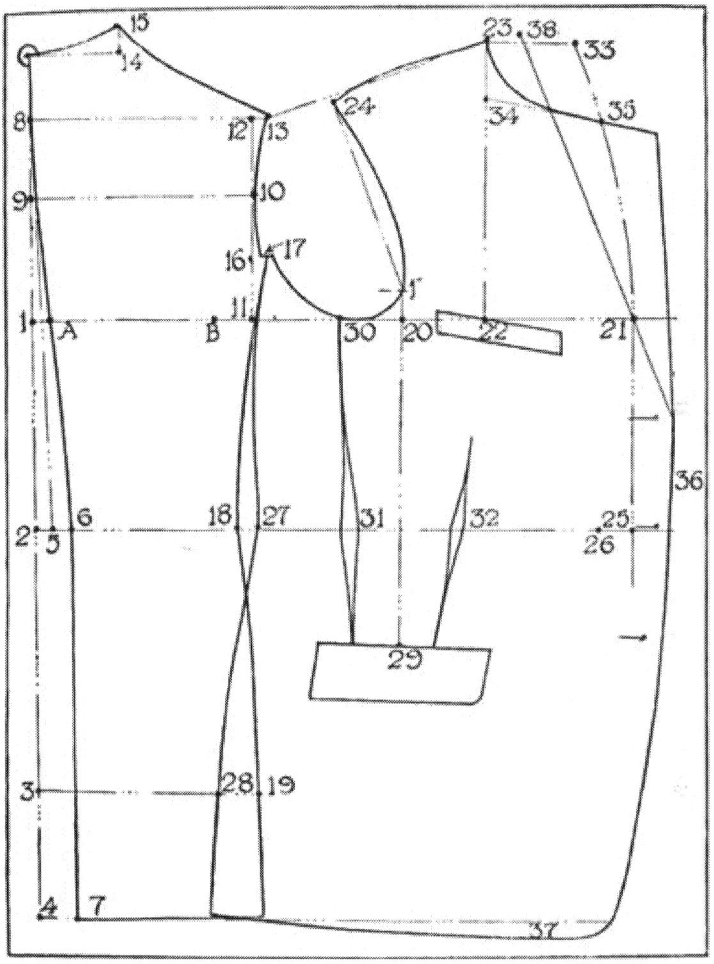

DIAGRAM 9.

This amount can be varied if a wider or narrower shoulder is desired.

14 from 0 = one-sixth scale plus 1/4⊠ (3 1/4⊠);

15 from 14 = 3/4⊠;

Join to 0 for back neck.

16 from 11 = 2⊠;

17 from 16 = 1/2⊠;

Mark a 1/4⊠ each way for seams from this point and shape back scye.

18 from 6 = 1⊠ less than back width (6⊠);

19 from 3 = 2 to 18 plus 1/2⊠;

Shape the side seam from 17 through 18 and down through 19, curving slightly below 18.

B from A = one-third half breast (6⊠);

20 from B = 1/4 half breast plus 2⊠ (6 1/2);

21 from A = half breast plus 2 1/2⊠;

22 from 20 = one-sixth scale;

Square up.

23 from 22 = half scale plus 1/4⊠;

Join 23 to 13;

24 from 23 = 13 to 15 less 1/4⊠;

Drop 1/4⊠ below line;

Mark up 1⊠ from 20 and join to 24;

Shape shoulder, giving a slight curve, and the scye, hollowing 1/2⊠ below 24;

25 is found by squaring down from 21 for sizes where the waist is not less than 3⊠ smaller than the breast.

26 from 6 = half the waist measure plus 2 1/2⊠;

27 from 18 = half the waist surplus shown between points 25 and 26;

28 from 19 = the difference between the half breast and half seat measures plus 1/2⊠ (1 1/2);

Curve forepart side seam through 27 and 28, giving a slight round over the hip.

29 is the centre of pocket and is located by squaring down 11⊠ to 12⊠ from 20.

Make the width of pocket 6 1/4⊠;

30 from 20 = 2 1/4⊠;

Shape the underarm dart to rear end of pocket, suppressing the waist at 31 one-half the waist surplus shown from 25 to 26.

The breast dart runs at a forward incline from the front end of the pocket and for proportionate figures should not be suppressed more than 1/4⊠ at 32.

33 from 23 = one-sixth scale;

Curve down to 21;

34 from 23 = 2⊠;

35 from 33 = one-sixth scale;

Join to 34.

Shape the neck, hollowing to within 1⊠ of 34.

Add 1 1/2⊠ beyond the centre line at 36 and extend the bottom of forepart 3/4⊠ below bottom construction line at 37;

38 for crease line is 1⊠ out from 23;

Draw the crease line to the front edge as shown.

NOTES ON THE DRAFT

In trades that cater for manual workers it may be found advisable to advance point 20 at the front of scye and the neck line at 22 to accommodate the muscular shoulder development in such figures.

For an easier fitting waist section the front dart will be left out and only a proportion of the waist surplus (26 to 25) will be taken out at the underarm dart and side seam.

Point 24 will vary in its position slightly to accord with the amount of wadding introduced and the degree of manipulation that the shoulder will be subject to.

The line 34 to 35 has only to be considered from a point of view of style and can be varied.

D.B. REEFER. BY DIRECT MEASURES. Diagram 10

FEATURES:—*Double-breasted fronts, buttoning two and showing three; moderately high and close-fitting waist; jetted hip pockets; welted outside breast pocket.*

MEASURES:—36″ *breast;* 32″ *waist;* 38″ *seat;* 9″ *scye depth;* 16 1/2″ *waist length;* 28 3/4″; *full length;* 13″ *front shoulder;* 17 3/4″ *over-shoulder;* 8″ *across chest;* 7″ *across back. Scale* 18″.

INSTRUCTIONS FOR DRAFTING

THE application of the direct measures to the ordinary S.B. Lounge will be identical with the procedure explained in this draft. The neck has been lowered to suit the particular style of step and the increased length of lapel. The overlap for the buttons is a variable feature and should be arranged in accordance with the build of the man.

BODY PART. SECTION A

Square lines from 0.

1 from 0 = scye depth (9⊠);

2 from 0 = waist length less, say, 1/2⊠ for the fashionable line.

3 from 2 = 1 to 2 plus 1 1/2⊠;

4 from 0 = full length plus making-up allowance.

5 from 2 = 3/4⊠: join to 0.

6 from 5 = 3/4⊠;

Curve gradually into the above line, above the breast line.

7 from 4 = 1 1/4⊠: complete back seam.

8 from 1 = one-third over-shoulder measure plus 3/4⊠: square out;

9 from 8 = 2 3/4⊠: square out;

10 from inside line at 9 = back width plus 1/2⊠;

Points 11 and 12 are located by squaring by line 9 to 10;

13 from 12 = 1/2⊠ or more if a wider shoulder is desired.

14 from 0 = one-sixth scale plus 1/4⊠ square up;

15 from 14 = 3/4⊠;

Shape to 0 and to 13;

16 is 2⊠ above 11;

17 is 1/2⊠ out from 16 for side seam;

Mark 1/4⊠ each way for seam.

18 from 6 = back width less 1⊠ (6⊠);

19 from 3 = 2 to 18 plus 1/2⊠;

Shape side seam of back as shown through 18 and 19;

20 from A = half breast plus 2 1/2⊠;

21 from 20 = across chest 8⊠;

22 from 21 = one-sixth scale (3⊠); square up.

23 by sweep from 21 = front shoulder measure less back neck 0 to 14;

Apply the over-shoulder measure less 1/2⊠ from A to 24 and then from 21 to 25 by sweeping.

25 is definitely located by applying the width of back shoulder seam (15 to 13) less 1/4⊠ from 23.

Join 25 to 1⊠ up from 21;

Hollow scye 1/2⊠;

26 is squared down from 20;

27 from 6 = half waist plus 2 1/2⊠;

28 from 18 = half the waist surplus shown from 26 to 27.

29 from 19 = half the difference between the breast and seat measures plus 1/2⊠.

30 is 2⊠ from 21 for underarm seam;

Square down to B from 21 for centre of pocket.

Shape underarm dart to rear of pocket, taking out half the waist surplus (26 to 27) at 31;

32 is the breast dart: take out 1/4⊠;

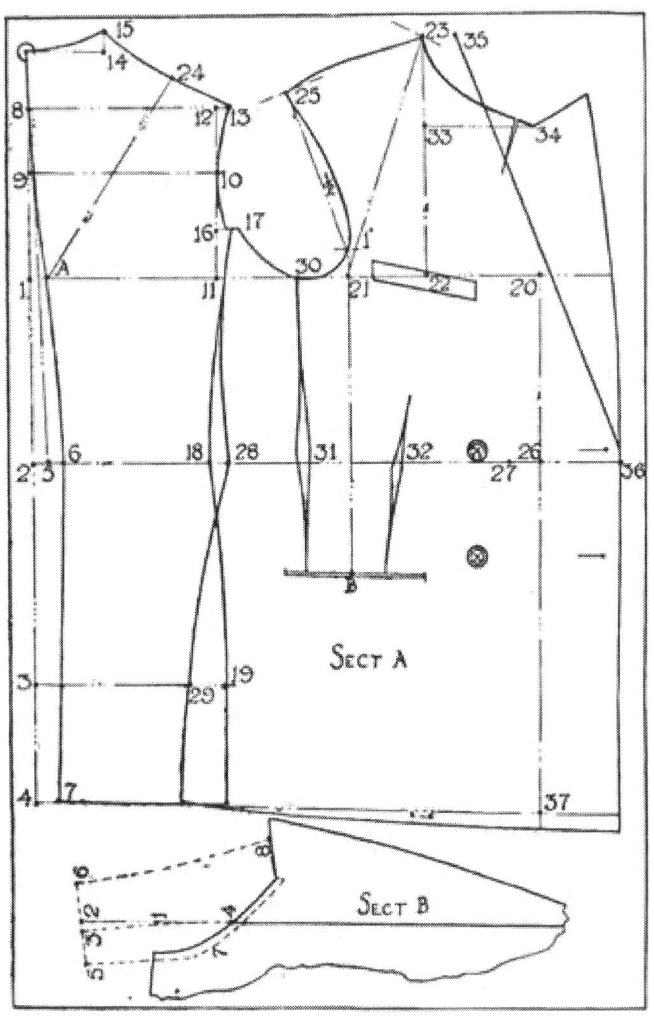

DIAGRAM 10.

33 from 23 = one-sixth scale plus 1/2⊠ (3 1/2⊠);

Square out for end of lapel step at 34.

35 for crease row is 1⊠ out from 23;

Allow 3″ to 4″ from 26 to 36 for the overlap, and shape front as shown.

Extend the bottom of forepart 3/4″ below bottom construction line at 37, and keep a straight run for a distance equal to twice the frontage given (26 to 36).

The vertical spacing of the buttons is arranged so that the lower set comes in line with the pocket. The distance back from the centre line is 3/4″ less than the amount of overlap on the front.

COLLAR CUTTING. SECTION B

The solid line shows the outline of the neck.

Point 35 in the big draft is represented here by point 1.

2 from 1 = 0 to 14 of neck.

3 from 2 = 1/2″ for spring;

Curve to 4.

Using line 3 to 4 as guide, square back of collar 5 and 6.

5 from 3 = 1 1/4″, the "stand";

6 from 3 = 2″, the "fall";

Curve the stand to follow the outline of the neck, allowing 1/4″ as shown at 7.

8 is arranged to agree with the style of step desired.

Where the collar is to be turned in previous to being felled, or where it is sewn on by machine, add 1/4⊠ round the stand: curve 5 to 7.

NOTES ON THE DRAFT

The instructions for giving ease to the scye laid down in the last draft can very well be ignored here, as the across chest should automatically regulate the position of the scye to accord with the build of the figure.

When the measures have been carefully taken, no further adjustment should be required for short or long-necked figures, sloping or square shoulders, or erectness of carriage.

THE SLEEVE DRAFT. Diagram 11

THE sleeve system demonstrated here is based on measurements taken from the scye. Therefore, if there is any variation from the normal shape produced in the drafting of the body part, these changes are automatically transferred to the sleeve draft.

The marking of both the pitches before the garment is sent out to the work-hand and checking up when it is returned is most strongly advised. Indifferent pitching of the sleeves in the workshop is largely responsible for the unsightly fullness at the hindarm of which customers so frequently complain.

POSITION OF THE PITCHES SECTION A

Point 1 in this section depicts the portion of the back pitch. In all sizes 36 breast and above this is located by squaring from point 2, which is 2 3/4⊠ from 3.

Below 36 breast point 2 should be situated half A B plus 1/2⊠ from A.

The front pitch at 4 is located 3/4⊠ above the breast line 5;

7 from 6 on the back line is the same distance as 5 to 4.

THE SLEEVE. SECTION B

Square lines from 0.

1 from 0 = 1 to 7 of scye plus 3/4⊠;

2 direct from 1 = the upper half of the scye as shown by wavy line from 1 to 8 and 9 to 4.

3 is midway between 0 and 2;

4 from 3 = 1 to 8 less 1 1/4⊠

5 is midway between 3 and 0.

Shape the crown of the sleeve from 1 through 5 and 4 and on to 2.

6 is the sleeve length and is found by applying the length measured less the netback width from 2 (31⊠ minus 7⊠).

7 from 6 = 1 1/2⊠; square out;

8 from 7 direct = one-third scale (as for coat) plus 1/2⊠;

9 from 1 = half 1 to 6 less 1/2⊠;

Square out for elbow line.

10 from 9 = 1⊠;

Connect to 6 and 1;

11 from 10 = one-third scale plus 2⊠.

This completes the top side.

For Underside 12 from 1 direct = the lower half of the scye (round the curve) from 1 to 4.

13 from 1 = half 5 to 6, the scye width.

Allow 1/4⊠ at 1 and 12 for seams and curve through 13, sinking 1/4⊠ below the line from 1.

The sleeve drafted in this fashion will allow a reasonable amount of fullness over the crown.

The underpart should be well eased in the region of the wavy line when putting the sleeve into the scye.

THREE-QUARTER SLEEVE SECTION C

This is popularly known as the "false forearm" finish and is introduced to bring the forearm seam well under the arm and out of sight.

Points 1, 5, and 8 would be the track of the seam as shown in the preceding draft.

The underside is curtailed 1⊠ as shown at 2, 6, and 9, 1/4⊠ being allowed from 2 to 3 for the seam.

4 is opposite point 3 and is 1⊠ from 1.

7 from 5 and 10 from 8 are also 1⊠.

Point 10 is slightly higher than 9; this allows for the stretching which is necessary in the region of 7 to get the sleeve to lie over nicely.

SPLIT PIVOT SLEEVE. SECTION D

This is a novel but very useful arrangement which provides a superabundance of ease when the arms are in action, and is chiefly confined to sporting coats, such as are used for shooting and golfing.

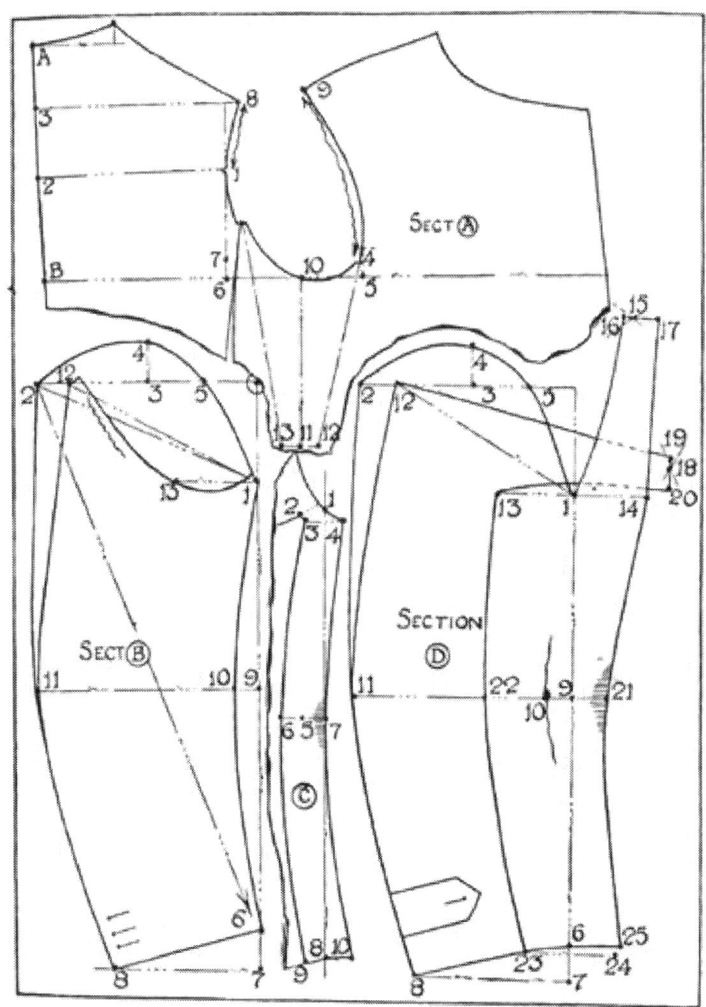

DIAGRAM 11.

Instead of the ordinary shaped underside, a wedge-shaped piece is introduced, to be sewn under the arms and down the side of the coat. The finished appearance is very much like the ordinary sleeve, excepting that a deep pleat is formed in. the underside at back scye.

The outline of the wedge-shaped piece is shown on Section A by dot and dash lines.

This is marked for the guidance of the work-hands, but must not be cut away.

10 from 5 = half 5 to 6 less 1/2⊠;

11 from 10 can be arranged to taste.

12 and 13 are each 1/2⊠ from 11;

Shape as shown.

SLEEVE DRAFT

Points 1 to 11 are located as described in Section B for the ordinary sleeve.

12 from 1 = the lower scye quantity 4, 10 to 1;

13 from 1 = 5 to 10 plus 1/2⊠;

14 from 1 is the same.

To locate point 15 take the distance 4 to 12 and sweep from 1; also the distance from 10 to 11 plus 1/2⊠ and sweep from 14.

16 from 15 = 1/4⊠;

17 from 15 = 11 to 12 plus 1/4⊠;

Join 16 to 1 and 17 to 14.

To locate 18 take the distance 1 to 13 (direct) and sweep from 12; also the distance 10 to 11 plus 1/2″, and sweep from 13.

19 from 18 = 1/4″;

20 from 18 = 11 to 13 plus 1/4″.

21 and 22 are each 2 1/2″ from 10.

23 and 24 are each 2″ from 6.

25 from 24 = 1/2″ to allow for stretching necessary in the region of 21.

When making, 17, 14, 21, and 25 are sewn to 20, 13, 22, and 23.

12 to 19 is turned in and stitched down on 1 to 13 of body part; in a like manner 1 to 16 goes to 4 and 12, on forepart.

DRESS LOUNGE. (SEMI-CORPULENT FIGURE.) Diagram 12

FEATURES:—*Single-breasted; link front; silk-faced lapels; jetted hip and welted outside breast pockets; close hips and shapely waist.*

MEASURES:—40" *breast;* 40" *waist;* 42" *seat;* 9 3/4" *scye depth;* 17 1/4" *waist length;* 29 1/2" *full length;* 13 7/8" *front shoulder;* 18 3/4" *over shoulder;* 8 3/4" *across chest;* 8" *across back. Scale* 19 1/2".

INSTRUCTIONS FOR DRAFTING

THIS draft illustrates how the waist is adjusted for figures slightly above normal. It is essential to have the amount of disproportion in order to regulate the distribution of the excess waist size. This is found by deducting 4⊠ from the breast measure and comparing the result with the actual waist size, viz. 40 B—4 = 36⊠: 36 from 40 W = 4⊠ disproportion.

The change from the ordinary to the dress lounge is very little and consists of reduction at the front overlap.

DRAFT

Square lines from 0.

1 from 0 = scye depth 9 3/4⊠;

2 from 0 = waist length 17 1/4⊠ less 1/2⊠; for the fashion line.

3 from 2 = 2 to 1 plus 1 1/2⊠;

4 from 0 = full length.

5 from 2 = 3/4⊠; join to 0.

6 from 5 = 3/4″: curve into line 5.

7 from 4 = 1 1/4″;

8 from 0 = one-sixth scale plus 1/4″;

9 from 8 = 3/4″: shape to 0.

10 from 1 = one-third over shoulder plus 3/4″:

11 from 10 = 2 3/4″: square out from 10 and 11.

12 from 11 E back width plus 1/2″;

13 and 14 are located by squaring from 12.

15 from 14 = 1/2″: join to 9.

16 from 13 = 2″;

17 from 16 = 1/2″: mark 1/4″ each side for seams.

18 from A = half breast plus 2 1/2″;

19 from 18 = across chest 8 3/4″;

B from 18 = 1/8 disproportion less 1/4″;

Join to 19.

20 from 19 on line to B = one-sixth scale: square up.

21 from 19 = front shoulder measure less back neck 0 to 8.

Apply the over-shoulder measure less 1/2″ from A to C and then from 19 to 22 by a sweep.

22 is definitely located by applying the back shoulder width 9 to 15 less 1/4″ from 21.

Mark up 1″ from 19 and join to 22;

Hollow scye 1/2″ at 23.

24 from 6 = back width less 1″ (7″);

25 from 3 = 2 to 24 plus 1/2″;

26 is squared down from 18.

27 from 26 = one-fourth disproportion less 1/4⊠: join to 18.

28 from 6 = half the waist plus 2⊠

29 from 24 = half 28 to 27;

30 from 25 = half the difference between the breast and hip plus 1/2⊠ (1 1/2⊠).

31 from 19 = 2 1/2⊠;

C is squared down from 19 and is 11⊠ down.

Shape the underarm dart from 31 to rear of pocket, taking out half the waist surplus (28 to 27) at 32.

33 from 21 = one-sixth scale;

34 from 21 = one-sixth scale;

Curve to B.

Shape the lapel as shown from 21 on to line 23.

Add 3/4⊠ beyond the centre line at 27 for the front edge and shape as shown to the bottom. Give 3/4⊠ below the bottom construction line at 35 and complete.

NOTES ON THE DRAFT

There are some figures which are very flat in the back waist and seat region. This will necessitate a slight adjustment in the distribution of the waist increment, a little more being placed at the front waist 27 and less at the side.

For the popular barrel effect the pattern can be pleated over at M (dot and dash lines) before being placed on the material. This will have the effect of opening the dart at 31. The space exposed will then be cut away in the material.

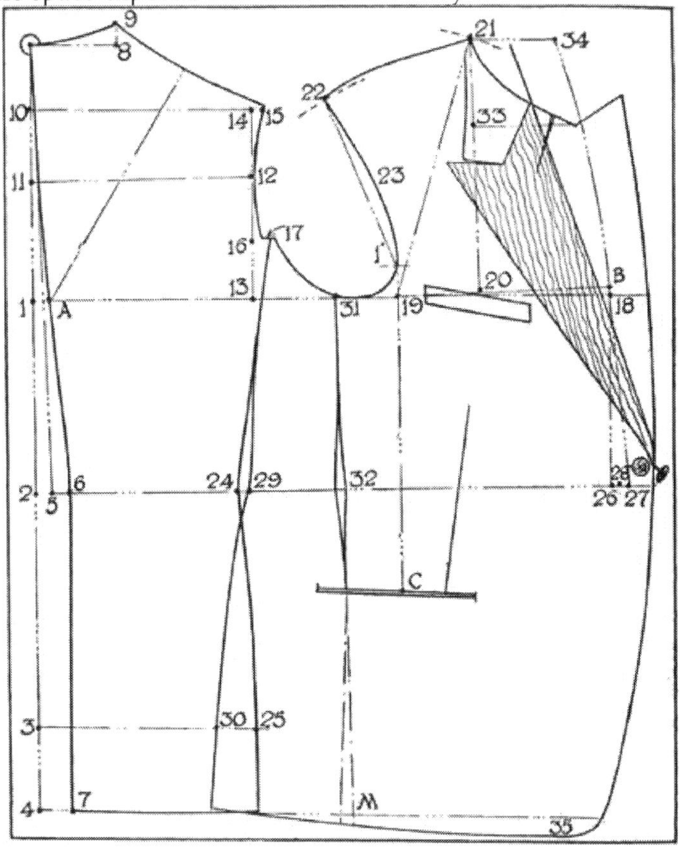

DIAGRAM 12.

MORNING COAT. Diagram 13

FEATURES:—*Button one; pointed lapel; close waist; high and straight waist seam. Cut-away skirt.*

MEASURES.—36" *breast;* 32" *waist;* 38" *seat;* 9" *scye depth;* 16 1/2" *waist length;* 38 1/2" *full length;* 13" *front shoulder;* 17 3/4" *over shoulder;* 7" *across back;* 8" *across chest. Scale* 18".

INSTRUCTIONS FOR DRAFTING

THE scale for body-coats is found in the same way as for lounges.

The system shown for the construction of the draft is the Direct Measure one, but where the additional measures are not available, the proportionate arrangement, given previously, can be used.

The length of the waist between points 2 and 3 can be varied in accordance with the prevailing fashion.

The ordinary S.B. step collar can be used in place of the pointed one shown; also the fronts may carry two or three buttons.

DRAFT

Square lines from 0.

1 from 0 = scye depth 9⊠;

2 from 0 = waist length 16 1/2⊠;

3 from 2 = 1⊠ or to taste;

4 from 0 = full length 38 1/2⊠;;

5 from 2 = 1 1/4⊠: connect to 0.

6 is squared down from 5.

7 from 0 = one-sixth scale plus 1/4⊠;

8 from 7 = 3/4⊠: shape to 0.

Mark out 1/2⊠ at 3 and square down for vent.

9 from 1 = one-third over shoulder plus 3/4⊠: square out.

10 from 9 = 2 3/4⊠: square out.

11 from the inside line at 10 = back width plus 1/2⊠;

12 and 13 are squared from 11;

14 from 13 = 1/2⊠;

Connect to 8 for shoulder seam.

15 from 5 = one-ninth scale (2⊠), but this can be made slightly larger where heavy tweeds are used.

Join 11 to 2 and shape the blade seam, giving 1⊠ of round at 16.

Square down from 15 to B.

17 from A = half breast plus 2 1/2⊠

18 from 17 = across chest 8⊠;

19 from 18 = one-sixth scale (3⊠) square up.

Sweep the front shoulder measure less back neck (0 to 7) from 18 to 20;

Deduct 1/2⊠ from the over-shoulder measure and apply from A to 21, then from 18 to 22, by a sweep.

22 is definitely located by applying the width of back shoulder 8 to 14, less 1/4⊠ from 20 to 22.

Mark up 1⊠ from 18 and join to 22.

Hollow the scye 1/2⊠ in front of the construction line.

23 is squared down from 17;

24 from 5 = half waist plus 2⊠;

25 from 15 = two-thirds the waist surplus shown from 24 to 23.

26 is 1 1/2⊠ from 12: go up 1 1/4⊠ for summit of underarm seam and mark a seam's width on either side.

27 from 25 = 16 to 26 less 3/4⊠;

28 from 27 = one-third the waist surplus (24 to 23).

When shaping the underarm seam give a little spring.

Using 11 as a pivot, sweep from B to C;

From C square out the lower waist line to 29 (parallel with line 5 to 23).

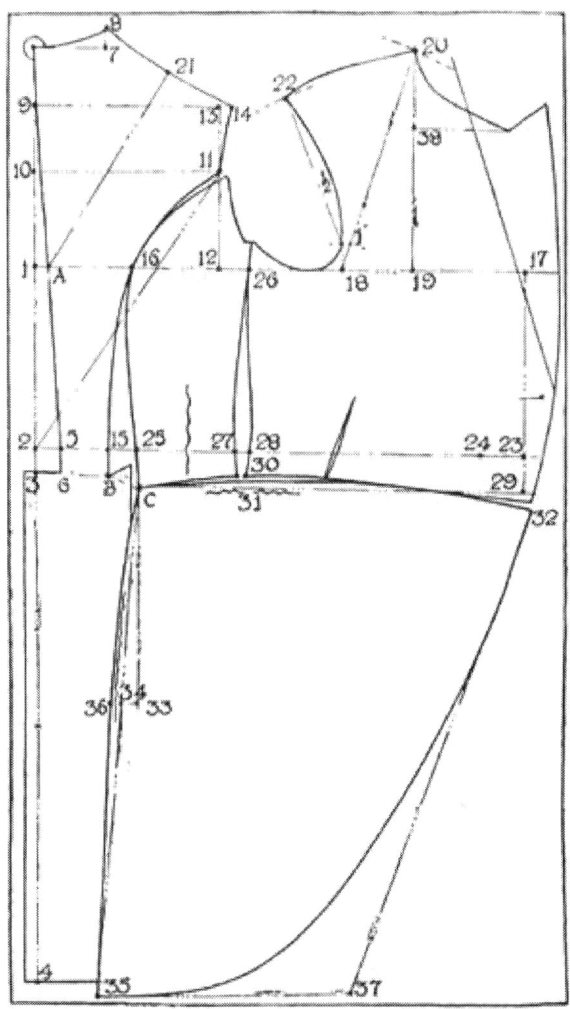

DIAGRAM 13.

Curve the waist seam of the body part from C up to 30 (1/2⊠ above the line) and down 1/2⊠ below 29 at the front.

Add 1 1/2⊠ beyond the centre line at the button hole.

When shaping the waist seam of skirt, take out 1/4⊠ between 30 and 31, and open a similar quantity at 32.

33 from C = 9⊠; squared by line C–29.

34 from 33 = 1⊠; the difference between the half seat and breast measures.

35 is 1/2⊠ below line from 4 and is located by drawing through 34 from C.

Give 1/2⊠ of round at 36 when shaping back skirt from C to 35.

37 from 35 = half 5 to 23 plus 1⊠.

Join 32 to 37 and curve front of skirt as shown.

38 from 20 = one-sixth scale: square out from depth of gorge. Mark out 1⊠ from 20 for crease line.

Take a small dart out at the waist directly below point 18. Add 1⊠ for pleat as shown at B and continue down to the bottom (parallel with line 3 to 4).

NOTES ON THE DRAFT

The distance 2 to 5 remains constant whatever the waist size.

For prominent blades the suppression at 15 to 25 should be increased and the underarm filled in a corresponding amount at 27.

In disproportionate waists the fronts are adjusted at 23 as in the lounge draft.

The sleeve is the same as for the lounge, point 11 representing the back pitch.

1 1/4⊠ should be added at C to 35 when marking out on the material to form the upper half of the pleat.

When making, the side body should be strained with the iron in the waist at 27 and 25 and shrunk in the centre as shown by wavy line.

The skirt is drawn in with a thread at 31 and 36, and the resulting fullness pressed back over the hip prominence.

DRESS COAT BY DIRECT MEASURES.
Diagram 14

FEATURES:—*High and straight waist seam; three buttons; revers moderately wide and rolling to second button.*

MEASURES:—36″ *breast;* 32″ *waist;* 38″ *seat;* 9″ *scye depth;* 16 1/2″ *waist length;* 39″ *full length;* 13″ *front shoulder;* 17 3/4″ *over shoulder;* 7″ *back width;* 8″ *across chest. Scale* 18″.

INSTRUCTIONS FOR DRAFTING

THE rear section of this draft is practically the same as that for the morning coat. The fronts are curtailed at the waist to expose the white vest when the garment is in wear. If the figure is at all full-chested, a cut or dart should be taken out up the button line and an allowance made at the front. This dart can be used to advantage in keeping the lower edge of the fronts nice and snug to the figure for stout men.

The sleeve is the same as for a lounge, with slightly narrower elbow and cuff.

DRAFT

Square lines from 0.

1 from 0 = scye depth (9);

2 from 0 = waist length (16 1/2);

3 from 2 = 3/4⊠;

4 from 0 = full length;

Square out from all points.

5 from 0 = one-sixth scale plus 1/4⊠

6 from 5 = 3/4⊠;

Shape to 0;

7 from 2 = 1 1/4⊠;

Square down to 8 and connect to 0.

9 from 1 = one-third over-shoulder measure, plus 3/4⊠;

10 from 9 = 2 3/4⊠; square out.

11 from the inside line at 10 = back width plus 1/2⊠ (7 1/2).

12 and 13 are located by squaring from 11.

14 from 13 = 1/2☒;

Join to 11 and shape shoulder seam to 6.

Join 11 and 2.

15 from 1 = one-ninth scale (2☒).

Shape blade seam giving 1☒ of round at 16.

17 from A = half breast plus 2 1/2☒;

18 from 17 = across chest 8☒;

19 from 18 = one-sixth scale (3);

Sweep the front shoulder measure less 0 to 8 from 18 to locate 20 on line up from 19.

Deduct 1/2☒ from the over-shoulder measure and apply the remainder from A to 21 and from 18 to 22 by a sweep.

22 is definitely located by applying the back shoulder width 6 to 14 less 1/4☒ from 20.

Mark up 1☒ from 18 and hollow scye 1/2☒.

24 from 17 = 3/4☒;

25 is located by squaring down from 24;

26 from 7 = half waist plus 1☒ (17);

27 from 15 = two-thirds 25 to 26;

28 from 12 = 1 1/2☒;

29 from 27 = 3/4☒ less than 16 to 28;

30 from 29 = one-third 25 to 26.

Mark up 1 1/4☒ above 28 for top of under-arm seam and shape to waist.

31 from 25 = 4 1/2☒;

32 from 31 = 1☒.

B and C are found as in the morningcoat draft.

Curve the waist seam from 32 to 33 which is 1/2″ above C line.

The skirt seam at 34 is only 1/4″ above C line.

Shape the front from 32 up to 35, which is 1″ above the waist line and 3/4″ out from the centre line.

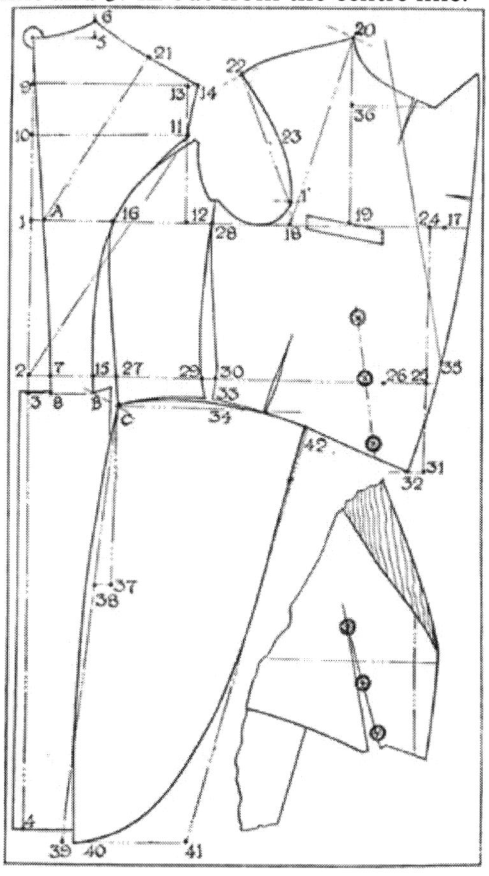

DIAGRAM 14.

36 from 20 is one-sixth scale;

Square out and shape lapel as shown.

The crease line for lapel is 1⊠ out from 20.

37 from C is 9⊠ squared by the waist line.

38 from 37 = the difference between half breast and half hip, viz. 1⊠.

Draw through 38 from C and extend 1/2⊠ below bottom line to 39.

40 is 1/2⊠ from 39;

Curve back skirt giving 1/2⊠ round at 38.

41 from 40 = one-eighth waist measure.

42 from 32 = one-third the forepart line from 32 to C.

Connect 42 and 41 and shape skirt as shown.

NOTES ON THE DRAFT

The manipulation for this coat is the same as prescribed for the morning coat.

A beneficial effect is obtained by working a round on the crease row of the lapel. This will require an extremely short outer edge in the lapel, and to obtain this either one or two small vees may be taken out as shown in the draft.

The small diagram depicts the dart through the buttons explained above. The amount taken out depends upon the figure.

D.B. FROCK COAT BY PROPORTION.
Diagram 15

FEATURES:—*Button two, showing three; pointed lapels; silk facing; moderately high waist seam.*

MEASURES:—36" *breast;* 32" *waist;* 38" *seat;* 16 1/2" *waist length;* 40" *full length;* 7" *half back. Scale* 18".

INSTRUCTIONS FOR DRAFTING

THIS garment, whilst not being very popular at the present time with the ordinary layman, forms the livery dress for most Nonconformist ministers. With a slight readjustment of the rever and in the number of buttons, it is also used as a general livery coat for servants employed by public bodies, banks, etc.

Compared with the morning coat, the skirt is cut much fuller in order to provide walking room. The hollowed waist seam to the skirt is responsible for the distribution of this extra width at the sides, but if this is overdone it will cause the back pleats and the fronts to gape open when the coat is being worn.

The lapel is cut separately and the front end laid to the fold of the material so that the facing is left on and a seam avoided down the edge.

DRAFT

Square lines from 0.

1 from 0 = half scale (9);

2 from 0 = waist length 16 1/2⊠;

3 from 2 = 1⊠;

4 from 0 = full length 40;

Square out from the above points.

5 from 2 = 1 1/4⊠;

6 is squared down from 5.

7 from 0 = one-sixth scale plus 1/4⊠;

8 from 7 = 3/4⊠;

9 from 0 = one-fourth 0 to 1;

10 from 9 = 2 3/4⊠;

11 from the inside line at 10 = back width plus 1/2⊠.

12 and 13 are located by squaring from 11.

14 from 13 = 1/2⊠;

Join to 8 for shoulder seam.

Connect points 11 and 22.

15 from 5 = one-ninth scale (2);

Curve blade seam, giving 1⊠ of round at 16 and continuing down from 15 to B.

17 from A = half-breast plus 2 1/2⊠.

E from A = one-third half breast (6⊠).

18 from E = one-fourth half breast plus 2⊠ (6 1/2);

19 from 18 = one-sixth scale;

Square up.

20 from 19 = half scale plus 1/4⊠;

Connect 20 and 14.

21 from 20 = 8 to 14, the back shoulder, less 1/4⊠

Drop 1/4⊠;

22 from 18 = 1⊠;

Join to 21 and shape scye as shown, hollowing 1/2⊠.

23 is squared down from 17.

24 from 5 = half waist plus 2⊠;

25 from 15 = two-thirds waist surplus, 23 to 24;

26 is 1 1/4⊠ from 12;

27 from 25 = 16 to 26 less 3/4⊠;

28 from 27 = one-third waist surplus, 23 to 24.

For the summit of the underarm seam mark up 1 1/4⊠ from 26 and allow a seam on either side. Using 11 as a pivot, sweep B to C.

Square out from C.

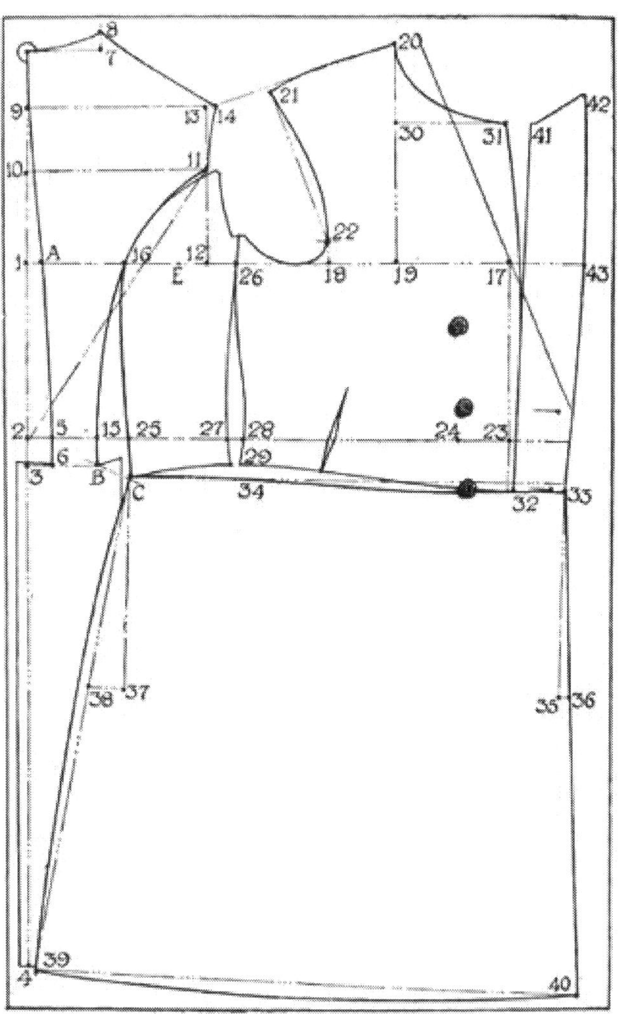

DIAGRAM 15.

Raise waist seam of body part 3/4⊠ above C line.

30 from 20 = one-sixth scale plus 1/4⊠;

31 from 30 = 5⊠ in this draft, but can be varied to suit lapel.

From 31 run lapel seam down to 32, allowing 1/4⊠ at 17 and 23.

32 is located 1/2⊠ down from C line.

33 is 2 1/2⊠ out from 32.

Shape waist seam of skirt passing through C line at 34.

35 is 8 1/2⊠ squared down from 33.

36 from 35 = 1/2⊠;

Draw through from 33.

37 is 9⊠ from C.

38 from 37 is 1/2⊠ more than half the difference between seat and breast measures.

Draw through 38 from C and down to 39.

39 from C = 1/4⊠ more than 3 to 4.

40 from 33 is 1/4⊠ more than C to 39.

41 from 31 = 1 1/4⊠ curve to the body part below 17. This quantity should be reduced when a shorter rever is required.

42 from 41 = 2 1/2⊠.

Make the width of lapel at 43, 3⊠.

Finish the draft by giving 3/4⊠ of round to the skirt from 39 to 40.

NOTES ON THE DRAFT

Provision for increased waist size is made on the lines prescribed for the morning coat.

No seam has been allowed down the skirt front, the facings being left "growing-on," when taking from the material.

When the waist is above normal, it is a wise policy to check up the width of top of skirt with the side-body and forepart and allow 3/4⊠ for easing-on in the region of 34.

BACK FINISHES FOR SPORTS COATS.
Diagram 16

THE fronts of Sports Coats, apart from the substitution of patches in place of the ordinary flaps, remain very much on the lines of the ordinary lounge. With the back section, however, it is different, for many features both ornamental and useful have been introduced from time to time to charm the younger generation.

The selection given here comprises the more modern ones that a cutter may be called upon to produce.

In each instance the back section is cut in the ordinary way, as for a lounge, and the adjustments made when marking out on the material, or, better still, when constructing a new back pattern.

SECTION A

This depicts one of the plainer finishes, frequently used in plus four suits.

Two pleats in the waist on either side of the centre may be used, or two small darts sewn out to produce a shapely waist effect.

The ordinary pattern is outlined by dot and dash lines.

4 from 3 is the amount allowed for pleat or dart at 1, and 5 to 6 for that at 2.

From 4 connect to the back neck at 7 and to the bottom of the coat.

From 6 run up to the breast line at 8 and down to the bottom of skirt.

SECTION B

This is rather a novel finish with a pleat extending from the shoulder seam to the waist.

A small strap emanating from the side seam covers the necessary seam at the waist.

2 is about 1 3/4⊠ from shoulder end.

1 is 3/4⊠ from the side seam.

Cut the back up the pleat line 1 and 2 and open out 3″ for the pleat allowance to 3 and 4.

Allow 1/2″ at 3 to 5 for seam.

In pleating line 4 and 3 falls under 1 and 2.

SECTION C

This depicts the short "knife pleat" at the side seam which is frequently used in shooting coats.

1 is 3″ above the waist.

2 is at the back pitch point.

Cut the pattern up the pleat line 1 to 2 and open out 2 1/4″ from 2 to 3 and 1 1/4″ from 1 to 4.

SECTION D

Here is a very ornamental finish with shoulder yoke and waist pleats.

The back is cut across on the waist line and allowance made at 3 to 4 and 5 to 6 for the three vertical pleats.

The yoke curves from 1″ to 1/2″ above the pitch at 2.

The centre section is extended 1″ to 2″ for gathering as shown.

Seams must be allowed on each side of the yoke and waist seams when marking out on the material.

A half belt usually covers the waist seam.

SECTION E

This is one of the standard back finishes and one that has been used universally for all purposes.

A straight shoulder yoke runs across 1/2⊠ above the back pitch level, and the waist is cut across.

A "knife pleat" is introduced over the blade on line 1 to 2.

The shaded lines between 2 and 3 and 1 and 4 show the extent of the pleat (3⊠).

This is allowed for by extending the back from 7 to 8 and 5 to 6.

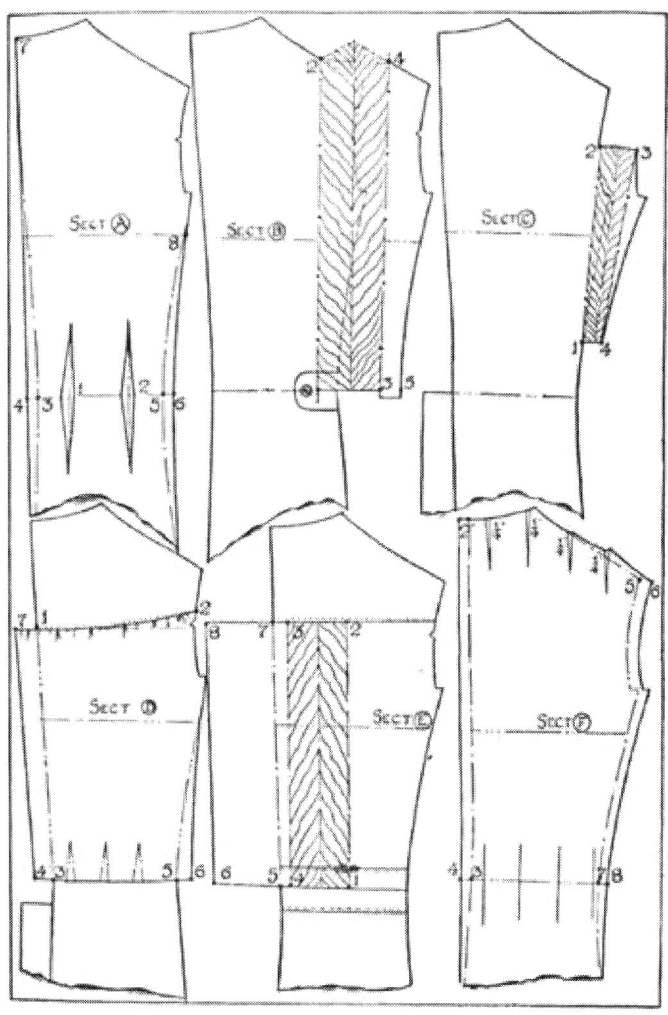

DIAGRAM 16.

When the pleat is formed line 1 to 2 will be under line 3 to 4. Allow seams at yoke and waist.

SECTION F

This depicts one of the latest varieties which has as its chief virtue the distribution of extra width over the whole blade region.

Featured in a golf or shooting coat it gives a very pleasing effect.

The outline of the ordinary back is shown by dash lines.

The back is cut without a centre seam and four pin tucks or seams are run down from the neck and shoulder on either side. The same number of tucks are run through the waist.

To provide for these the centre back is extended 1/2⊠ at 1 to 2 and 3 to 4, and the back scye side seam a similar quantity from 5 to 6 and 7 to 8.

CUTTING OF OVERGARMENTS

S.B. CHESTERFIELD BY PROPORTION.
Diagram 17

FEATURES:—*Single-breasted; close-fitting waist; centre seam and vent; pointed lapel; to button three.*

MEASURES:—36″ *breast;* 32″ *waist;* 38″ *seat;* 7 3/8″ *back width;* 16 1/2″ *waist length;* 40″ *full length.*

INSTRUCTIONS FOR DRAFTING

IT must be understood that all measures are taken as for the lounge coat, that is, the breast and waist are taken over the vest and the remainder over the jacket. The ordinary back width would be 7⊠; the measure given above has 3/8⊠ added to it for the overgarment.

The scale is found by taking one-third breast plus 6⊠, viz. one-third of 36 = 12 plus 6 = 18 scale. Below 36 breast half the measure gives the scale.

The fronts as shown are intended to be made to button through, but if a fly finish is preferred, the same method of drafting can be adhered to.

BODY PART. SECTION A

Square lines from 0.

1 from 0 = half scale (9);

2 from 0 = waist length plus 1/4⊠;

3 from 2 = 2 to 1 plus 1 1/2†;

4 from 0 = full length plus making-up allowance.

5 from 2 = 3/4⊠: 6 from 5 is the same.

Join 5 to 0 and curve gradually into 6 from the blades.

7 from 4 = 1 1/4⊠: join to 6;

8 from 0 = one-sixth scale plus 3/8⊠;

9 from 8 = 3/4⊠: join to 0;

10 from 0 = 1/4th 0 to 1: square out;

11 from 10 = 2 3/4⊠: square out;

12 from the inner line at 11 = back width plus 1/2⊠ (7 7/8);

13 and 14 are located by squaring from 12;

15 from 14 = 1/2⊠: join to 9 for shoulder;

16 from 13 = 1 1/2⊠;

17 from 16 = 3/4⊠: mark a seam each way;

18 from 6 = width of back less 1⊠ (6 3/8);

19 from 3 = 2 to 18 plus 1/2⊠;

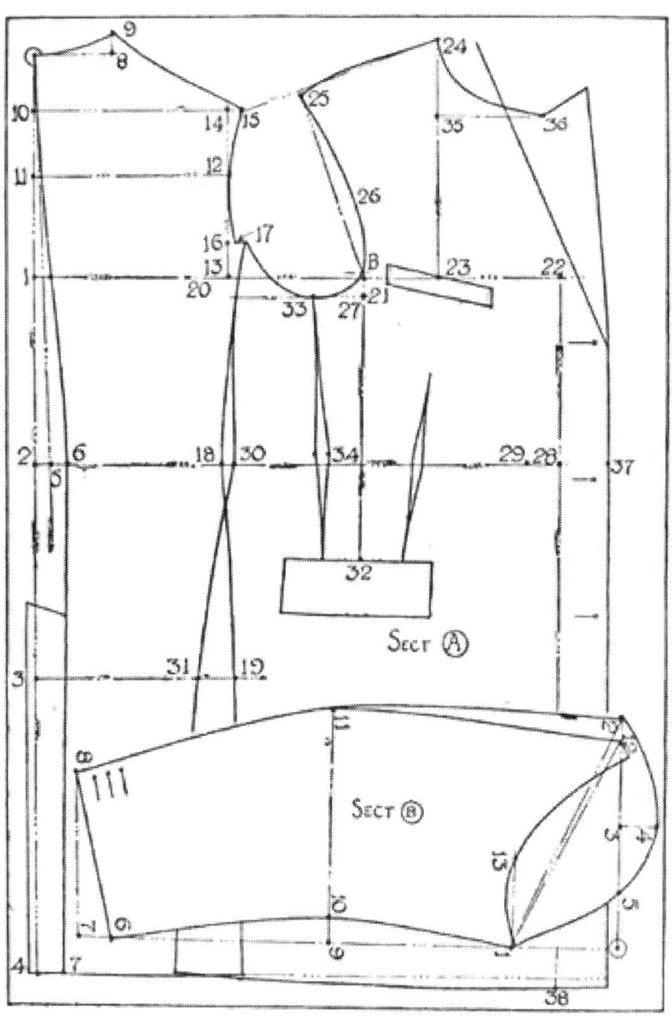

DIAGRAM 17.

Shape side seam from 17 through 18 and 19.

20 from A = one-third of half breast (6);

21 from 20 = one-fourth of half breast plus 2 3/4⊠ (7 1/4);

22 from A = half breast plus 3 3/4⊠ (21 3/4);

23 from 21 = one-sixth scale plus 1/4⊠;

24 from 23 = half scale plus 1/2⊠;

Join 24 and 15.

25 from 24 = 9 to 15 less 1/4⊠: drop 1/4⊠ below the line;

B from 21 = 1/4⊠: join to 25 and hollow scye 1/2⊠ at 26.

27 is 3/4⊠ down from 21 for scye base: complete scye as shown.

28 is squared down from 23.

29 from 6 = half waist plus 3 3/4⊠;

30 from 29 = half 28 to 29, the waist surplus;

31 from 19 = half the difference between the breast and seat measures plus 1/2⊠.

Shape fore part side seam as shown from 17 through 30 and 31.

32 for centre of pocket is 11 1/2⊠ down from 21: make pocket 6 1/2⊠ wide.

33 from 27 = 2 1/2⊠

Shape the dart to rear of pocket, suppressing at the waist 34, half the waist surplus, 28 to 29.

The breast dart running from front end of pocket towards the breast is suppressed 1/4⊠.

35 from 24 = one-sixth scale plus 1/4″;

Square out.

Shape neck, letting the collar end come at 36 on line from 35.

37 from 28 = 2″ for button stand.

Drop foreparts 3/4″ at 38.

The crease line commences at 1 1/4″ out from 24.

THE SLEEVE. SECTION B

Length of lounge sleeve = 31″;

Back width 7 3/8″.

The preliminary preparation on the body part for the location of the pitches is similar to what was laid down for lounges. The back pitch being placed at 12 and the front one 3/4″ above 27 (at 21).

Square lines from 0.

1 from 0 = 12 to 13 plus 3/4″;

2 direct from 1 = 12 to 15 plus 25 to 21;

3 is midway between 0 and 2;

4 from 3 = 12 to 15 less 1 1/4″;

5 is midway between 0 and 3;

Shape crown through 5, 4, and on to 2;

6 from 2 direct = sleeve length less back width plus 1″ for overcoat (31 minus 7 3/8 plus 1″);

7 from 6 = 1 1/2″;

8 from 7 = one-third scale plus 1 1/4⊠;

9 from 1 = half 1 to 6 less 1/2⊠;

10 from 9 = 1⊠;

Curve forearm to 1 and 6;

11 from 10 = one-third scale plus 2 3/4⊠;

Shape hindarm seam to 2 and 8;

12 from 1 direct = 12 to 21, round lower half of scye;

13 from 1 = half 13 to 21, the width of scye.

Shape undersleeve, dropping 1/4⊠ below line 1 and 13.

NOTES ON THE DRAFT

If an easier-fitting waist is required, the front dart can be omitted, and, in heavy materials, the underarm dart also.

Where a full skirt is desired, and at the same time a shaped waist, extend point 31 a further 1/2⊠ to 1⊠.

No wadding has been provided for in the shoulders. Where it is essential that the shoulders should be built up raise the scye end at 25 and allow a little on the sleeve crown at 4.

A wider or narrower shoulder effect should be regulated after the completion of the ordinary draft. This will automatically increase or decrease the height of the shoulder ends to agree with the position of the scye seam on the body.

SAC CHESTERFIELD. BY DIRECT MEASURES. Diagram 18

FEATURES:—*Single-breasted; step lapel; loose-fitting, with draped back; patch or slit pockets; seam and vent in back.*

MEASURES:—36" *breast;* 32" *waist;* 9" *scye depth;* 16 1/2" *waist length;* 40" *full length;* 13 3/8 *front shoulder;* 17 3/4" *over shoulder;* 8 3/8" *across chest;* 7 3/8" *across back. Scale* 18".

INSTRUCTIONS FOR DRAFTING

THE above direct measures are taken as for the lounge coat and carry the following additions for the overgarment:—Front shoulder 3/8⊠; across chest 3/8⊠; back width 3/8⊠.

If the draft is required by proportion the system laid down for the Close-fitting Chesterfield can be used, without alteration to width and height quantities.

If the back is required without a centre seam, the material for the back should be cut out on the large size, then shrunk over the blade to the shape of the pattern.

The sleeve for this coat will be drafted as described for the ordinary Chesterfield, but due attention must be paid to the overlap at the side seam (25 to 27) when measuring round the scye for the undersleeve.

DRAFT

Square lines from 0.

1 from 0 = scye depth (9⊠);

2 from 0 = waist length plus 1/4⊠;

3 from 0 = full length (40⊠);

4 from 1 = one-third over-shoulder measure plus 3/4⊠: square out.

5 from 4 = 2 3/4⊠: square out;

6 from 2 = 3/4⊠;

To locate 7, draw through 6 starting at point 5.

Round the back centre gradually from A to 0.

8 from 0 = one-sixth scale plus 3/8⊠;

9 from 8 = 3/4⊠: join to 0;

10 from the inner line at 5 = back width plus 1/2⊠ (7 7/8);

11 and 12 are located by squaring from 10;

13 from 12 = 1/2⊠: join to 9 for shoulder seam;

14 from A = half breast plus 3 3/4⊠. (21 3/4⊠);

15 from 14 = across chest measure 8 3/8⊠;

16 from 15 = one-sixth scale plus 1/4⊠: square up.

Apply the front shoulder measure less 0 to 8 from 15 by sweep to 17.

Apply the over-shoulder measure less 1/2⊠ from A to 18 and then by sweep from 15 to 19.

19 is definitely located by applying the back shoulder width 9 to 13 less 1/4⊠ from 17.

20 is 1/4⊠ above 15: join to 19.

Hollow scye 1/2⊠ at 21.

22 from 15 = 3/4⊠ for scye base;

Square across.

23 from 11 = one-third the scye width 11 to 15.

24 is located by squaring down from 23.

25 is 1/4⊠ out from line 23 and is situated midway between the breast line and the base of scye.

26 from 24 = 1 1/4⊠: draw through from 25;

27 from 23 line = 1/2⊠ and is in line with point 25;

28 from 24 = 1 1/4⊠: draw through from 27;

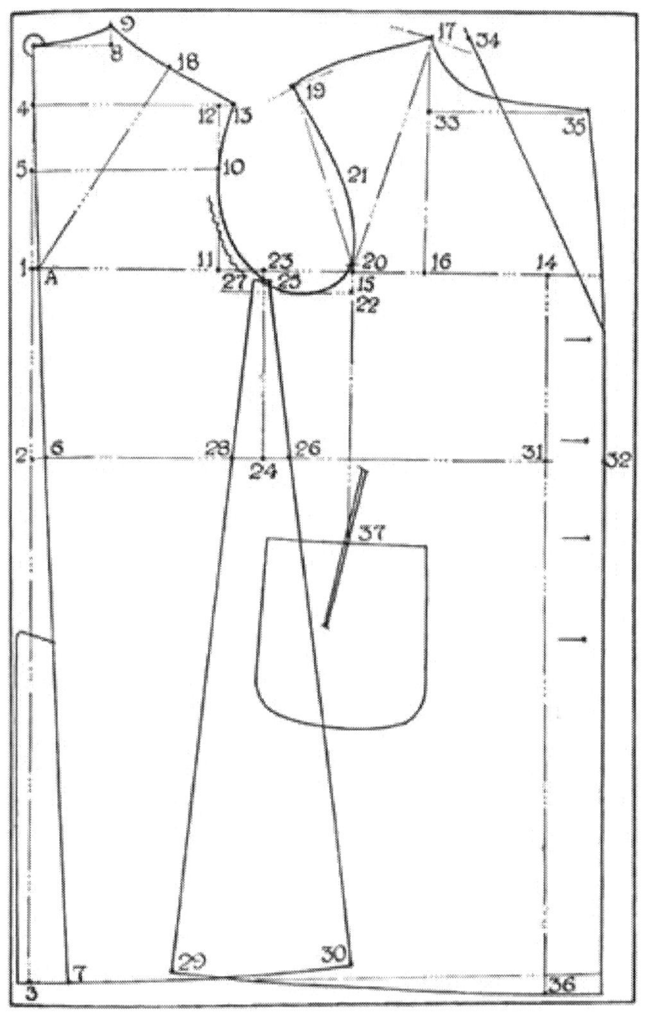

DIAGRAM 18.

29 from 23 = A to 7;

30 from 23 is the same.

31 is squared down from 14.

32 from 31 = 2☒ for front edge.

33 from 17 = one-sixth scale (3☒);

Square out.

34 for crease line is 1 1/4☒ out from 17.

35 is on line from 33 and forms the guiding point for the shape of the neck. The distance out from crease line depends on the width of lapel required.

Extend the bottom of forepart 3/4☒ below the bottom construction line at 36 and join to 29.

Join 7 to 30 for base of back-part.

The centre of pocket at 37 is found by squaring 11 1/2☒ down from 15.

NOTES ON THE DRAFT

In order to ensure a well-draped back scye, the back must either be drawn in well or shrunk in the region of the wavy line.

The amount of skirt given in the draft will be found suitable for average purposes, but if more is desired, points 27 and 28 should be extended further from line 23–24.

There is no fixed position for the vent, the depth being regulated to accord with the prevailing fashion, but for a safe guide, at the present time one-third the full length plus 2☒ up from the bottom should be sufficient.

PLEATED BACK CHESTERFIELD. Diagram 19

FEATURES:—*Double-breasted, buttoning two; centre seam with box pleat from waist; side pleats; half belt.*

MEASURES:—36" *breast;* 32" *waist;* 38" *seat;* 9" *scye depth;* 16 1/2" *waist length;* 40" *full length;* 13 3/8" *front shoulder;* 17 3/4" *over shoulder;* 7 3/8" *across back;* 8 3/8" *across chest. Scale* 18".

INSTRUCTIONS FOR DRAFTING

WITH the ordinary back as given with the close-fitting style, this draft can be used for a semi-fitting model.

The allowance for the quantity taken up in the knife pleat under the belt is allowed on either side of the ordinary back outline.

Additions have already been made to the Direct Measures to allow for the overgarment. (See Sac Chesterfield draft.)

DRAFT

Square lines from 0.

1 from 0 = scye depth (9⊠);

2 from 0 = waist length plus 1/4⊠

3 from 2 = 1 to 2 plus 1 1/2⊠

4 from 0 = full length (40⊠);

5 from 2 = 3/4⊠: join to 0.

6 from 5 = 3/4⊠: curve gradually into the above line.

7 is squared down from 5 by waist line and forms the centre back line.

8 from 0 = one-sixth scale plus 3/8⊠;

9 from 8 = 3/4⊠: connect to 0 for back neck;

10 from 1 = one-third the over-shoulder measure, plus 3/8⊠: square out;

11 from 10 = 2 3/4⊠: square out;

12 from 11 (inner line) = back width plus 1/2⊠;

13 and 14 are located by squaring up and down from 12;

15 from 14 = 1/2⊠: join to 9 for shoulder seam;

16 from 13 = 1 1/4⊠: square out;

17 from 16 for top of side seam = 1⊠;

Mark a seam on either side.

18 from 6 = back width less 1⊠ (6 3/8⊠);

19 from 18 = two-thirds of the amount taken up by the pleat, 1 1/2⊠: the remaining third for pleat is given at 6 to 5;

20 from 3 = 2 to 18 plus 1/2⊠;

21 from 20 = 18 to 19;

Shape side seam of back through 19 and 21;

22 from A = half breast plus 3 3/4⊠;

23 from 22 = across chest 8 3/8⊠;

24 from 23 = one-sixth scale, plus 1/4⊠.

Sweep the front shoulder measure, less back neck (0 to 8) from 23 to 25.

Deduct 1/2⊠ from the over-shoulder measure and apply the remainder from A to 26 and then by sweep from 23 to 27.

27 is definitely located by applying the back shoulder width, 9 to 15, less 1/4⊠ from 25.

28 is 1/4⊠ above 23;

Join to 27 and hollow 1/2⊠;;

29 is 3/4⊠ down from 23;

Square across for base of scye;

30 is squared down from 22;

31 from 6 = half waist plus 3 3/4⊠;

32 from 18 = half the waist surplus shown from 30 to 31;

33 from 20 = half the difference between the breast and seat measures plus 1/2⊠;

Shape side seam from 17.

34 for centre of pocket is 11 1/2″ down from 23;

35 is 2 1/2″ from 29;

Shape underarm dart to a point 1/2″ in the rear of pocket and suppress the waist half the waist surplus (30 to 31) at 36;

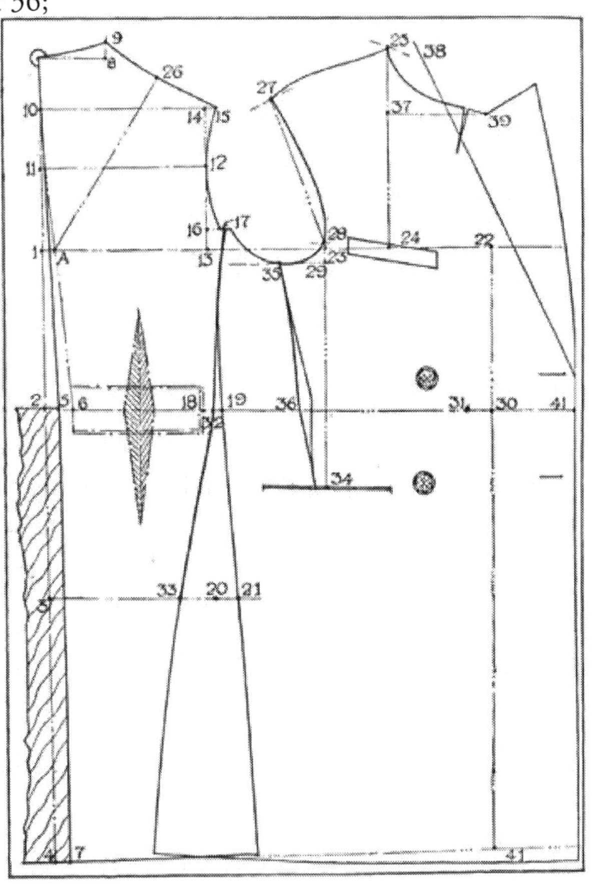

DIAGRAM 19.

37 from 25 = one-sixth scale plus 1/4⊠: square out.

38 from 25 for crease line is 1 1/4⊠;

41 from 30 = 4⊠ to 4 1/2⊠ for the front overlap.

Arrange the position of first button-hole 1 1/2⊠ above the waist and draw crease row from 38.

39 is squared out from 37.

Shape neck as shown and take a small vee out.

Give 3/4⊠ below bottom construction line at 41 and complete draft.

NOTES ON THE DRAFT

The length of the half belt is shown on the draft and extends the width of normal back from 6 to 18.

When the material is thick and clumsy the dart at 35 can be run out a little below the breast line. This would have the effect of giving ease in the scye region.

The allowance for the back pleat from 5 should be not less than 4⊠ and not less than 6⊠ at the base from 7.

RAGLAN OVERCOAT. Diagram 20

FEATURES:—*Single-breasted; pointed lapel; very loose-fitting; draped back scye; three-piece sleeve.*

MEASURES:—36" *breast;* 32" *waist;* 16 1/2" *waist length;* 40" *full length;* 7 3/8" *back width. Scale* 18".

INSTRUCTIONS FOR DRAFTING

THIS draft is based on the Proportionate System, but where Direct Measures have been taken they can be applied as laid down in previous drafts.

The Raglan effect in the body part is obtained by cutting away the shoulder section of the ordinary sac coat. The amount of curve given to the diagonal seams is purely a matter of taste, but care must be taken to see that they enter the scye at the back and front sleeve pitches.

BODY PART. SECTION A

Square lines from 0.
1 from 0 = half scale;
2 from 0 = waist length plus 1/4⊠;
3 from 0 = full length;
4 from 0 = one-fourth 0 to 1;

5 from 4 = 2 3/4⊠;

6 from 2 = 3/4⊠;

Draw through 6 from 5, thus locating 7 on bottom line;

8 from 5 = back width plus 1/2⊠;

10 and 9 are located by squaring up and down from 8;

11 from 10 = 1/2⊠;

12 from 0 = one-sixth scale plus 3/8⊠;

13 from 12 = 3/4⊠: join to 0;

14 from A = one-third of half breast (6⊠);

15 from 14 = one-fourth half breast plus 2 3/4⊠;

16 from A = half breast plus 3 3/4⊠;

17 from 15 = one-sixth scale plus 1/4⊠: square up;

18 from 17 = half scale plus 1/2⊠;

Join to 11;

19 from 18 = 1/4⊠ less than 11 to 13;

20 is 1/4⊠ above 15;

21 from 15 is 1⊠ down;

Square across for base of scye;

22 is midway between 9 and 15, but can be varied to suit the laying-out on the material.

B is squared from 22;

23 from 22 = 1/4⊠;

24 from 22 = 1/2⊠;

25 and 26 are each 1 1/4⊠ out from B.

Draw through 26 from 23 and 25 from 24;

C and D are located on the base line from 21;

27 from 18 = one-sixth scale plus 1/4⊠;

Square out and shape lapel.

ADJUSTMENT FOR RAGLAN EFFECT

28 from 18 = 1/2⊠;

Join to 15 by a graceful curve;

29 from 8 = 1/4⊠: curve from 13 through this point and into scye at W;

W is 1 1/2⊠ down from 8;

The front pitch of the sleeve is located on the breast line.

SLEEVE. SECTION B

Square lines from 0.

1 from 0 = 8 to 9 plus 3/4⊠;

2 from 1 direct = 8 to 11 plus 19 to 15;

3 from 0 = 8 to 11 less 1 1/4⊠;

Square out;

5 from 1 direct = 15 to 19 less 1/4⊠;

6 from 2 direct = 8 to 11 plus 1 1/4⊠;

4 is on line from 1 and from 2 = the amount 8 to 29.

Take the distance on the straight line from 15 to 28 and sweep this from 1 to 7.

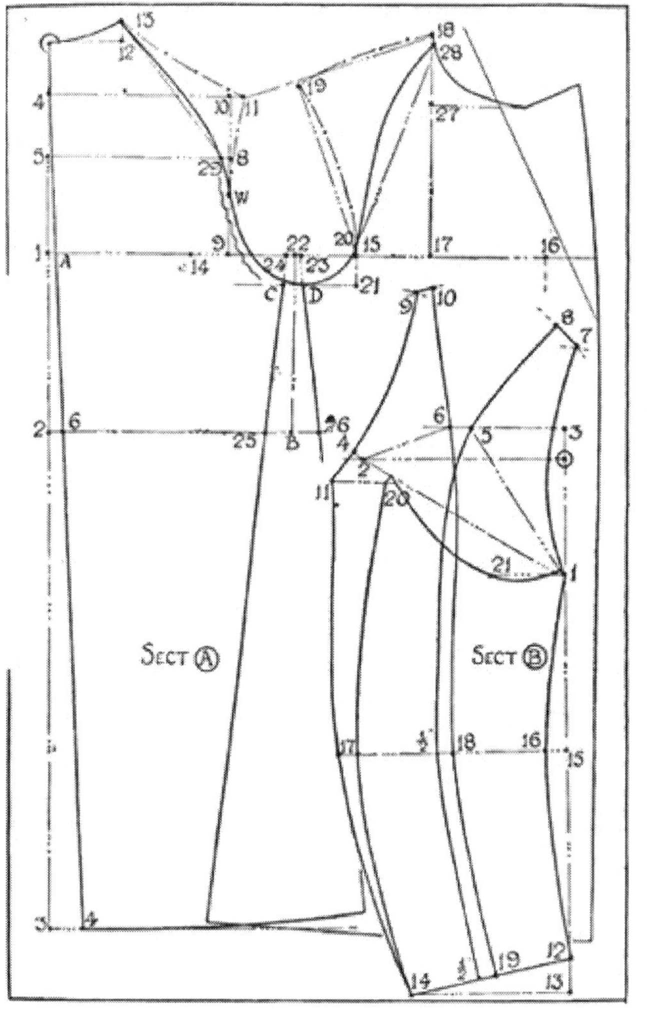

DIAGRAM 20.

Take the distance 29 to 13 and sweep this from 4 towards 9.

Take the distance 13 to 11, less 1/4⊠, and sweep from 5 definitely to locate 7.

Using the same quantity (11 to 13 minus 1/4) sweep from 6 to locate point 9.

7 to 8 on sweep from 5 = 1⊠, comprising 1/2⊠ for seams and 1/2⊠ lost at 18 to 28;

9 to 10 on sweep from 5 = 1/2⊠ for two seams.

Curve from 7 to 1 to compare with 28 to 15.

Curve from 9 to 4 to compare with 13 to 29 and continue down to 11, 1 1/2⊠ or the amount the pitch has been dropped from 29 to W.

12 from 2 = the sleeve length less back width (7 3/8) and plus 1⊠ for the overgarment.

13 from 12 = 1 1/2⊠: square out;

14 from 12 = one-third scale plus 1 1/2⊠;

15 from 1 = half 1 to 12 less 1/2⊠;

16 from 15 = 1⊠;

17 from 16 = one-third scale plus 3 1/4⊠;

18 from 16 = half the distance to 17 less 1/4⊠;

19 from 12 = half the distance to 14 less 1/4⊠;

Curve back half of sleeve from 10 through 5, 18, and 19.

Curve the front part of the sleeve from 8 through 5 and on to the bottom, allowing 1/2⊠ for seams beyond 18 and 19.

21 from 1 = half the width of scye (9 to 15) plus 1/2⊠;

20 direct from 1 = W to D plus C to 15, the lower half of the scye;

Shape the undersleeve coming inside point 17, 3/4⊠.

NOTES ON THE DRAFT

No adjustment must be made to the sleeve draft to accommodate irregularities in form or attitude. These must be embodied in the coat draft before the sleeve is constructed.

This sleeve is arranged to give a natural shoulder-width effect, but if a fuller and wider top part is desired, this can be obtained by overlapping the centre a little more below points 5 and 6.

The back should be drawn in, in the region of the wavy line at back scye.

VARIETIES OF RAGLAN SLEEVES. Diagram 21

THIS diagram demonstrates how the one and two-piece Raglan sleeves are constructed. The former is used mostly for slip-on coats in rainproof materials and requires very careful treatment in order to procure a graceful hang.

The two-piece is a much more elegant sleeve and can be used for almost any purpose.

The ordinary sac coat is drafted as for the three-piece sleeve and the scye deepened.

BODY PART. SECTION A

For a Prussian collar finish the neck is carried forward 1/2″ as shown from A to B. This adjustment is also essential in coats that are cut extremely deep in the scye.

B to C = one-sixth scale plus 1/4″;

D from C = one-sixth scale plus 1/2″;

Curve neck as shown.

The buttonhole side extends 1″ beyond the centre line to E and the button side 2″ to F.

Points 1 up to 7 remain as in the previous draft.

8 from 3 = half 3 to 9 less 1/2″.

Shape the scye, dropping 2″ or more below the breast line at 10 and 11.

TWO-PIECE SLEEVE. SECTION B

Square lines from 0.

1 from 0 = 1 to 9 of scye plus 1/2″;

2 from 1 direct = 1 to 6 and 3 to 17;

3 from 0 = 1 to 6 less 1 1/2″;

4 from 1 = 3 to 17 less 1/4″;

5 from 2 = 1 to 6 plus 1 1/4″;

Take the distance on the straight line from 3 to 5 and sweep this from 1 to 6.

Take the distance 2 to 1 and sweep this from 2 to 7.

Take the distance 2 to 6 less 1/4⊠ and sweep this from 4 to locate definitely point 6 of sleeve.

Using the same quantity sweep from 5 to locate definitely point 7.

6 to 8 on sweep = 1⊠;

7 to 9 = 1/2⊠;

10 from 1 = half the distance 8 to 11;

11 from 10 squared out = 6⊠ always;

12 from 11 = 1/4⊠: draw through 10;

13 from 1 = 3 to 10 of scye;

14 from 2 = 1 round to 11 of scye.

15 is midway between 13 and 14;

16 is squared down from 15 and from 2 = the sleeve length less back width.

Square out on either side of 16.

17 and 18 are one-third scale plus 1/2⊠ from 16 for width of cuff.

When shaping from 17 to 18, give a little round between 16 and 18 and hollow above line 16 to 17.

Shape back part of sleeve from 9 through 5 and down to 16.

Shape front part from 8 through 4 and down to 16, overlapping 3/4⊠ at 15 and 1/2⊠ at the cuff.

Curve 6 to 1 to agree with forepart shoulder and continue down to 13.

Join 7 and 2 and continue down to 14.

ONE-PIECE SLEEVE. SECTION B

(Dot and dash lines.)

This sleeve below points 1 and 14 is the same as the two-piece, excepting, of course, that there is no centre seam.

To form the single horn of the sleeve, take the distance 3 to 5, add 3/4″ for fullness and sweep from 1 towards A.

Take the distance 1 to 2, add 3/4″ and sweep from 2 towards A.

A is definitely located where the two sweeps above intersect.

Mark out 1/2″ on either side of A as shown at B and C.

Connect B to 2 and C to 1.

The lower part of the sleeve continues from 1 to 13 and 2 to 14. The sleeve fullness is introduced in the region of the wavy line.

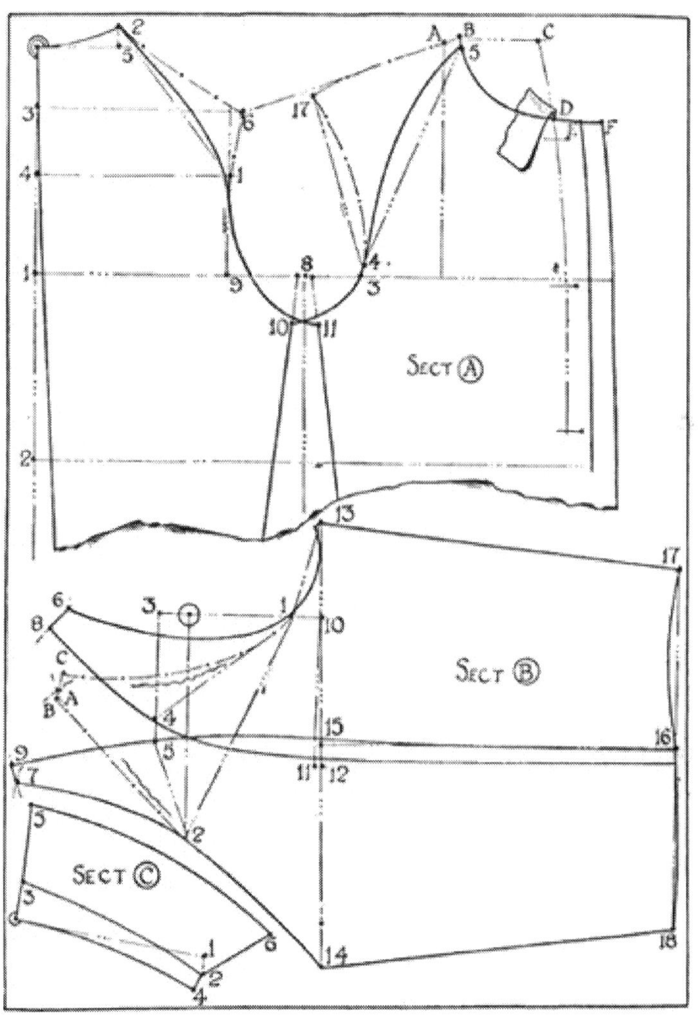

DIAGRAM 21.

PRUSSIAN COLLAR. SECTION C

Square lines from 0.

1 from 0 = 0 to 2 and B round to D less 1/2⊠.

2 from 1 = 3/4⊠;

3 from 0 = 1 1/2⊠, the "stand";

4 from 2 = 3/4⊠;

5 from 0 = 3 1/2⊠;

Shape the front end of collar, making the distance from 2 to 6, 1/2⊠ more than the back.

SPLIT-SLEEVED CHESTERFIELD. Diagram 22

FEATURES:—*Single-breasted; loose-fitting; single-breasted lapel; slit pockets; three-piece sleeve.*

MEASURES:—36" *breast;* 32" *waist;* 38" *seat;* 7 3/8" *back width;* 16 1/2" *waist length;* 40" *full length. Scale* 18".

INSTRUCTIONS FOR DRAFTING

IN order to connect with the centre seam of the sleeve, the shoulder seam is moved to the summit of the shoulder.

This entails an addition of 1⊠ on the back part and a corresponding reduction at the forepart shoulder end.

The underarm seam of body part can be moved nearer the centre of the scye, if it will help when taking the pattern from the material.

The sleeve heads of these coats are usually stitched over, so an inlay will be required round the sleeve crown.

BODY PART. SECTION A

Square lines from 0.
1 from 0 = half scale (9);
2 from 0 = waist length (16 1/2);
3 from 0 = one-fourth 0 to 1;
4 from 3 = 2 3/4⊠;
5 from 2 = 3/4⊠;
Draw through from 4 and curve back up to 0;
6 from 0 = one-sixth scale plus 3/8⊠ (3 3/8);
7 from 6 = 3/4⊠;
8 from 4 = back width plus 1/2⊠;
9 and 10 are found by squaring from 8;
11 from 10 = 1/2⊠;
Join to 7;
12 from A = one-third of half breast measure;
13 from 12 = one-fourth of half breast plus 2 3/4⊠;
14 from A = half breast plus 3 3/4⊠;

15 from 13 = one-sixth scale plus 1/4″;

16 from 15 = half scale plus 1/2″;

Connect 16 and 11.

17 from 16 = 7 to 11 less 1/4″;

Mark up 1/4″ from 13 and join to 17;

18 is 1″ from 13;

19 from 9 = one-third the distance across scye from 9 to 13.

20 is squared down from 19.

21 and 22 are each 1 1/4″ from 20.

23 is 1/4″ from line 19.

24 is 1/2″ from line 19.

Shape scye and side seam as shown.

B is squared down from 14.

C is one-sixth scale plus 1/4″ from 16: square out.

Add 2″ on the front beyond B line.

26 is found by continuing the back scye 1″ above 11;

Join to 7.

25 is 1″ down from 17.

T is 3/4″ above 18.

W is 1 1/2″ below 8.

The top of pocket is 9″ down from 13.

THE SLEEVE. SECTION B

Square lines from 0.

1 from 0 = 8 to 9 plus 3/4⊠;

2 direct from 1 = 8 to 26 plus 25 to T;

3 from 0 = 1 1/4⊠ less than 8 to 11: square out;

Take the distance from T to 25 plus 3/4⊠ and apply from 1 to locate point 4 on top line;

Take the distance 8 to 26 plus 1/2⊠ and apply from 2 to 5;

Connect 1 to 4, giving 1⊠ of round and 5 to 2, giving 1/2⊠ of round;

Continue the sleeve crown 1 1/2⊠ from 2 to 6;

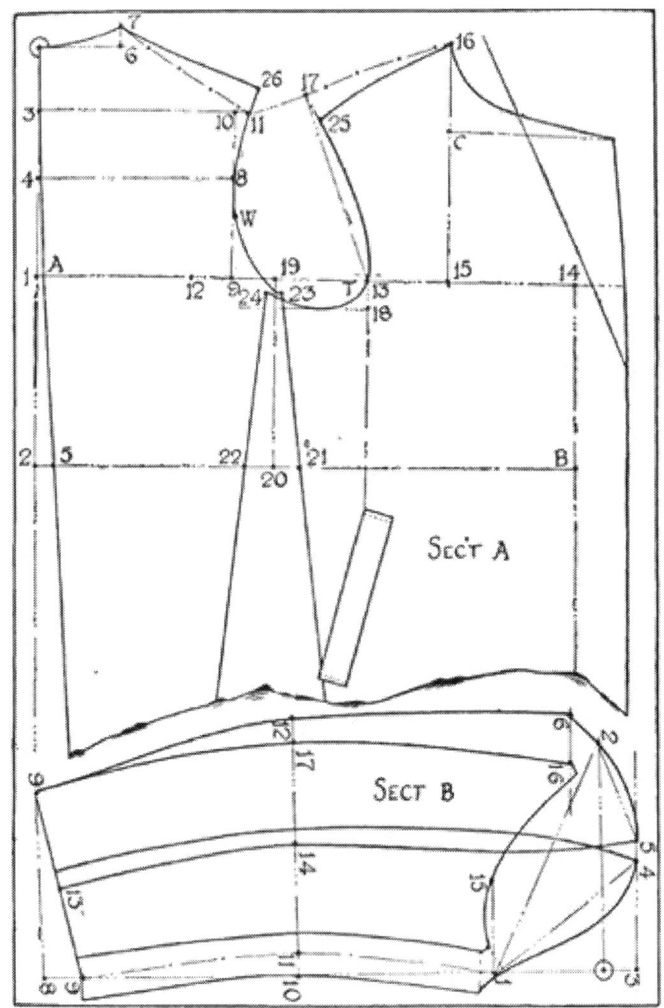

DIAGRAM 22.

7 from 2 direct is the sleeve length plus 1″ and less the back width 7 3/8;

8 from 7 = 1 1/2″: square out;

9 from 7 = one-third scale plus 1 1/4⊠;

10 from 1 = half 1 to 7 less 1/2⊠;

Square out;

11 from 10 = 1⊠;

12 from 10 = one-third scale plus 3 1/4⊠;

13 from 7 = half 7 to 9 less 1/4⊠;

14 from 11 = half 11 to 12;

15 from 1 = half scye width 9 to 13 plus 1/2⊠;

16 from 1 direct = W to 23 plus 24 to T;

17 from 12 = 3/4⊠.

Complete draft by joining 5, 14, and 13, and allowing 1/2⊠ for seams when drawing from 4 to cuff.

Alter for false fore-arm as described in article on Sleeve Construction.

NOTES ON THE DRAFT

When sewing in the sleeve, see that the hindarm seam at 6 joins back scye at W.

The back scye requires nicely drawing-in, in order to obtain a straight and clean hang to the skirt at the sides.

CUTTING FOR CORPULENT FIGURES

LOUNGE JACKET. Diagram 23

FEATURES:—*Single-breasted; button two; pointed lapels; close-fitting waist; centre seam; no vent.*

MEASURES:—48″ *breast;* 52″ *waist;* 51″ *seat;* 11″ *scye depth;* 18 1/4″ *waist length;* 31″ *full length;* 16″ *front shoulder;* 22″ *over shoulder;* 10 1/4″ *across chest;* 9″ *across back. Scale* 22″.

FORMULA FOR ASCERTAINING AMOUNT OF DISPROPORTION

IN order to distribute correctly the waist increment in the draft, it is essential to know the amount of disproportion; in other words, the amount the waist is above the proportionate size. This is found as follows:—Deduct 4⊠ from the measured breast to find the proportionate waist; compare the result with the actual waist measured on the figure and the difference will register the amount of disproportion, i.e. 48 breast less 4⊠ = 44 P.W. 52 actual waist minus 44 P.W. gives 8⊠ disproportion.

INSTRUCTIONS FOR DRAFTING

No alteration is required in the method of finding the scale for corpulent figures. Apart from the slight alteration shown at 20 to 22, no change is necessary in drafting by the proportionate system previously described.

The "belly cut" described in the instructions below should not be included for any figure that does not show a waist measure larger than the breast size.

BODY PART. SECTION A

Disproportion 8⊠.
Square lines from 0.
1 from 0 = scye depth 11⊠;
2 from 0 = waist length 18 1/4⊠;
3 from 2 = 1 to 2 plus 1 1/2⊠;
4 from 0 = full length;
5 from 2 = 1/2⊠: join to 0;
6 from 5 = 1/2⊠;
Curve gradually to line 5;
7 from 4 = 6 from 2;

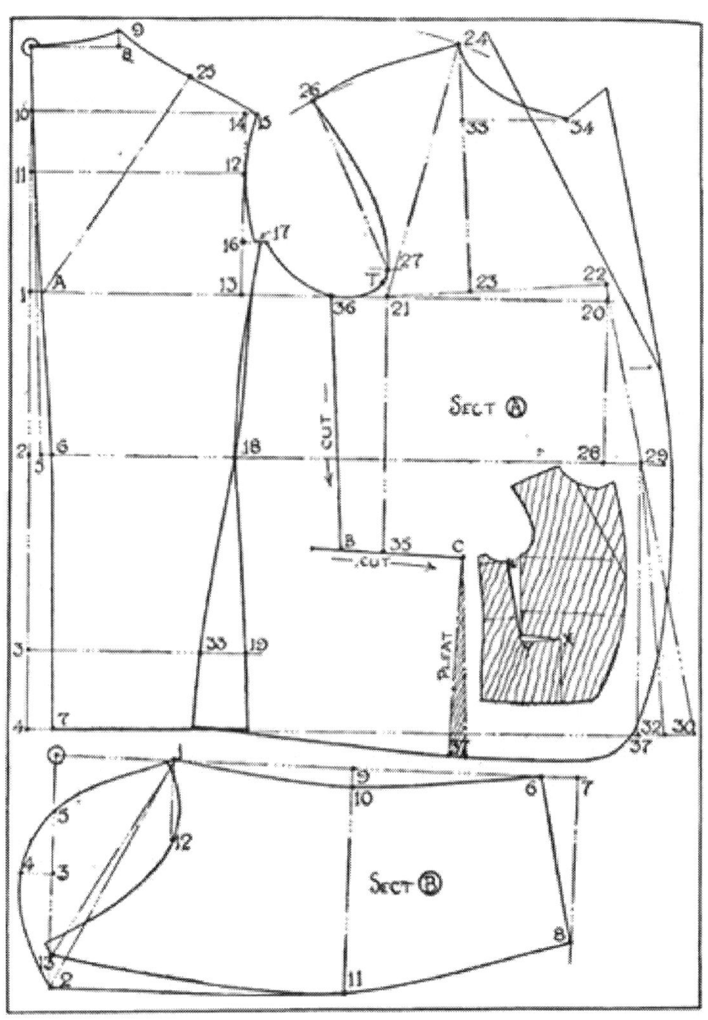

DIAGRAM 23.

Join to 6;

8 from 0 = one-sixth scale plus 1/4☒;

9 from 8 = 3/4☒; join to 0;

10 from 1 = one-third over-shoulder measure plus 3/4⊠;

11 from 10 = 2 3/4⊠: square out;

12 from the inside line at 11 = back width plus 1/2⊠;

13 and 14 are located by squaring up and down from 12.

15 from 14 = 1/2⊠;

Join to 9 for shoulder seam;

16 from 13 = 2 1/4⊠: square out;

17 from 16 = 3/4⊠;

Mark a seam on either side;

18 from 6 = width of back (9) less 1⊠;

19 from 3 = 2 to 18 plus 1/2⊠;

Shape side seam of back (from 17) as shown;

20 from A = half breast plus 2 1/2⊠ (26 1/2);

21 from 20 = across chest (10 1/4);

22 from 20 = one-eighth disproportion less 1/4⊠ (3/4): join to 21;

23 from 21 = one-sixth scale;

Square up by line 21–22.

24 from 21 = front shoulder measure less 0 to 8.

Apply the over-shoulder measure less 1/2⊠ from A to 25 and then by sweep from 21 to 26.

26 is definitely located by applying the back shoulder width 9 to 15 less 1/4⊠ from 24.

27 from 21 = 1⊠;

Join to 26 and shape scye as shown.

28 is squared down by breast line from 20.

29 from 28 = 1/4 disproportion less 1/4″ (1 3/4).

Draw through 29 from 22, thus locating 30 on base line.

37 is squared down from 29.

32 is midway between 30 and 31;

Join to 29 for centre line.

Apply half the waist measure plus 2″ from 6 towards front. In this instance it falls on 29, so there is no waist surplus.

33 from 19 = half the difference between the breast and seat measures plus 1/2″.

Seeing that there is no waist surplus the side seam of forepart will run through point 18.

33 from 24 = one-sixth scale;

Square out;

34 is on line 33;

Shape neck as shown.

Add 1 1/2″ button stand and complete front.

36 from 21 = 2 1/2;

35 is 11 1/2″ from 21 for centre of pocket;

Draw a straight line from 36 to rear of pocket centre at B.

Square down from front end of pocket for pleat line 37.

The amount taken out in the pleat at 37 = 37 to 32 less 1/4⊠.

Before laying pattern on the cloth cut on line 36 to B, then along pocket mouth to C.

Pleat the bottom over as shown by shaded lines.

The effect of this operation is shown in the shaded inset diagram, which depicts the pattern as it would be laid on the material. The space at W and Y is cut away.

When the cuts at W and Y are sewn up, a receptacle is formed for the prominence of the figure at X.

THE SLEEVE. SECTION B

Square lines from 0.

1 from 0 = 12 to 13 of scye;

2 from 1 = 12 to 15 plus 26 to T;

3 is midway between 0 and 2;

4 from 3 = 12 to 15 less 1 1/4⊠;

5 is midway between 0 and 3;

Shape crown.

6 is the length less back width from 2;

7 from 6 = 1 1/2⊠;

8 from 6 = one-third scale plus 1/2⊠;

9 and 10 are found as before.

11 from 10 = one-third scale plus 2⊠;

12 from 1 = half scye width 13 to 21;

13 from T = lower scye (12 round to T).

NOTES ON THE DRAFT

In the case of a D.B. front, the overlap allowed on the front should follow line 22–29 and 32.

In larger waists the application of the measure on the waist line may go beyond the centre front at 29, thus showing a deficiency. When this occurs, the deficiency must be made up by overlapping the side seam of forepart over back at 18 and not by extending the fronts. Common sense must be used in arranging the back waist suppression at 5 and 6.

S.B. VEST BY DIRECT MEASURES. Diagram 24

FEATURES:—*Single-breasted; no collar; medium opening.*

MEASURES:—42" *breast;* 44" *waist;* 10" *scye depth;* 17 5/8" *waist length;* 14" *front shoulder;* 19 1/2" *over shoulder;* 8 1/2" *across chest;* 13" *opening;* 28 3/4" *full length. Scale* 20". *Disproportion* 6".

INSTRUCTIONS FOR DRAFTING

THE front shoulder is 1/4⊠ and the across chest 1/2⊠ less than the measures as taken for the lounge jacket.

Disproportion and scale quantities are found as described in the lounge draft.

Provision for the figure prominence is arranged by the introduction of a horizontal dart running across the lower end of the pocket.

Dress and D.B. vests are cut on the same lines, the front overlap being based on line 21 to 26.

DRAFT

Square lines from 0.

1 from 0 = scye depth, 10⊠;

2 from 0 = waist length 17 5/8⊠;

3 from 2 = 1/2⊠: join to o;

4 from 3 = 1/2⊠: curve gradually into the above line as shown;

5 from 0 = one-sixth scale plus 1/4⊠;

6 from 5 = 3/4⊠;

Join to 0 for back neck;

7 from 1 = one-third over-shoulder measure plus 3/4⊠: square out;

8 from 7 = one-third scale plus 1 3/4⊠;

9 is located by squaring down from 8;

10 from A = one-fourth breast plus 1⊠;

11 from A = half breast plus 1 1/2⊠;

12 from 11 = across chest, 8 1/2⊠;

13 from 11 = one-eighth disproportion less 1/2⊠;

14 from 12 = one-sixth scale;

Square upwards by line 12 to 13;

15 from 12 = the front shoulder measure less 0 to 5;

Apply the over-shoulder measure less 1/2⊠ from A to 16; then from 12 to 17 by sweep.

17 is located definitely by applying the back shoulder width (6 to 8) less 1/4⊠ from point 15.

18 is 1 1/2⊠ above 12;

19 is 3/4⊠ from 18: join to 17;

Hollow scye 1/2⊠ and curve round to 8;

20 is squared down from 11;

21 is one-fourth disproportion less 1/4⊠ from 20;

22 from 15 = one-sixth scale;

Curve down to 11;

23 from 15 = opening measure plus 1/2⊠, but less 0 to 5;

24 from 15 = full length plus 3/4⊠, but less 0 to 5;

25 is squared down from waist line.

26 is midway between 24 and 25.

Starting at 3/4⊠ out from 15, shape the front edge, giving 3/4⊠ beyond centre line 11–21–26.

Square down from 10;

Curve side seam of forepart slightly as shown.

C from 4 = half waist plus 1 1/2⊠.

In this instance the waist is deficient to the extent shown from 21 to C.

28 from 27 for the side seam of back = 21 to C.

29 from 27 = 2 1/2⊠ for side length.

30 from 29 = two-thirds 20 to 21 and forms the allowance for the pocket vee.

The amount taken out of the vee above 27 is 1/2⊠ less than 29 to 30. 31 from 28 = 27 to 29 plus 1/2⊠.

NOTES ON THE DRAFT

When difficulty in getting the suit out of the material is experienced, some relief can be obtained by moving the side seam at 10 more towards the front. This increases the back part which is made from lining and correspondingly decreases the cloth space the forepart will take up.

Very little stretching is needed in the shoulders.

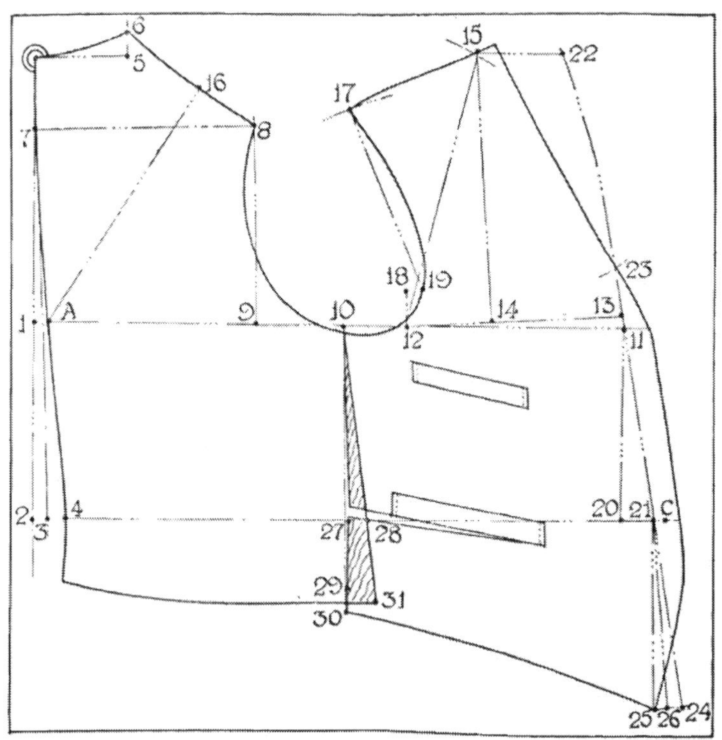
6
5
16
17
15
22
7
8
18
19
23
1
A
9
10
14
13
12
11
2
3
4
27
28
20
21
C
29
31
30
25
26
24

DIAGRAM 24.

MORNING COAT BY PROPORTION.
Diagram 25

FEATURES:—*Single-breasted; button two; step collar; high-waisted; cutaway fronts.*

MEASURES:—44" *breast;* 46" *waist;* 8 1/2" *back width;* 18" *waist length;* 39" *full length. Scale* 20 3/4". *Disproportion* 6".

INSTRUCTIONS FOR DRAFTING

APART from the treatment at the waist, the construction of this draft is very similar to the ordinary normal draft.

The waist suppression at 15 to 28 to a great extent influences the room over the seat, therefore the standard allowance of 3/4⊠ for spring to the skirt is substituted instead of using the seat measure as in former drafts. Care must be taken in arranging the length of the waist seam of skirt; this must compare with the body part plus a small allowance for fullness that will be introduced at the hip.

DRAFT

Square lines from 0.

1 from 0 = half scale (10 3/8);

2 from 0 = waist length (18);

3 from 2 = 1⊠;

4 from 0 = full length;

Square out from above points.

5 from 2 = 1⊠: join to 0;

6 from 3 = 1⊠;

7 from 0 = one-sixth scale plus 1/4⊠;

8 from 7 = 3/4⊠: join to 0;

9 from 0 = one-fourth 0 to 1;

Square out;

10 from 9 = 2 3/4⊠: square out;

11 from inside line 10 = back width plus 1/2⊠;

12 and 13 are located by squaring from 11;

14 from 13 = 1/2⊠: join to 8;

15 from 5 = one-ninth scale plus 1/4⊠;

Connect 11 and 2 and shape blade seam, giving 1⊠ of round at 16;

Continue from 15 to B.

17 from A = one-third of half breast measure;

18 from 17 = one-fourth of half breast measure, plus 2⊠;

19 from A = half breast plus 2 1/2⊠;

20 from 21 = 1/8 disproportion less 1/4⊠: join to 18;

21 from 18 = one-sixth scale;

Square up;

22 from 21 = half scale plus 1/4⊠: join to 14;

23 from 22 = 8 to 14 less 1/4⊠;

24 from 18 = 1⊠;

Join to 23 and hollow scye 1/2⊠;

25 is squared down from the breast line at 19;

26 from 25 = one-fourth disproportion less 1/4⊠ (1 1/4);

27 from 5 = half waist plus 2⊠;

28 from 15 = 1/2⊠.

NOTE.—The blade suppression 15 to 28 must never be made less than 1/2⊠. In this instance the waist surplus shown from 27 to 26 is only 1/8⊠. Therefore the extra 3/8⊠ has to be made up by overlapping at the underarm seam 30 to 31.

29 from 12 = 1 1/2⊠: mark up 1 1/2⊠ for top of underarm seam.

30 from 28 = 16 to 29 less 1/2⊠ for width of side body;

31 from 30 = 3/8⊠, found as described above.

Sweep B to C by point 11 and square out parallel with waist line from C;

32 from C = 9⊠;

33 from 32 = 3/4⊠: draw line C to 34;

34 is 1/2″ below line from 4.

Shape back skirt giving 1/2″ of round at 35;

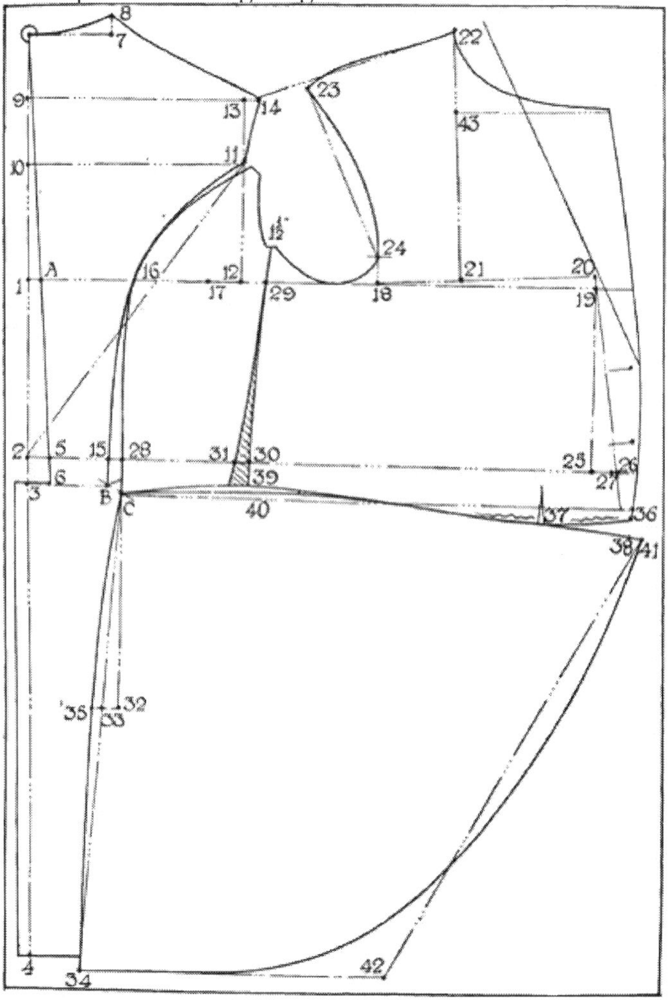

DIAGRAM 25.

Allow 1 1/2⊠ button stand at top hole and run off as shown;

36 is 1/2⊠ below C line;

37 is 1⊠ below C line;

38 from 36 = half 25 to 26.

Shape waist seam of body part to 39, which is 3/4⊠ above C line.

Take out 1/4⊠ between body part and skirt at 40;

38 to 41 is the amount that the body part has been overlapped at 39;

42 from 34 = half 5 to 26 plus 1⊠;

Join to 41 and use this as a guide line when shaping skirt front.

43 from 22 = one-sixth scale plus 1/4⊠;

Square out and shape neck as shown;

The back pleat is finished by marking out 1⊠ from B and squaring down to 4 line.

NOTES ON THE DRAFT

The waist seam of forepart in the region of 37 should either be drawn in and the resulting fullness pressed upwards over the prominence, or a small vee can be taken out. The amount the waist seam is reduced by this process will enable the skirt to be eased on over the hips.

In a larger waist point 27 may be situated outside of or in front of point 26, thus showing a deficiency. This will not affect the suppression at 28, for the 1/2⊠ will still have to be taken out. The overlap, however, at 31 will be greater, as it will consist of the amount the waist is short at the front plus the 1/2⊠ suppression at 28.

CHESTERFIELD OVERCOAT. Diagram 26

FEATURES:—*Single-breasted; step lapel, rolling to* 1 1/2″ *below breast line; medium-fitting waist; centre seam, but no vent.*

MEASURES:—42″ *breast;* 44″ *waist;* 47″ *seat;* 10″ *scye depth;* 17 1/2″ *waist length;* 42″ *full length;* 14 5/8″ *front shoulder;* 19 1/2″ *over shoulder;* 9 3/8″ *across chest;* 8 5/8″ *across back. Scale* 20″. *Disproportion* 6″.

INSTRUCTIONS FOR DRAFTING

THE above measures carry the additions for the overcoat as follows:—Front shoulder plus 3/8⊠; back width and across chest plus 3/8⊠.

The proportionate method of drafting is the same as prescribed for the ordinary Chesterfield. Disproportion is found as for other garments.

For sac coats the disproportion only affects the fronts, the sides remaining the same.

THE DRAFT

Square lines from 0.
1 from 0 = scye depth 10⊠;
2 from 0 = waist length plus 1/4⊠;
3 from 2 = 1 to 2 plus 1 1/2⊠;
4 from 0 = full length;
Square out from the above points;
5 from 2 = 1/2⊠;
Join to 0;
6 from 5 = 1/2⊠;
Curve gradually into the above line;
7 from 4 = 2 to 6;
Connect to 6;

8 from 1 = one-third over-shoulder measure plus 3/4☒: square out;

9 from 8 = 2 3/4☒;

10 from 0 = one-sixth scale plus 1/4☒;

11 from 10 = 3/4☒: join to 0;

12 from 9 = back width plus 1/2☒ (9 1/8);

13 and 14 are located by squaring from 12;

15 from 14 = 1/2☒: join to 11;

16 from 13 = 1 1/4☒;

17 from 16 = 3/4☒:

Mark a seam on either side.

18 from 6 = the net back width less 1/4☒;

19 from 3 = 2 to 18 plus 1/2☒;

Shape side seam of back as shown.

20 from A = half breast plus 3 3/4☒;

21 from 20 = across chest 9 3/8☒;

22 from 21 = 1/8 disproportion less 1/4☒: join to 21;

23 from 21 = one-sixth scale plus 1/4☒;

Square up by line 21 to 23;

24 from 21 by sweep = the front shoulder measure less back neck 0 to 10;

Apply the over-shoulder measure less 1/2☒ from A to 25; then by sweep from 21 to 26;

26 is located definitely by applying the back shoulder width 11 to 15 less 1/4☒ from 24;

Mark up 1/4⊠ from 21 and join to 26: hollow scye 1/2⊠;

27 from 21 = 3/4⊠ for scye base.

28 is squared from 20 on breast line;

29 from 28 = 1/4 disproportion less 1/4⊠;

Apply waist measure plus 3 3/4⊠ from 6 towards front. In this instance it falls on point 29, therefore there is nothing to take out nor anything to be overlapped at the side seam at 18.

30 from 19 = half difference between breast and seat measures plus 1/2⊠: draw side seam from 17 through 18 and 30;

Draw through 29 from 20 extending 9⊠ down to 31.

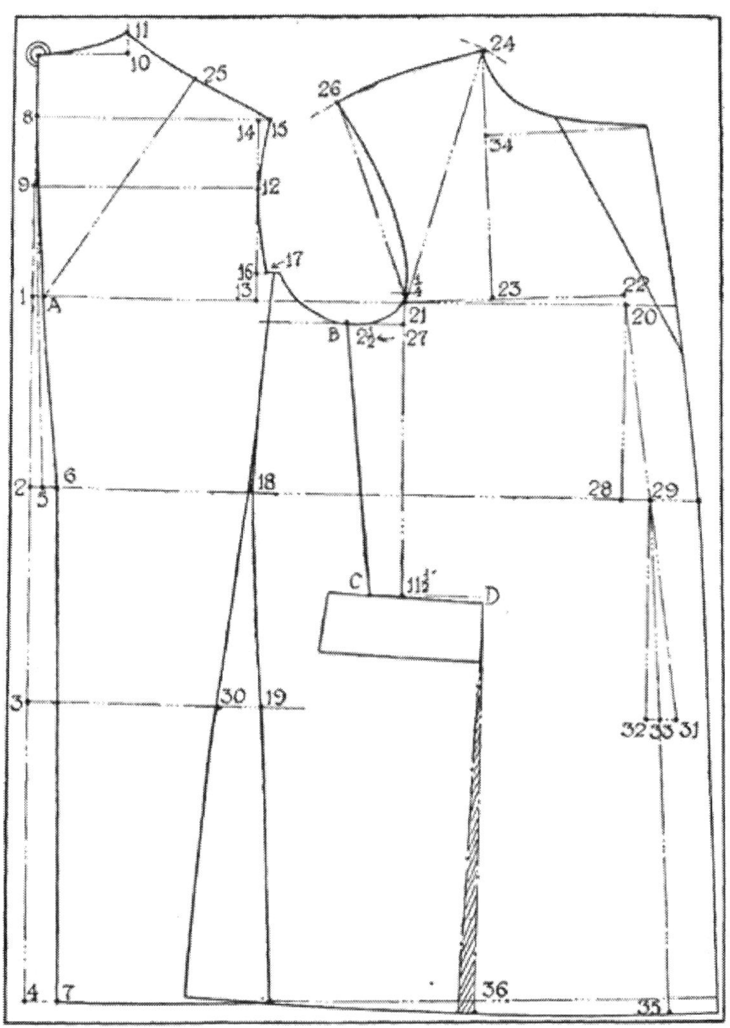

DIAGRAM 26.

32 is squared from 29;

33 is midway between 32 and 31;

Draw through 33 from 29 for actual centre front line;

Give 2⊠ overlap beyond centre line;

34 from 24 = one-sixth scale plus 1/4⊠;

Shape lapel and neck on to this line;

Give 3/4⊠ below bottom construction line and complete outline.

Mark down 11 1/2⊠ from 21 for centre pocket.

Run the underarm seam from a point 2 1/2⊠ back from 27 to rear of pocket.

Square down from front end of pocket at D and mark a pleat at 36. The amount taken out in the pleat is equal to 32 to 33.

The pattern is arranged on lines described for the lounge. The seam from B to C and the pocket mouth from C to D are cut before the pleat is taken out at 36.

NOTES ON THE DRAFT

Where a looser fitting but still slightly shaped waist is desired, a little more overlap can be given at the waist 18 and seat 30.

If a double-breasted front is required, 4⊠ to 4 1/2⊠ is added beyond centre line, care being taken to follow line 29 to 33 below the waist.

The sleeve is the same as for the ordinary Chesterfield.

VARIATIONS FROM THE NORMAL DRAFT

Diagram 27

THE accompanying page of diagrams illustrates how the normal pattern will have to be adjusted to meet the requirements of irregular figures. It is assumed that the original block has been constructed on a proportionate basis and is one that will provide a satisfactory fit for the normal type of figure. When making the adjustments it is advisable to work on a low estimate and not make the alteration from the block too pronounced.

Especially is this precaution necessary when one is working from descriptions provided by travellers or agents.

It is possible to have a combination of the examples shown here, such as a "stooping figure with square shoulders," or a "short stocky figure that is very erect."

When this occurs, it is better to make the adjustment for size before that for attitude.

If Direct Measures are taken, most of the changes will be automatically embodied in the process of drafting. In the diagrams shown, the normal block is outlined by solid lines and the deviations by dash or dot and dash lines.

SECTION A. LONG NECK OR SLOPING SHOULDERS

The alteration for this figure is shown by dash lines.

Vertical lines are drawn through back and front neck points, and the extra height added to accord with the figure as shown from 1 to 2 and 3 to 4.

Connect 4 and 5; also 2 and 6.

Raise the neck back at 7 to agree with the quantity raised at 4.

SECTION A. SHORT NECK OR SQUARE SHOULDERS

The alteration for this figure is shown by dot and dash lines and is executed in the reverse way described for the long neck figure.

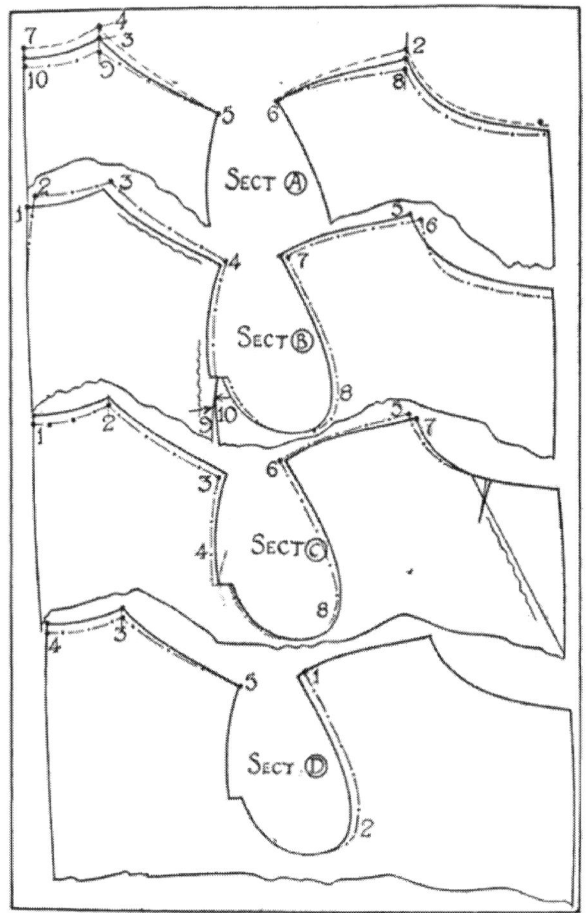

DIAGRAM 27.

Lower the front from 1 to 8 and the back from 3 to 9. Lower centre at 10 to agree with the drop at 9.

SECTION B. STOOPING FIGURE

Raise the back from 1 to 2 and bring in point 2 half the quantity raised to give the necessary round over the blade. Point 3 is raised and advanced to agree with the position of 2.

Raise point 4, and if the figure requires a wider back extend down the back scye as shown.

Drop the front the same amount the back has been raised and carry it forward a corresponding amount.

Drop shoulder end at 7 and hollow scye at 8.

Full on the shoulder of back and shrink the back scye in the region of wavy lines.

If the coat has been cut out, the backs can be passed up to obtain the necessary length. To do this balance marks are placed at the side seams as shown at 9 and 10. These go together when sewing the side seam.

SECTION C. ERECT FIGURE

Shorten the back right across as shown at 1, 2, and 3 and narrow the back scye at 4.

Raise the front shoulder seam right across as shown at 5 and 6.

Crooken the shoulder by receding the neck point from 7 to 5.

Widen the across chest at 8 and take out a small vee in the neck and through the crease line as shown.

SECTION D. SHORT STOCKY FIGURE

This particular type is generally blessed with a very large upper arm section. Other features are: a narrow shoulder and very upright carriage.

Advance the scye, say 1/2″, from the shoulder seam (1 to 2).

Lower the back at 3 and 4 and run out to the shoulder end at 5 as set down for square shoulders.

MOTOR LIVERIES

By THE EDITOR

A MOTOR LIVERY OVERCOAT. Diagram 35

IN former days the making of livery garments for the house and for carriage wear was within the province of most tailors, especially in country districts. But the advent of the motor-car has revolutionised the livery trade, and nowadays uniforms for chauffeurs have displaced the coatees, frock coats, and box coats of coachmen, footmen, and grooms. There is quite a good trade to be done in chauffeurs' liveries, and it is worth the tailor's while to cultivate it.

Motor livery overcoats do not vary much in style. It is true that some are made with a waist seam and others with a roll and step collar; but usually the form takes that of a double-breasted coat, loose-fitting but held in at the back with a belt and pleats, and a Prussian collar. The style here shown may be used exactly as given, or used as a foundation to vary as required. If desired the fronts may be cut much wider at the top, in plastron fashion; pockets may be made with flaps, and so on.

Some of the points connected with this coat are: 2 1/2″ is allowed beyond the collar measure for crease; the overlap at top is 6″, at waist 4″, and at bottom 6″—all quantities which may be varied for style or size. The collar is of the deep Prussian style. A belt about 12″ in length is placed at the back and serves to hold the pleats. The top button is half hidden by the collar. The cuff has a strap, which can be used to tighten the sleeve in windy weather; the alternative is to have buttons at hindarm.

The measures are as follows: 36″ breast; 32″ waist; 9″ depth of scye; 18″ fashion waist; 45″ full length; 13″ front shoulder; 17 1/2″ over-shoulder; 8″ across chest; 7 1/4″ across back; to elbow 20″; sleeve length 32″; neck 15″. 3/8″ is added to across back and across chest; 1/4″ to depth of scye; 1/2″ to front shoulder; 3/4″ to over-shoulder, for overcoat allowances. Scale 18″.

THE DRAFT. SECTION A

To reproduce, draw line 0, 6.

1 from 0 is 2 1/2″;

2 from 0 is 5″;

3 from 0 is 9″;

4 from 0 is top of belt, 15 1/2″;

5 from 0 is fashion waist, 18″;

6 from 0 is full length.

Square lines from these points.

7 from 0 is one-sixth of scale (18⊠) plus 1/2⊠ 3 1/2⊠;

From 7 mark up 3/4⊠ and curve back neck.

8 from 2 is across back 7 1/4⊠ plus 1/2⊠ for seams, and 3/8⊠ for overcoat allowance, 8 1/8⊠.

Square up and down from 8.

Spring out 3/8⊠ beyond 9 and draw back shoulder.

11 is 1 1/4⊠ above the line.

12 from 5 is half scale.

13 is 6⊠ from 12.

14 is 3/4⊠ (or more or less).

Rule a line from 14 to 12.

15 is obtained by squaring from line 14, 12.

16 is half breast plus 3 1/2⊠ to 4⊠.

17 from 16 is, in the usual way, the across chest measure plus 3/8⊠ for overcoat allowance; but for a chauffeur's coat it is as well to cut this a little more forward in the scye, therefore this may be made the ordinary across chest measure plus 1/8⊠ only, 8 1/8⊠.

Deepen scye 1/2⊠ to 3/4⊠ and mark line 10.

19 is squared from 10.

18 is 1 1/2⊠ above 19.

20 from 17 is one-sixth of scale.

Square a line up from 20.

To locate 21, sweep the front shoulder measure 13 plus 1/2⊠ for overcoat allowance, less the distance from 0 to 7 on back; the point on line 20 where the sweep strikes, fixes the neckpoint at 21.

The sweep must be taken from point 17.

22 is located by sweeping the over-shoulder measure, from point 17 plus 3/4⊠ for overcoat allowance, and less the distance from 3 to X on back.

The distance from 21 to 22 is 1/4⊠ less than the back shoulder seam; 22 should be dropped 3/8⊠ below the sweep.

Rule a line from 22 to 18 and hollow 1/2⊠.

23 from 21 is one-sixth scale plus 1/4⊠.

Draw a line connecting 23 with 16.

24 from 23 is one-sixth of scale.

Make up neck to measure, allowing 3 1/4⊠ over linen collar, including seams.

25 is 1/2⊠ from 24.

26 is found by squaring down from 16.

27 is 1/4⊠ in front of 26.

Draw a line from 16 through 27 to 28.

29 is 6⊠ from 25.

30 is 5⊠ from 16.

31 is 4⊠ from 27.

32 is 6⊠ from 28.

Drop front 1⊠.

35 from 12 is 2⊠ to 2 1/2⊠ according to taste.

Overlap forepart a little at 11 and draw side seam through 35 to 36.

33 is 2⊠ from 17.

34 is 8⊠ from 33.

Six buttons are placed down the fronts.

THE SLEEVE. SECTION B

To reproduce sleeve, square lines 0, 2 and 0, 7.

1 from 0 is the same distance as 10 to 8 on back.

2 from 1 is found by measuring from 8 to 9 on back, placing that at shoulder point 22, and continuing in a straight line to forearm pitch.

3 is midway between 0 and 2.

4 is 1 1/2⊠ up from 3.

Draw sleeve head through these points.

Apply sleeve measure in the usual way, or make the forearm from 1 to 6 18 1/2⊠.

5 is 9⊠ from 1.

7 is 1 1/2⊠ from 6.

Square from 5 and 7.

8 from 5 is 3/4⊠.

9 from 8 is 8 3/4⊠;

10 from 6 is 7 1/2⊠.

11 from 1 is obtained by measuring the underpart of scye from 8 to forearm pitch, noting the overlap at 11.

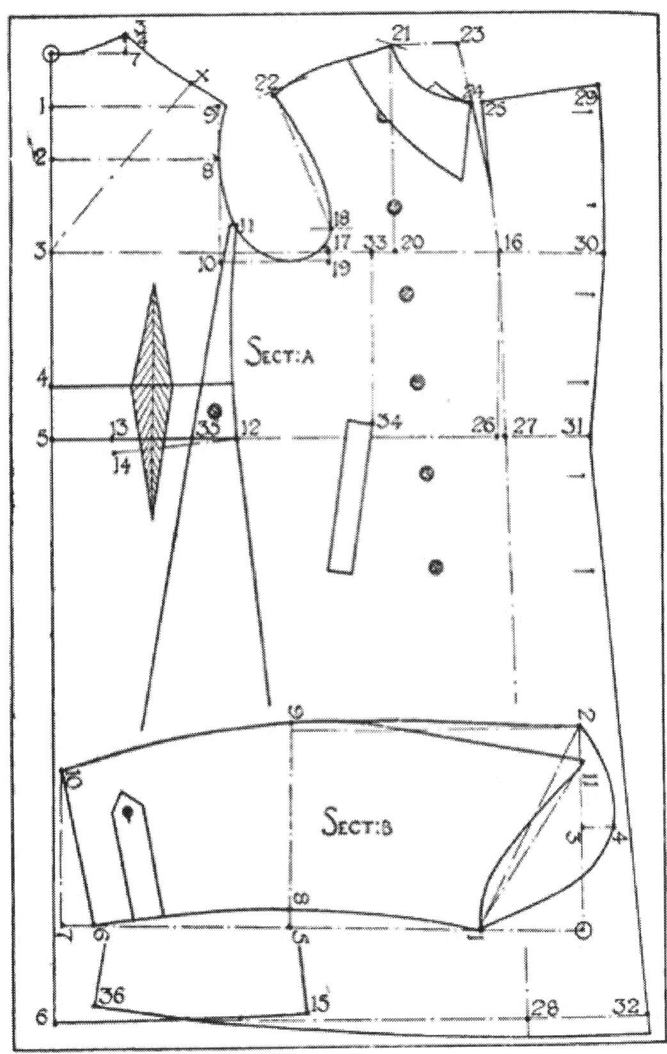

DIAGRAM 35.

A CHAUFFEUR'S JACKET. Diagram 36

Chauffeurs' jackets are made up in various ways. They may be single-breasted with patch pockets; double-breasted with roll and step collar; or D.B. with Prussian collar. The back may be made lounge style or patrol fashion. Some firms, it may be said, have their own styles of front; and, of course, customers may express their views on the subject.

The type selected for the accompanying draft is one with a D.B. front, patrol back, and Prussian collar. Some of the points about the draft are: A forward scye is given; the crease edge of collar is made 1 1/2⊠ more than the linen collar; five buttons are placed down the front, the top one about 1 1/4⊠ down, and the bottom one 2 1/2⊠ below the waist; the Prussian collar has a 2 1/4⊠ fall.

The measures are: 36⊠ breast; 32⊠ waist; 16 1/2⊠ natural waist; 29⊠ full length; 7 1/4⊠ across back; 19 1/2⊠ elbow; 31 1/2⊠ sleeve length; 13⊠ front shoulder; 17 1/2⊠ over-shoulder; 9⊠ depth of scye; 8⊠ across chest; 15⊠ collar. Scale 18⊠.

THE DRAFT. SECTION A

To reproduce, draw line 0 5.

1 from 0 is 2 1/2⊠.

2 from 0 is 4 1/2⊠;

3 from 0 is 9⊠, depth of scye;

4 from 0 is 16 1/2⊠, natural waist.

5 from 0 is the full length.

From these points square lines.

6 from 0 is one-sixth of scale, 3⊠.

From 6 mark up 3/4⊠ and curve back neck.

7 from 2 is across back measure plus 1/2⊠.

Square up and down from 7.

Spring out 3/8⊠ beyond 8 and draw back shoulder.

10 from 3 is 3 3/4⊠.

11 from 4 is 2⊠.

12 from 5 is a little more than 11 from 4.

13 from 11 is 1 1/2⊠.

14 is dropped 1/2⊠ below 12, and is 1/2⊠ from 12.

15 is half scale (9⊠) from 3.

A is one-twelfth scale from 9.

Square aline down from 15.

17 from 16 is 1/2⊠.

18 from 16 is also 1/2⊠.

20 from 19 is 3/4⊠.

21 from 19 is also 3/4⊠.

Take 1/4⊠ out between back and side-body at 7.

The back and side-body may now be completed by taking 1/4⊠ off all the way down centre of back, as it is made without a seam.

22 from 3 is half breast plus 2 1/2⊠.

23 from 22 would be in the usual way the across chest measure 8☒; but in this case 1/2☒ is deducted, to give a forward scye, because of the attitude of a chauffeur when driving.

From 23 square up 1 1/2☒.

24 is one-sixth of scale from 23.

Square a line up from 24.

25 is located by sweeping the front shoulder measure from 23, less back neck. The point where the sweep strikes line squared from 24, fixes the neckpoint at 25.

26 is located by sweeping the over-shoulder measure, less the distance from 3 to X on back, from point 23.

25 to 26 is made 1/4☒ less than the shoulder seam of back.

Rule a line from 26 to 1 1/2 and hollow 1/2☒.

27 is one-sixth of scale from 23.

Draw a line from 27 to 22.

28 is one-sixth of scale from 27.

29 is 1/2☒ from 28.

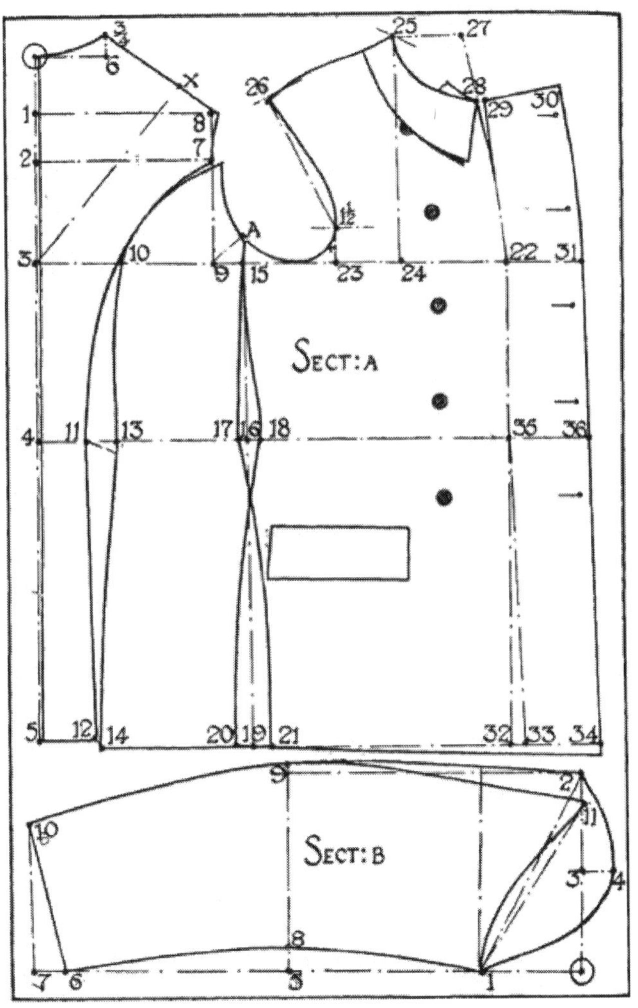

DIAGRAM 36.

Square a line down from 22 fixing 35 and 32.

30 from 29 is 3 1/2";

36 from 35 is also 3 1/2";

33 from 32 is 3/4⊠;

34 from 33 is 3 1/2⊠.

Drop front 1/2⊠, and complete.

THE SLEEVE. SECTION B

To reproduce the sleeve, square lines 0, 2 and 0, 7.

1 from 0 is the same distance as 9 to 7 on back.

2 from 1 is the same quantity as 7 to 8 on back and 26, in a straight line, to forearm pitch.

3 is midway between 0 and 2.

4 is 1 1/2⊠ up from 3.

Apply the sleeve length in the usual way, or make the forearm from 1 to 6, 18⊠.

5 from 1 is 8 1/2⊠.

7 is 1 1/2⊠ below 6.

Square from 5 and 7.

8 from 5 is 1⊠.

9 from 8 is 7 3/4⊠

10 from 6 is 6 1/2⊠.

11 from 1 is the same amount as a measure taken between the two pitches underneath, following the scye.

Hollow about 3/4⊠ only.

HOW TO MAKE TROUSERS

By PHILIP DELLAFERA

THE stitch marks indicating inlays, etc., must first be put in, as shown by Diagram 37.

SECTION A is the topside; this is cut without inlays at leg and side seams, but a pocket facing is sometimes left on at top of side seam; if this is not cut on, it must be sewn on when making up the pocket mouth.

The notches at leg and side seams are balance marks, which will be explained later.

SECTION B is the underside which is provided with inlays at leg seam, side seam and seat seam, the notches corresponding with those on topside.

Before starting the actual sewing of tops, it is necessary to cut out certain pieces of lining and linen; first of all, there is a crutch stay—SECTION F, Diagram 38—which is a square piece of linen folded over cornerwise; then there are two pieces of lining the same shape as the fly, one being used to line the fly itself, whilst the other piece is sewn to the right topside and forms the fly facing; a piece of linen is also cut this shape and used for buttonhole stays in the fly.

The button catch must also be lined with some kind of material, and in addition to this, a strip of linen or canvas must be included, which will serve as a stay for the buttons.

In addition to these items, two strips of linen must be cut for the pocket stays: these pieces are about 1⊠ in width and 10⊠ in length.

PREPARING THE TOPS (TOPSIDE). Diagram 38

The crutch stay must first of all be basted at the fork of both topsides, care being taken that it comes well above the fly tack, which is usually about 2 1/4⊠ above fork point and is indicated by a notch.

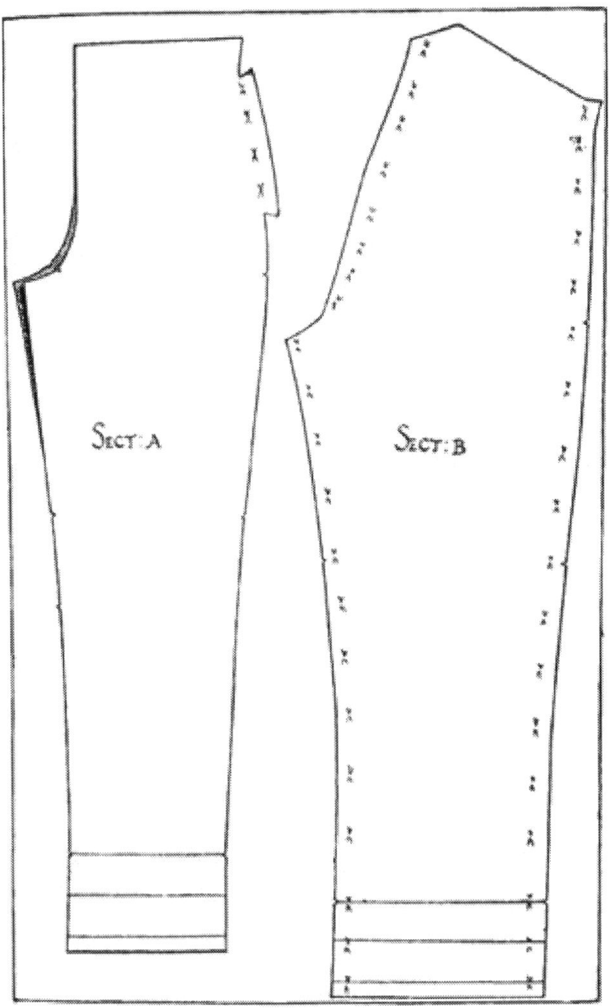

DIAGRAM 37.

The strip of linen must then be basted along the pocket mouth, holding it fairly tight so that the cloth is drawn in as shown by SECTION A, which illustrates the inside view of right topside: the linen is put on from a couple of inches above hip balance marks and reaches almost to the top of side seam.

This diagram plainly shows the crutch stay in position and the button catch is seamed on and pressed open, in readiness for lining, which must also include a piece of linen or canvas for button stay. The loose material which is produced at the pocket mouth must be carefully pressed away.

SECTION B

Here is illustrated the outside view of left topside; the pocket mouth has been drawn in with linen, this, of course, being on the wrong side cannot be seen from the outside; a piece of lining is seamed on the fly, after which it is turned over on the inside and forms the fly facing.

When sewing on this piece of lining it must be kept fairly tight in the hollow of fork, otherwise it will not get its proper shape.

The fly must now be prepared; it must be lined with Italian cloth or similar material and must also have a piece of linen put through as shown by SECTION C, which illustrates the fly with the right side facing downwards on to a piece of lining and then at the bottom the piece of linen is shown.

These three pieces are sewn together by means of a seam in the hollow of fly and finally it is turned out and produces a shape as shown by SECTION D, which illustrates the fly complete with holes; the material is uppermost, whilst the lining is facing downwards.

This should now be basted on to the fly facing of SECTION E, which shows the inside view of left topside; when basting in the fly the tacks must be together and the edge kept back about 1/8″ so that it will not show on the outside.

Sometimes the topsides are made with one or two pleats; this is allowed for in the cutting and waistbands are usually put on, or sometimes top welts are sewn on topsides only; but whichever method is adopted, the topsides must be pleated in to the actual size and this is indicated by SECTION G, which shows a portion of left topside with two small pleats facing the side seam. Of course, these may be made either way, as desired.

Having completed the preliminary stages of the topsides, they must be sewn to the undersides; but before doing so, the hip pocket (if required) should be put in whichever side it is ordered.

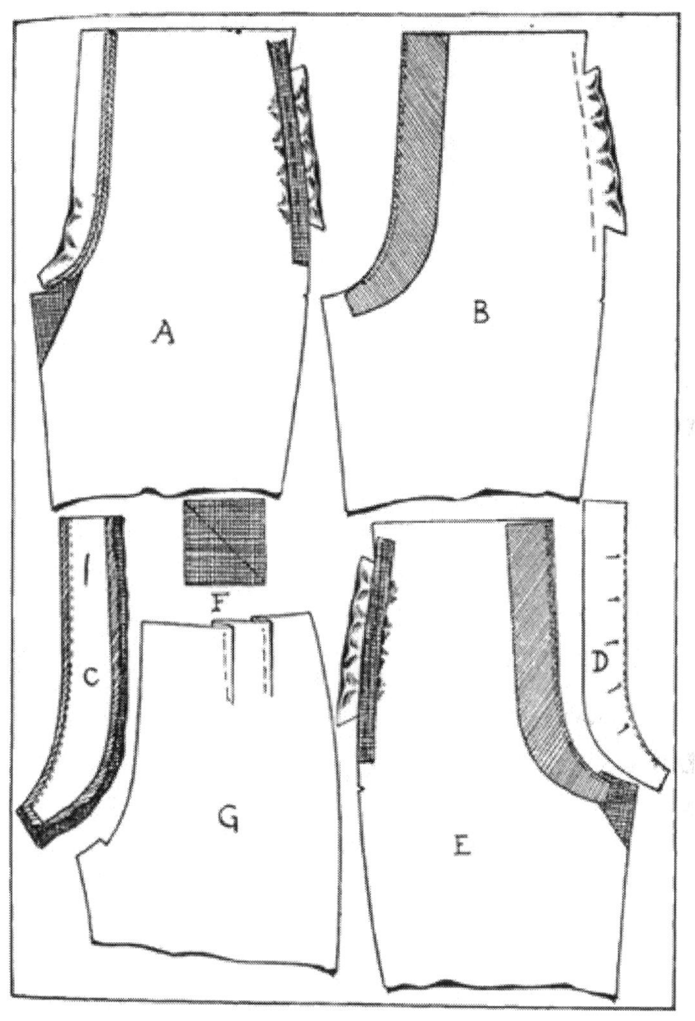

DIAGRAM 38.

DIAGRAM 39, SECTION A

This illustrates the left leg; the topside is stitched on to the underside at side seam from top to bottom with the exception of about 6 1/2⊠ for pocket mouth. It will be seen that the stitching is taken through the linen pocket stay at both top and bottom of the pocket opening.

It will also be seen that there are three notches on the topside and a corresponding number on the underside, and that they are exactly opposite each other. This is their correct position, for they are balance marks and must always be kept together. If this is not done, the legs will get twisted and after a little time, look most unsightly.

Sometimes these balance marks may be altered. For instance, a man with a prominent calf may require a little fulness over this part of the leg; in order to do this, the balance mark on the underside may be passed up about 1/2⊠ and the extra length thus obtained could be eased on over the calf. But, of course, the passing up of the underside balance mark will cause the topside to be a little longer than the underside between the knee and hip line; this must be eased on and pressed away.

This alteration is also made for corpulent figures, but is usually allowed for in the cutting, and details to this effect are always given with other particulars.

SECTION B

This shows the right leg; the side seam is sewn up; the button catch is seamed on and pressed open; the crutch lining is marked and the balance notches are also plainly indicated.

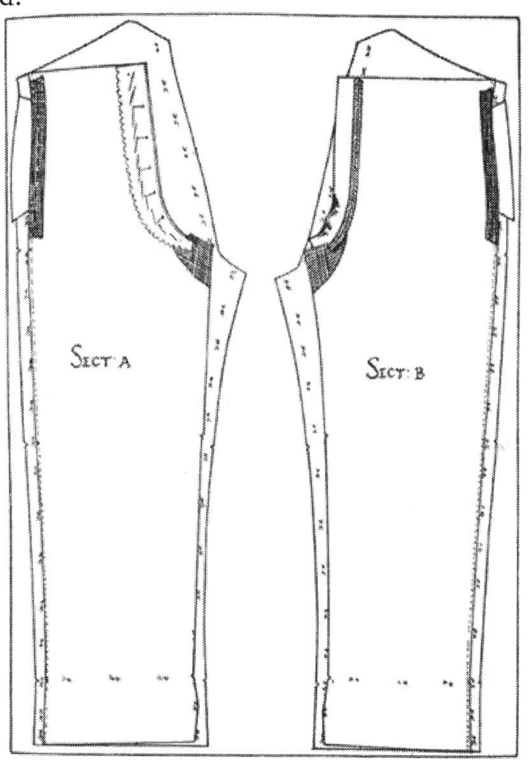

DIAGRAM 39.

PUTTING IN POCKETS AND TOP STAYS

DIAGRAM 40, SECTION A

After the side seams have been seamed up they should be pressed open as shown by accompanying diagram, which represents the top portion of left leg; the opening of pocket is plainly indicated.

Sometimes the side seam is "lapped," in which case it is not necessary to press it open, as it is just turned over with the topside overlapping the undersides and stitched down on the outside according to requirements. For a loose "lap" it is necessary to leave on a small inlay down topsides and instead of seaming up the side seam in the first place before it is turned over, it is just basted up and turned over right away and then stitched on the outside, after which the row of basting may be pulled out, thus leaving the loose "lap" as required.

This diagram shows the seam pressed open at the pocket mouth as well as the side, but before it is possible to put the pocket in, the inlay of underside must be turned over so that it covers the opening; but, if desired, the top portion may be cut across as shown by dot and dash line, in which case the seam is just left open at the top, the object being to get it as thin as possible at the top edge.

SECTION B. THE RIGHT LEG

This illustrates the completed side pocket; the hip pocket is shown and a portion of the fob pocket is also indicated.

The canvas or linen "stay" is shown along the top edge and also down the button catch.

The actual making up of the pocket is a little complicated, but I will endeavour to explain the main operations.

The pocket, which is cut about 13⊠ wide, is doubled over and stitched round, forming the bottom portion, leaving about 8⊠ open at the side, which eventually is fastened to the pocket mouth.

After it has been seamed round, it is turned out and seamed round again, so that the seam is neatened.

It is now ready to be inserted into the pocket mouth of trousers, and, looking at the diagram of pocket in SECTION B, the bottom half, which is not visible, is sewn to the facing of topside and reaches to within 1/4⊠ of the actual opening. The top half of pocket, which is seen on the diagram, is sewn to the back of the underside inlay, which has already been turned over the pocket mouth.

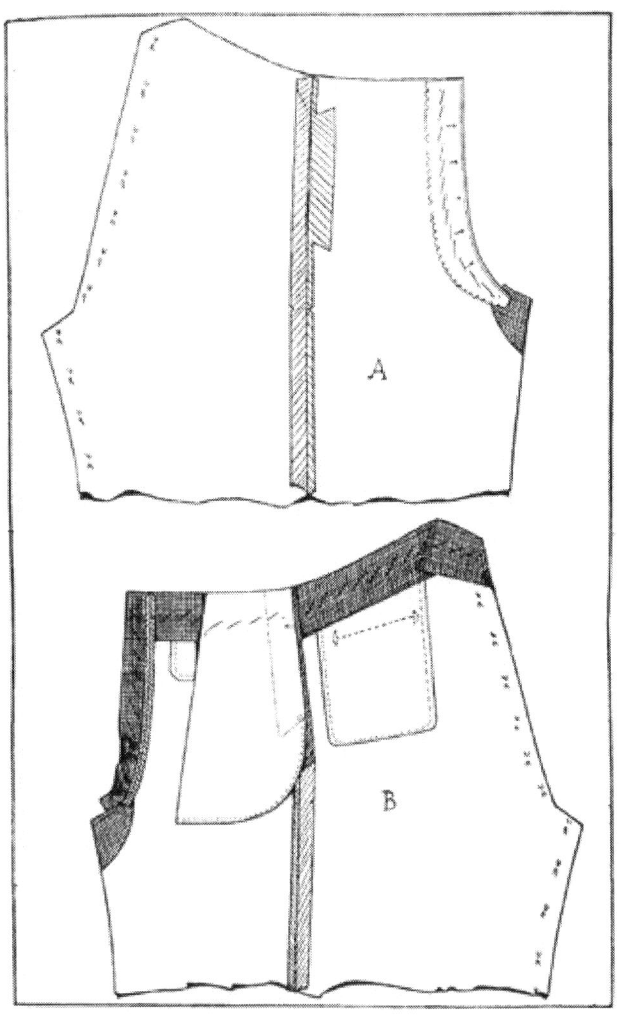

DIAGRAM 40.

It will now be seen that when the hand is placed through the pocket mouth into the actual pocket, that part which touches the back of the hand is fastened to the pocket facing of topside, whilst the part which touches the palm of the hand is fastened to the inlay of underside.

Before securing the pocket at the back, it is necessary to insert a strip of linen under the pocket and between the inlay of underside; the pocket is then felled on to this strip of linen, which serves as a stay not only for the pocket itself, but also for the tacks which are made at top and bottom.

If the pocket is now looked into, it will be found that the underside inlay is quite loose on the inside; this must be fastened, and is side-stitched from the outside of the pocket, the stitching of which is plainly indicated on the diagram from top to just below the bottom tack and about 1 1/2⊠ away from the back edge of pocket.

Having finished the pockets, the tops must either be turned in or bound. Both methods are used, but if the latter is adopted the canvas at top edge must be cut away so that the material can be turned over it and fastened; while if the former plan is preferred, a strip of lining must be sewn on the outside through both cloth and canvas; then the edge must be trimmed evenly, and finally, the binding turned over and fastened to the canvas, which has been placed on the inside for button stay.

The edge of button catch may be turned in and the lining felled on to it; or if desired, the lining may be seamed on the right side and turned over, so that the hollow edge just covers the fly seam, which is pressed open.

DIAGRAM 41, SECTION A

Here is shown the upper portion of right leg; the top edge has been turned over and fastened on the inside; the various details of pockets are indicated; the fly buttons are sewn on; the brace buttons are also put on and a hook fastening is indicated at top of button catch.

The position of top buttons is a matter which must not be overlooked; the back brace button, of course, is fixed at the point, which should not be more than two inches from seat seam, so that when it is seamed up, the two buttons at back are not more than 4⊠ apart. If these two buttons are too far apart, the brace will not pull evenly and there will be a tendency for a pleat to form at centre back between the buttons.

The front buttons are placed about 3 1/2⊠ to 4⊠ apart, the one at side being about 1 1/2⊠ in front of side seam. In corpulent trousers these are placed nearer the front, so that the front button is almost in line with the front crease.

SECTION B

This shows the upper portion of left leg; the pocket opening is marked; the buttons are placed in harmony with those on the right leg; the fly is stitched together with the top. The top stitching is made about 1⊠ from the edge and runs parallel with it, whilst the fly is stitched about 1 1/2″ or 1 3/4″ back from the edge.

Although a "hook" fastening is illustrated at top of button catch, this is not essential. Sometimes a buttonhole is made in the top of fly, which will necessitate a button on the catch; on the other hand, the buttonhole may be made right through the top, so that the button shows through on the outside.

Another plan is to put a button at the top of fly, in which case the buttonhole would have to be worked at the top of button catch in place of the eye already shown.

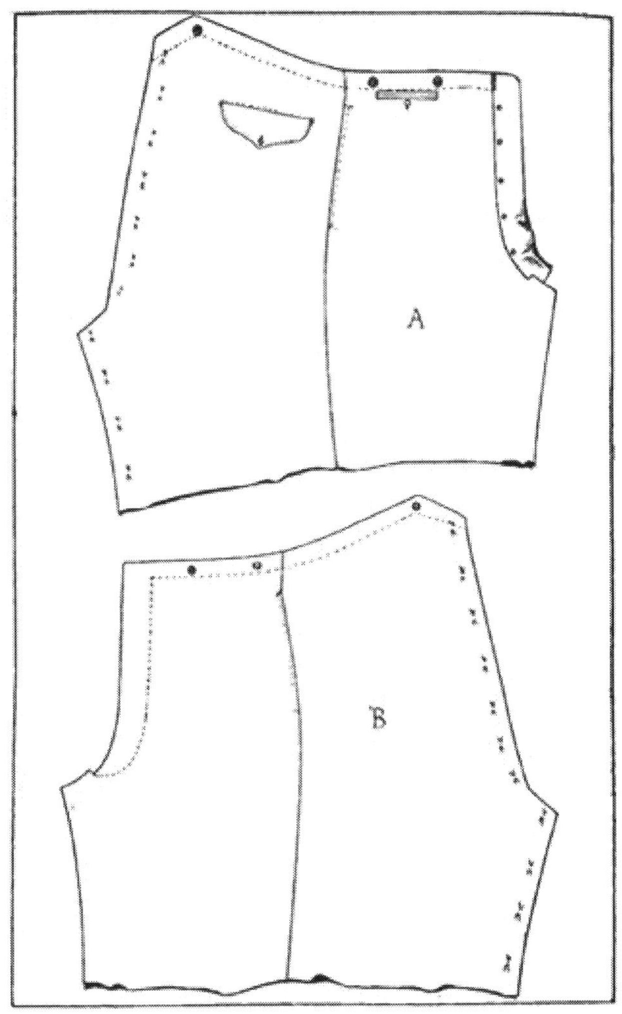

DIAGRAM 41.

CLOSING LEG SEAM AND MAKING BOTTOMS

DIAGRAM 42, SECTION A

The leg seam must now be sewn up, special care being taken that the balance marks are kept level at the knee and bottom, after which it should be pressed open.

In the next place the trousers should be "shrunk": this means that a certain shape has to be put into them, shrinking away any loose material that may show itself under the hams at back and also below the knee at the front.

This section gives a good idea of the desired shape; the fronts are hollow below the knee; there is also a hollow shape from seat to knee at the back, and there is also a slight round on the calf.

When laying trousers out for shrinking purposes or for putting in the crease, they must be laid so that the fly tack is over the side seam at the top and the side seam about 3/4☒ in front of the leg seam at the bottom. This diagram illustrates the tack in its correct position, but of course the side seam cannot be seen.

The next operation is marking off the length of leg and turning up the bottom, this being done by marking off the full length of leg plus 2☒ from a 1/4☒ below the top of leg seam to bottom, the 2⊠ being turned up afterwards to form the permanent turn-up, and the 1/4⊠ taken off at top for seam.

SECTION B

This illustrates the bottom portion of trouser leg which has been turned up to the mark indicating length of leg plus 2⊠, and the stitch marks across the turn-up show the actual length required.

The trouser leg is now inside out with the outside of turn-up showing and the length is 2⊠ more than required.

SECTION C

In order to get the correct length of leg, it will be necessary to turn up this extra 2⊠, thus forming a "cuff" of 2⊠ on the outside and a facing of about 3/4⊠, which must be felled or cross-stitched on the inside as indicated by diagram.

SECTION D

This diagram shows a finished portion of trousers; this is the turn-up completed; the plain seam is the leg seam, whilst the seam which is pressed open indicates the side seam and is slightly in advance of the leg seam.

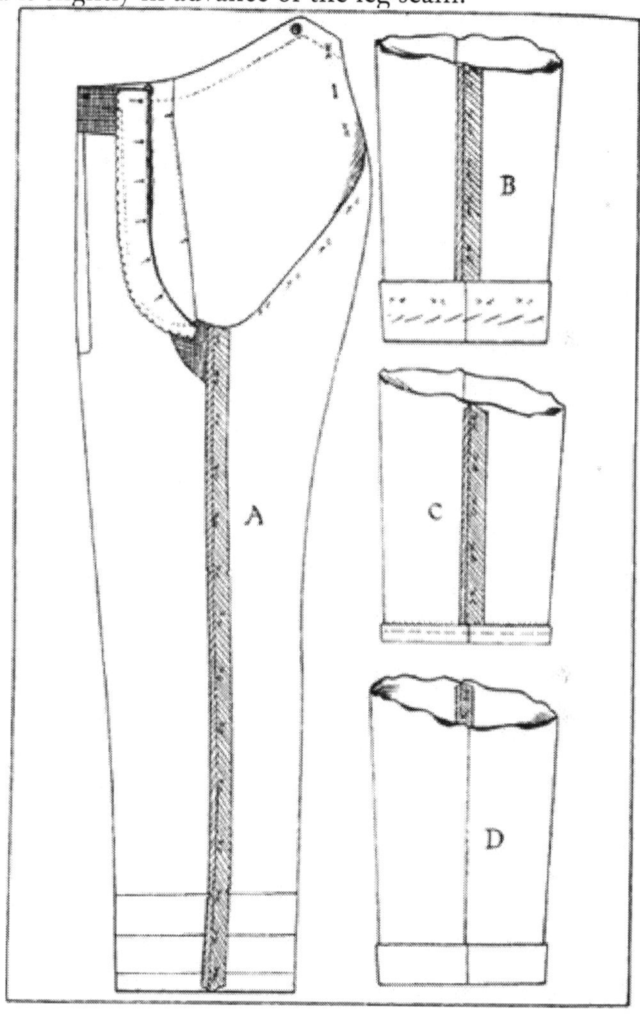

DIAGRAM 42.

FINISHING TOPS AND PLAIN BOTTOMS

DIAGRAM 43, SECTION A

Plain bottoms require hollowing at the front and if the material will not stand stretching, it must be slit for about 3/4″ and then the space made by opening this slit must be filled in with a small piece of material.

This method of finishing the bottom is more difficult because the felling must be done more carefully, so that the stitches do not show through; also, the shaping of the bottom requires more skill, the permanent turn-up being perfectly straight.

SECTION A illustrates the bottom portion of trouser leg inside out; the bottom is turned up and the wedge inserted in the hollow of front.

SECTION B shows the outside finish of the bottom of a plain trouser leg; it is hollow at the front and there is a slight dip at the back.

When both legs are completed the seat seam should be joined; this must be done with thread, and must be very strong, as there is always a great strain at this seam.

There should be a small vent at the top, about an inch being sufficient to ensure that it does not "tie" at the back.

After the seam has been pressed open, the fly must be firmly tacked at the bottom, and then the "curtains" and waistband linings put in.

The "curtains" are usually made from the same material as waistband linings, viz. striped silesia, and are put across the top of undersides, from the side seam to seat seam.

They are made about 3⊠ deep at the side seam and carried straight across to the seat seam, where they would measure about 6⊠ deep; but in any case, if there is a hip pocket, the "curtain" must cover the tackings of the pocket mouth.

The waistband linings themselves are cut on the bias, so that they go nicely round the hollow at top of side seam; this is not absolutely essential, but is certainly an advantage.

A small piece of sleeve-lining must also be used for a crutch lining to cover the seams at the fork point.

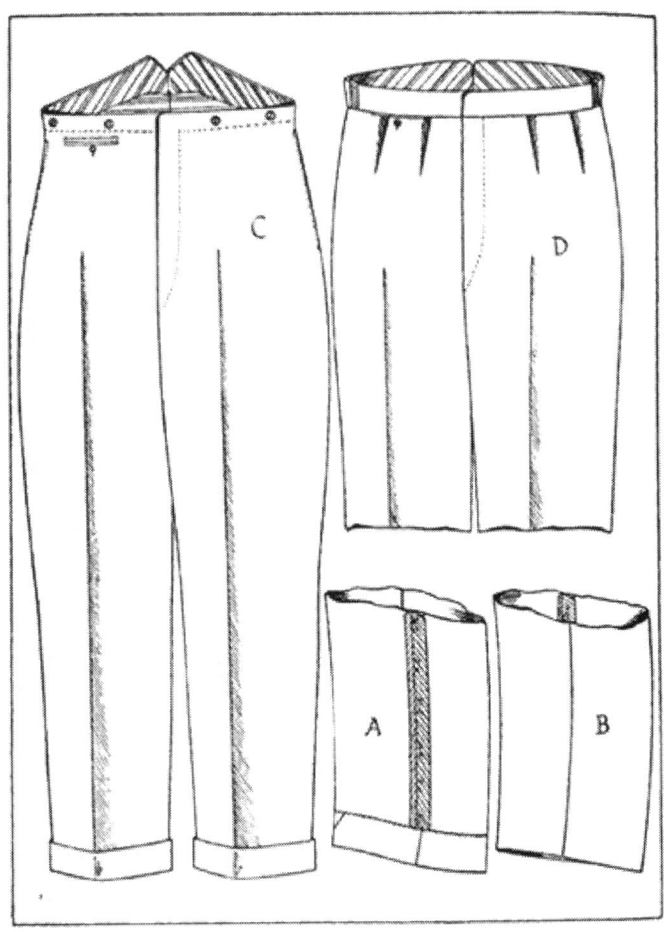

DIAGRAM 43.

SECTION C

This illustrates the finished top and also shows how the trousers should hang when held up by the top.

Trousers with pleats at the top are usually cut with waistbands right round or across the front only; this type of finish is a little different from the ordinary style; the back is not made quite as high as the others; loops are usually put at the sides for a belt, and sometimes a small strap with buckle is placed at each side. The ordinary method, of course, is for the strap and buckle to be in the centre of back.

SECTION D

This portrays the upper portion of a pair of trousers finished with waistbands, loops and two pleats on each topside.

HOW TO MAKE A LOUNGE JACKET

By PHILIP DELLAFERA

THE stitch-marks indicating the various inlays, position of pockets, number of holes, etc., must first be put in; then the facings, linings, flaps and all the other parts required to make the complete garment must be fitted up.

The facings are usually cut out first and the forepart lining fitted, allowing a fair margin at side seam and also plenty of material at scye; that is to say, the lining must not be cut as deep as the actual forepart.

The back lining should be provided with a small pleat down the centre and an extra 1/2⊠ should be allowed round back scye and shoulder.

The flaps and out-breast welt should be matched if there is a pattern or a stripe in the material; and special care should be taken with check material, so that the checks match in both directions.

The sleeve linings should be cut the same width as the sleeves, the length being made to reach to the actual length plus about 1/2⊠ at the top; in any case, it is advisable to have them on the long side, as they are easily shortened if too long.

DIAGRAM 44, SECTION A

This illustrates the back with stitch-marks across the back neck and along the bottom, the latter indicating the amount to be turned up and the former representing the sewing edge of collar.

A notch is also made for back pitch, whilst another at the hollow of waist indicates the waist line.

SECTION B shows the forepart; stitch-marks are placed down side seam; round the shoulder; along the bridle; both pockets are indicated; the holes are marked and the turn-up at bottom is also shown. The dart under the arm is cut out, so there is no need to mark this. The front pitch is notched and the waist-line is notched at side seam; this being used as a balance mark must correspond with the notch at back. SECTION C shows the top-sleeve with stitch-marks along the cuff indicating the actual length and a notch representing the front pitch.

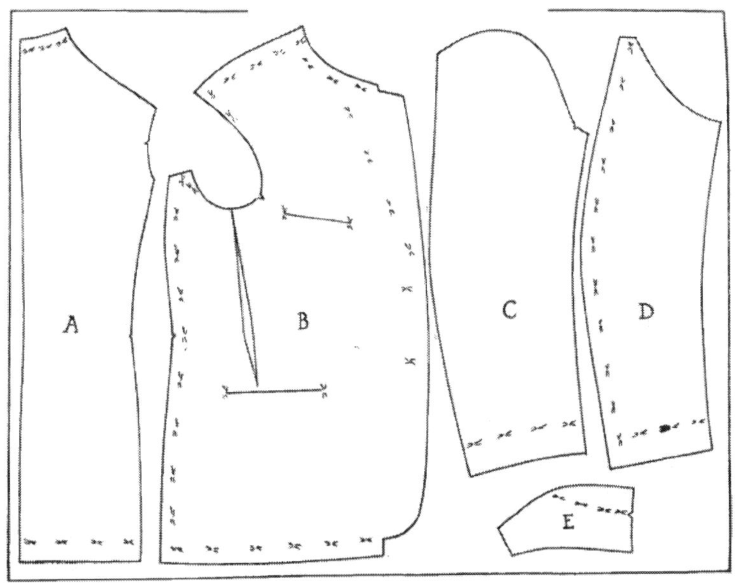

DIAGRAM 44.

This sleeve is cut with a false forearm; therefore the seam will go below the actual pitch which is indicated by a notch.

SECTION D portrays the under-sleeve; this is cut with an inlay down hind-arm seam and consequently a row of stitch-marks will be required so that both sleeves are made the same size; but in addition to this, the inlay may be used if a wider sleeve is required.

The length is indicated in the same way as topsleeve.

SECTION E shows the under-collar which is cut on the bias; this has a seam at the centre of back and the stitch-marks indicate the crease edge.

Having completed the fitting up it is advisable to "damp" the back, foreparts and sleeves before putting in the pockets, because it will be found that when pressing the flap or out-breast pocket the "gloss" will be removed, whilst it remains on the surrounding parts, and extra time and care will be entailed to get it off evenly.

The "damping" should be done with a fairly wet rag and hot iron and must be continued until the gloss is taken off both layers of material.

PUTTING IN THE POCKETS

DIAGRAM 45

The flaps should be cut out and matched; then lined with the same lining as used for the coat, cut a shade smaller than the flaps.

When seaming on the lining it is necessary to keep it tight, so that when it is turned out the lining will not be seen on the outside.

The edges of flaps must be stitched in harmony with the edges of coat. Before inserting the flaps in forepart, the underarm cut must be seamed up and pressed open. This is shown by SECTION A; the seam is made from the armhole to the level of pocket mouth and in doing this the bottom end must be tapered off nicely, so that when the seam is pressed open there will not be a "bubble."

Having done this, the next step is to baste on a piece of linen across the back of pocket mouth as illustrated on SECTION B. The linen should be about 2⊠ in width and of sufficient length to reach from side seam to about an inch or so in front of pocket mouth.

SECTION C shows the outside of right forepart; the underarm seam has been pressed open and the pocket jetting is stitched on to the bottom of pocket mouth, the correct position being ascertained by placing the flap on the forepart and marking both ends, the actual seam being made a shade shorter at each end.

The silesia or pocketing may be seamed on to the jetting before the latter is sewn to the forepart, or afterwards as desired.

After this, the pocket mouth may be cut open and basted out, making a small piping on the outside, this being stitched down so as to make it firm and thin.

The flap is now ready to be inserted and this is seamed in from the inside; it should be placed with the lining uppermost, the bottom of flap pointing upwards whilst the top should be inserted into the pocket mouth. In this way it will be possible to turn the forepart over so that the right side is facing downwards and then the seam made from end to end of pocket mouth.

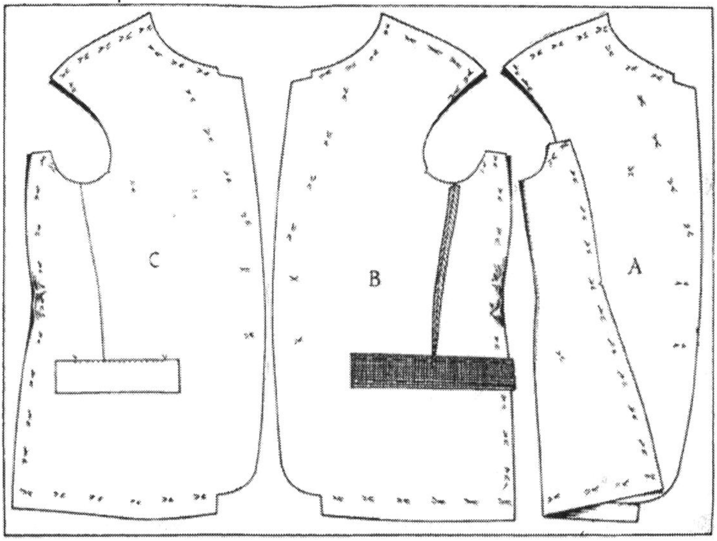

DIAGRAM 45.

DIAGRAM 46, SECTION A

This shows the right forepart; the stitching of jetting is plainly illustrated; the flap is turned upwards with the lining showing and the linen, which has been basted on the wrong side, is also indicated, a portion of which is seen protruding at side seam.

Having stitched the flap, it should be turned down in its proper position and basted along the seam on the outside in readiness for stitching and tacking. This should not be done until the pocketing has been sewn on, the bottom section being brought right up over the pocket mouth so that it catches the outside stitching and tackings of flap.

In addition to the piece of linen across the pocket mouth, an extra strip should be basted on so that it catches the back pocket tack and runs in an upward direction towards side seam, this being eventually fastened to the side seam.

The out-breast pocket is usually made with a welt; this is a strip of material about an inch in width and 6⊠ in length.

SECTION B illustrates the welt stitched on and in addition to this a facing is sewn on.

This type of pocket is rather complicated; it is made on the slant, the ends being perpendicular, therefore special care should be taken when stitching on the strips of material. The seam of the lower portion or welt should be a little longer than the seam of facing and the front end should be so arranged that the top row of stitching is at least 1/4⊠ farther back than the bottom row. This is necessary owing to the fact that the front end of welt really runs in a backward direction, and if both seams were the same length the opening would be seen beyond the end of welt and it would be impossible to cover it.

The back end of welt is made at a different angle; that is, taking the line of welt as a basis, but of course the back and front are parallel.

When cutting through the pocket mouth, the correct procedure is to snip the ends as illustrated on this section, the actual opening being made shorter than the seam of welt and the snips made at the angle shown on the diagram.

The front snip of welt must face towards the front edge of forepart, whilst the back snip must face towards the side seam. The snipping of the facing is not so important, providing the seam is made shorter than the actual seam of welt at both ends.

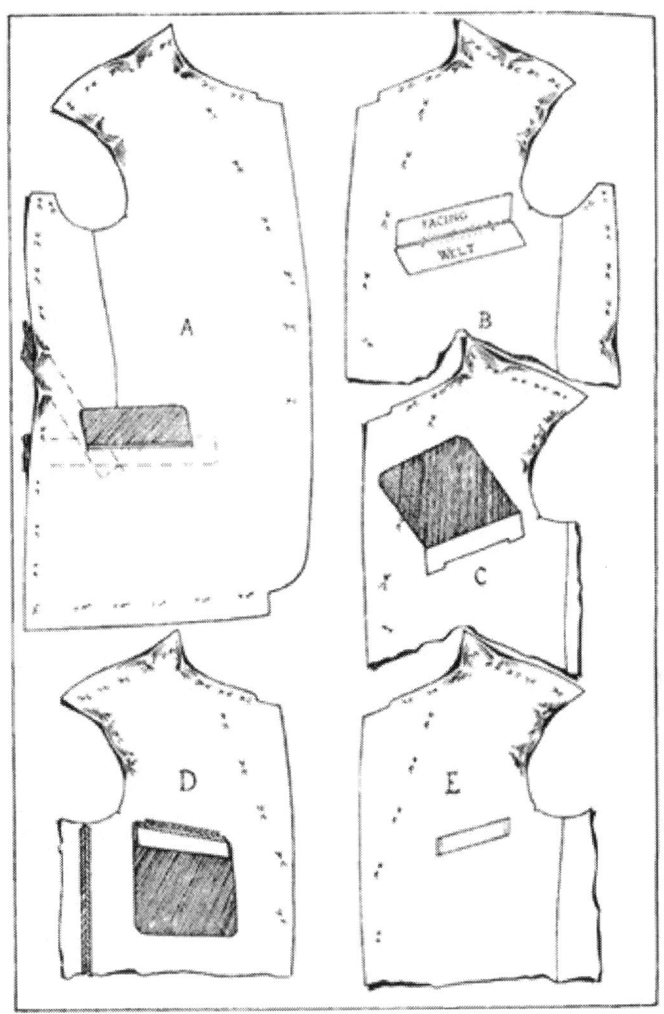

DIAGRAM 46.

Both seams are pressed open; linen must be put through the welt, and then the pocket should be seamed on; this, of course, may be done before the welt is sewn on.

If there is a stripe in the material or a pattern which requires matching, the welt will require special treatment, as it is cut on the slant and when the seam is taken off it gets a quarter of an inch lower down, thus throwing the pattern out unless this has been allowed for. Therefore, when basting on the welt it will be advisable to allow for this seam by dropping the welt, or by allowing an extra seam and then adjusting it to its proper position when basting it on.

The end must be tacked through the pocketing, and in addition a piece of linen may be included at the back; sometimes they are tacked through the canvas; this is not a very satisfactory method, as it is liable to drag across the fronts.

SECTION C illustrates the welt turned up in its proper position with a piece of silesia sewn on; this must be turned over and basted to the welt, making the latter about 1⊠ in width.

After this, the silesia should be snipped at each end so that it may be passed through the pocket opening; but at the same time a portion of the pocketing must be left outside to line the welt; this is done by folding it over and cutting it from the sides to the actual ends of pocket mouth.

SECTION D shows the inside of left forepart; the welt pocketing has been passed through and the seam of pocket facing is clearly illustrated. Another piece of silesia is now placed over the first piece; it is joined to welt facing and then seamed round.

SECTION E illustrates the finished welt; both ends must be turned in very carefully and tacked, as shown on this diagram.

CUTTING AND MAKING CANVAS

DIAGRAM 47, SECTION A

This is a very important part in the making of a jacket, and it is worth while spending a little extra time in preparing the canvas, which is really the mainstay of the garment.

It must be remembered that a man's shoulder is hollow, and in order to get a good fitting garment, the shoulder must be made to fit this hollow by shaping not only the outside material, but also the interlining or canvas, which is put between the forepart and the facing.

There are various ways of producing this effect, but the method I shall deal with is that usually adopted, viz. by stretching the shoulder end, shoulder seam and the hollow of neck slightly.

First of all, the canvas must be cut out as shown by solid line of SECTION A, this being the same shape as forepart at shoulder reaching as far as front pitch; it must then be cut down to bottom, making it about 4⊠ or 5⊠ at the latter point.

The upper portion is usually provided with an extra layer of canvas or horsehair, the shape of this being as indicated by dot and dash line, these two portions being fastened together either by a padding stitch by hand, or, if desired, it may be stitched out by machine. In order to get the shape at shoulder, cuts should be made at scye and shoulder as indicated by dotted lines for the main piece of canvas and dot and dash lines for the extra piece of canvas or horsehair. The cuts must be opened out when the two parts are being joined, so that extra length is produced both at scye and shoulder seam.

SECTION B plainly shows the canvas with the extra layer of horsehair well padded, the edge of same being bound with a strip of lining to prevent it fraying; the shoulder is stretched at scye and shoulder seam, and, in addition to this, the neck is slightly stretched, this latter being done by giving it a gentle pull under the iron.

This is the correct shape of shoulder and the cloth forepart must be stretched to fit this shaped canvas, otherwise all the work that is put into the canvas is useless. It is quite an easy matter to get this effect by pressing the shoulder in all directions after the forepart has been basted on to the canvas.

SECTION C illustrates the right forepart basted on to the canvas; the shoulder is well stretched in the various directions; the silesia pocket is plainly shown; the linen stay from the back of pocket to side seam is marked; the front tack is taken through the canvas; linen is basted on the edges and along the bridle; linen is also fastened to catch the buttons and the lapel is well padded.

This also is an item which should not be treated too lightly; a well-shaped lapel is only produced by padding it carefully and making it roll over gracefully. Both foreparts should be treated in this way and well pressed before attempting to put in the facings and linings.

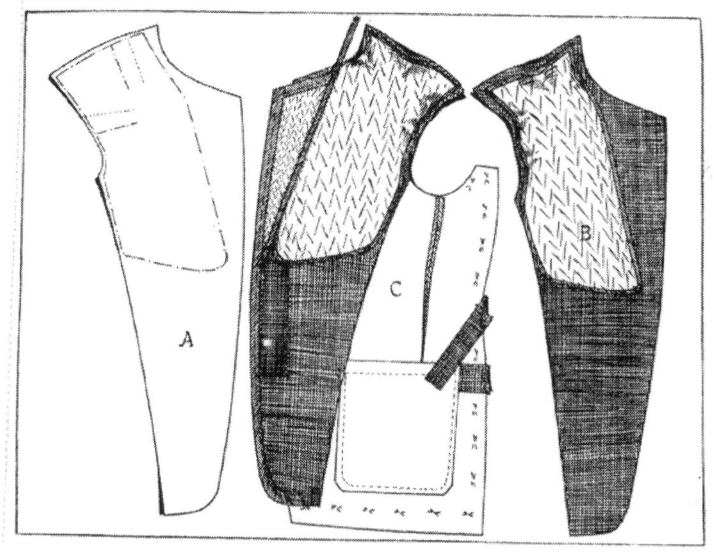

DIAGRAM 47.

MAKING UP THE LININGS

DIAGRAM 48, SECTION A

The facings and lining should be fitted to the foreparts and then the lining seamed on; this may just be pressed over or, if desired, stitched on the outside. Three pockets are usually made in the lining, two breast and one ticket, the latter being made in the left side.

First of all, the jettings which are made from the lining must be cut out and sewn on, as shown by SECTION A. The length of the breast pocket is about 6⊠ and the ticket pocket is made about 3 1/2⊠. Having stitched the jettings on as illustrated, the pocket mouth must be cut open; then the pieces must be passed through so that they are on the inside; finally, both edges must be basted, thus forming a piping, these being stitched down.

A strip of lining is also required to place at the back, so that it forms a facing; then the silesia pocketing must be put on and seamed round, the depth of the pockets being made to taste. The breast pocket is about 7⊠ deep, whilst the ticket pocket is about 3 1/2⊠ to 4⊠ deep.

The shoulders of facings must be shaped in harmony with the foreparts, and this is usually done by letting in a wedge as illustrated, this being covered with a piece of lining after the shoulders have been basted round, the amount of wedge being automatically fixed when the facing takes the shape of the forepart which has been previously stretched.

Sometimes a pleat is made under the arm to compensate for the dart; but a dart or seam may be made if desired.

When the facings are completed they should be basted to their respective foreparts. SECTION B shows the right facing basted to the forepart; the latter cannot be seen, as the lining completely covers it.

The facing should be eased on at the point of lapel, so that when it is seamed on and turned over, the seam will come under the facing at the back of lapel. This is very important, for if the facing is at all tight at this part, the lapels will not lie nicely; in fact they will curl upwards and look very unsightly. This is quite a common fault with pointed lapels and care should be taken to allow plenty of material in both directions of step of lapel when this style is being made up. Of course, the nature of material must be taken into consideration; for instance, a fine cashmere will not require as much as a tweed, and it is only with experience that the exact amount may be judged.

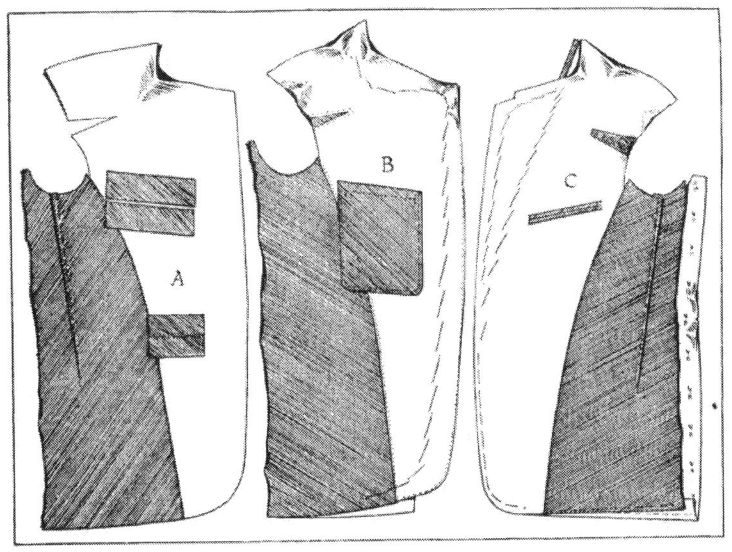

DIAGRAM 48.

After the facing has been stitched on to the forepart, the edges must be basted out. Here again, care must be taken to get the edge as thin as possible. The best method is to press the seam open before it is turned over, as this gives a very nice edge. Of course it is not absolutely necessary, and if not adopted, the edges must be well "rolled" between finger and thumb before being basted down.

SECTION C represents the right forepart laid out flat with the facing and lining uppermost; the edges have been basted; the shoulder is shown with the "puff" of lining over the wedge previously explained; the finish of breast pocket is plainly shown; the pleat is arranged from the scye terminating at the level of the outside flap pocket, and the bottom has been turned up to show the method of finishing.

After the foreparts have been lined, the edges should be well pressed; then the lapels must be turned over and pressed along the bridle or crease edge. They should be pressed quite flat in the first place and finally the crease should be taken out for a few inches above the bottom of lapel.

DIAGRAM 49, SECTION A

This represents the right forepart with the lapel turned over in its proper position; the bottom is turned up in line with the stitch-marks; the shoulder has taken its hollow form; the bridle is seen in line with the crease edge of lapel, and in addition to this, the lining is plainly indicated down side seam and around the bottom of armhole. This latter item is very important, because if there is insufficient lining at the bottom of scye, there will be a "drag" when the garment is finished.

The position of buttons is indicated by stitch-marks; these, of course, must be located after the holes have been worked.

SECTION B shows the back basted on to the back lining; the centre seam has been sewn up and pressed open; a pleat is arranged down the centre of lining, this being necessary owing to the fact that the cloth stretches more than the lining and the pleat would compensate for any strain that may be put on the back. It is also advisable to allow a fair margin of lining, especially round the shoulders, as this is usually taken up when wadding is placed round the back scye or at the shoulder point.

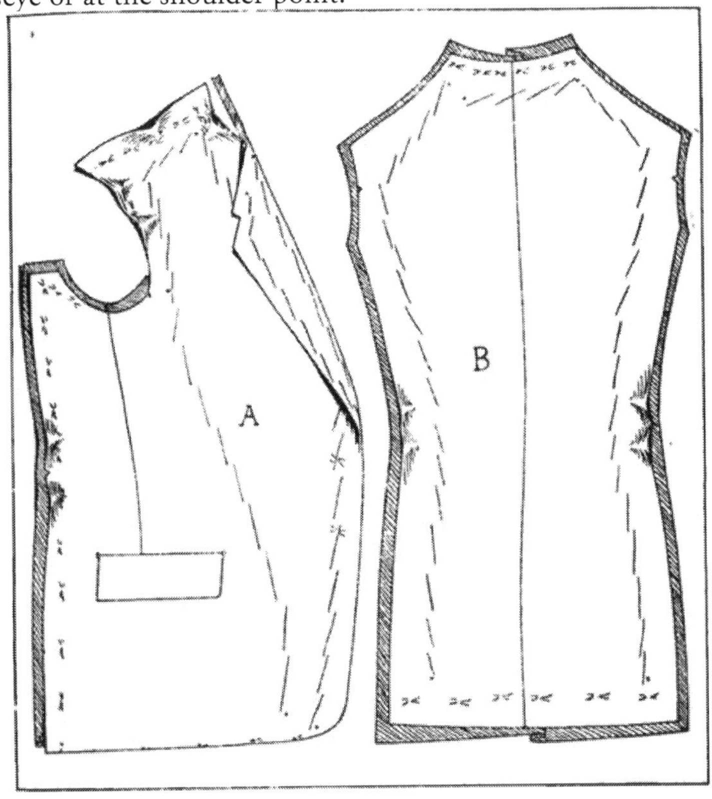

DIAGRAM 49.

DIAGRAM 50

This diagram illustrates both foreparts and back joined at the side seam. This is known as the "closing" stage, and when basting the side seam the balance marks at waist must be kept together if a well-balanced garment is to be obtained.

In some cases it may be necessary to alter these balance marks. For instance, if a man has a round back or stoops slightly, the back may be allowed to go up about 1/2⊠ or more according to the amount of deformity; on the other hand, the figure may be erect, in which case the back may be dropped according to requirements. The first instance would be lengthening the back balance and the latter would be shortening it.

No doubt these alterations would be provided for in the cutting, but I quote them to show the importance of keeping to the balance marks.

After the side seam has been pressed open, the lining must be basted, and it is the usual plan that the back lining overlaps the forepart lining.

The bottom must also be turned up evenly all round and the lining basted in position ready to be felled.

The shoulder seams may be basted, seamed up and pressed open and the back lining basted over the shoulder seam of facing.

When this is completed, the stitch-marks across the back neck and those in the neck of foreparts should form one continuous line, this being the line of neck to which the under-collar is sewn.

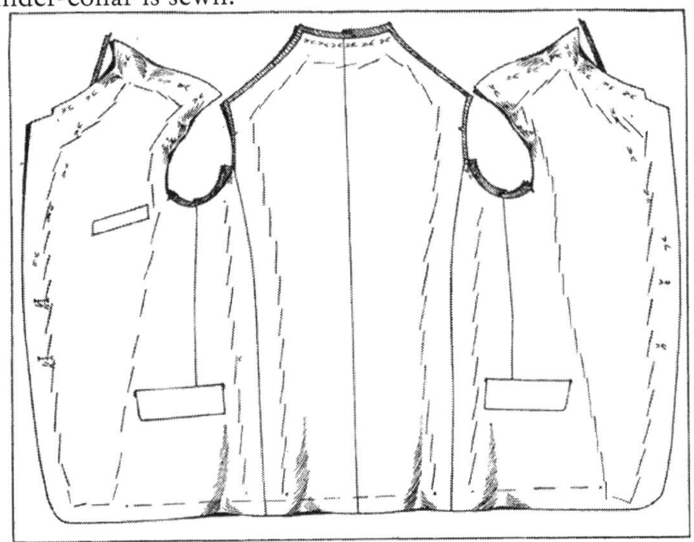

DIAGRAM 50.

DIAGRAM 51

This diagram illustrates the making-up of collar in various stages.

Collars are made up in many ways by different workmen. Sometimes the under-collar (SECTIONS B and C) is made up first of all and fastened to the neck of coat when it is shaped and finally the outside collar (SECTION D) is put on.

Another method is the one adopted in this case. The collar is made up completely before it is joined to the coat. The method of cutting the canvas is a matter of great importance; it must be on the bias so that it sets nicely round the neck, but the part of collar which is joined to the end of lapel must be on the straight. On SECTION A the outline of collar is clearly shown on a piece of canvas and the arrow indicating the part which must be placed on the straight of the material. When the canvas is cut in this way, it will be seen that the collar is well on the bias in every direction, with the exception of the collar end, which, of course, must be made in accordance with shape of lapel.

Another point which must not be overlooked is that the canvas must have a seam at the centre back, so that both ends of collar are on the straight. If the canvas is cut in one piece, the ends will not be alike; one will be on the straight, whilst the other will be on the bias, and it will be found that the end which is on the bias will not fit as nicely as the end which has been cut on the straight.

The back seams of canvas and under-collar must be seamed up, basted together and then the fall padded as illustrated on SECTION B. The stand of collar may be padded like the fall; or, if desired, may be stitched out by machine, or even side-stitched by hand.

After the collar has been padded, it should be shaped with the iron; this is done by slightly stretching both the edges as shown in this section, thus making the crease edge shorter.

The crease edge must also be drawn in slightly with a "draw thread" and then the stand should be pressed over as illustrated by SECTION C.

I now come to a most important part. The collar must be fitted to the neck; it must hold the lapel in the desired position; it must be the right height and last, but not least, it must not be too short, as this will spoil any garment.

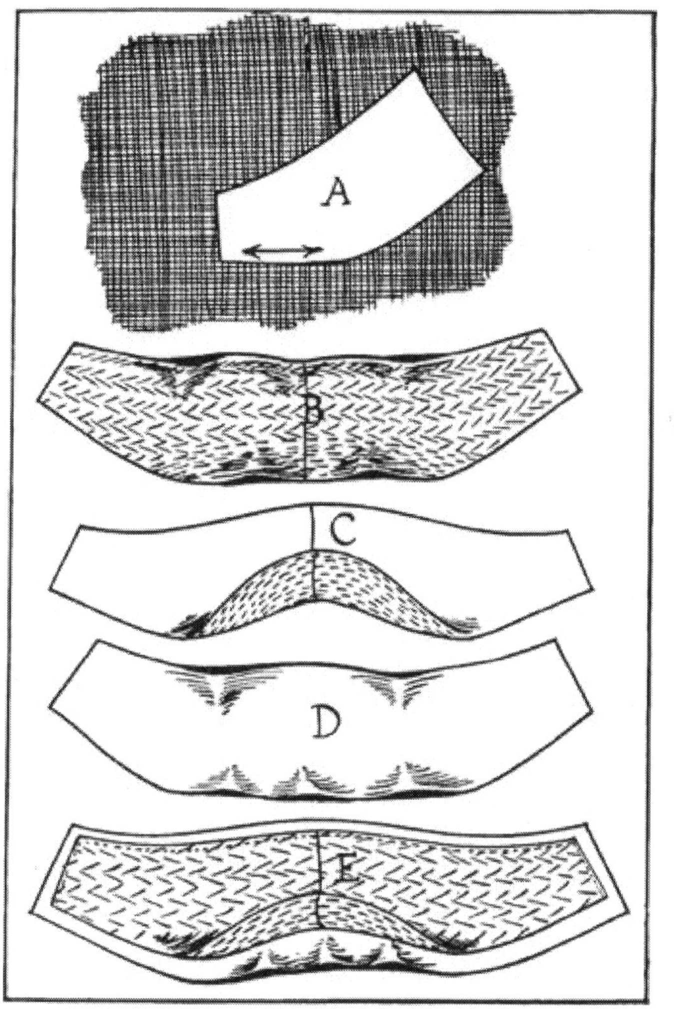

DIAGRAM 51.

Having decided that these points are correct, the outside collar, which is usually cut in one piece, must be prepared; the edges must be stretched sufficiently to ensure that it almost corresponds with the shape of under-collar, and any excess of material, which may show itself at the crease edge, must be shrunk away.

SECTION D shows the outside collar stretched at both stand and fall edges, whilst SECTION E illustrates the under-collar stitched on to the outer collar before it is trimmed and turned out.

The collar may now be joined to the neck of coat; sometimes the seam is made "raw" edge, and sometimes it is turned in; either way is correct and depends upon the nature of the material used.

The outside collar is "drawn" across the lapel by hand, this operation being done very neatly, as it shows on the outside.

The stand and fall must be pressed separately; then the crease edge of collar and a section of the lapel must also be pressed, after which the coat is ready for the sleeves. The buttonholes may be worked before the sleeves are made and put in.

DIAGRAM 52

This diagram illustrates the neck section of coat; a portion of back is shown joined to the foreparts; the crease edges of lapels and collar are plainly indicated by stitch-marks, and the stand of collar is stitched.

DIAGRAM 53

This diagram illustrates the jacket ready for the sleeves; the fronts have been well pressed; the lapels and collar are complete and the armholes have been shaped out a shade.

DIAGRAM 54

This diagram portrays the right section of a jacket with the sleeve sewn in, the hang of which is plainly illustrated. It must have a forward hang, the front being about half-way across the flap.

This diagram also shows the pointed lapel, which has been referred to previously.

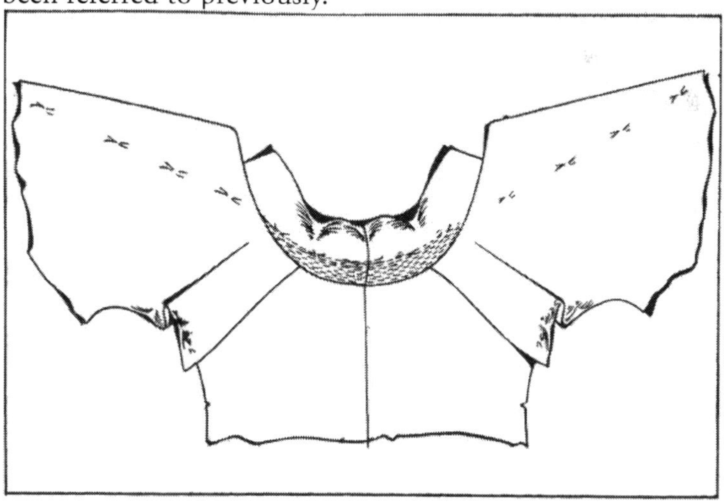

DIAGRAM 52.

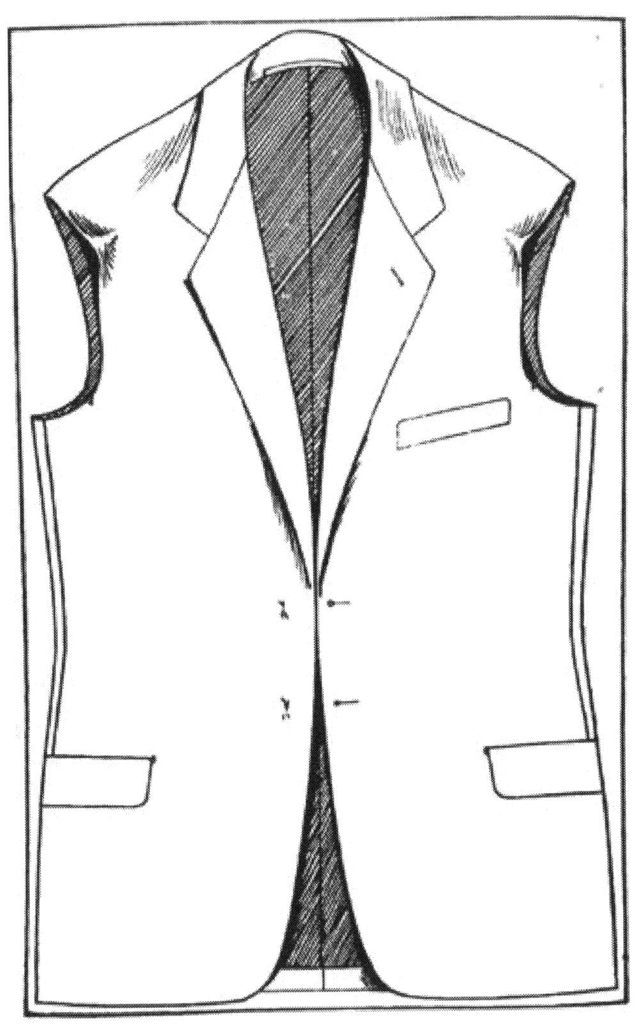

DIAGRAM 53.

DIAGRAM 54

MAKING THE SLEEVES

DIAGRAM 55

Jacket sleeves are invariably made with open cuffs and finished with two, three, or four holes and buttons, the holes in many cases being imitation ones.

To make the openings or slits it is necessary to sew on small pieces of lining or cloth on the cuff-facing, so that they reach to the top of the opening.

SECTIONS A and B show the top and under-sleeve with this piece seamed on and the slit is stitched from the actual length of sleeve upwards, the length of this seam being about 3 to 3 3/4⊠. The cuff facing, of course, is turned up before it is seamed.

After these portions have seen seamed up they should be turned out and basted, so that they appear as shown on SECTIONS C and D, which illustrate the wrong sides of top and under-sleeve.

DIAGRAM 56

The hindarm seam must be seamed up as shown by SECTION A; the seam is then pressed open and the top of slit tacked. The forearm seam must then be seamed up and pressed open; after which the cuff facing is turned up and fastened to the seam.

Sometimes canvas is put through the cuff, in which case it is usually cut on the bias so that it fits nicely.

The sleeve linings must now be seamed up and inserted into their respective sleeves and the cuffs felled round. (Section C illustrates the inside finish of cuff.) At least 1/2⊠ of lining must be allowed at the top as shown by SECTION B, as this amount is usually taken up when turning in the sleeve-head for felling.

SECTION D portrays one method of finishing the cuff; it has four holes and buttons.

Another important item is basting in the sleeves; these must have a certain amount of fulness at the top and also a little under the arm.

The pitch or hang of sleeve is also very important; it must not be too backward-hanging and at the same time must not be too forward.

SECTION E illustrates the upper portion of the left sleeve; it is drawn in so that the position of fulness may be seen at a glance. To baste this into the scye, start at front pitch, easing the topsleeve gradually at first, increasing slightly at the crown, then decreasing gradually at the hindarm seam and finally giving a little ease under the arm.

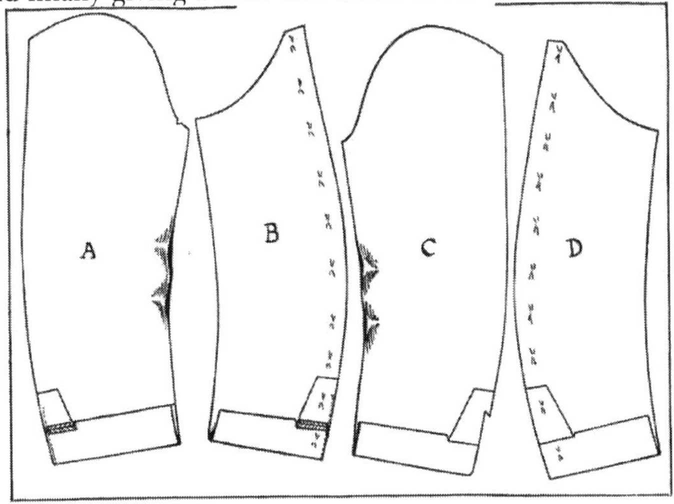

DIAGRAM 55.

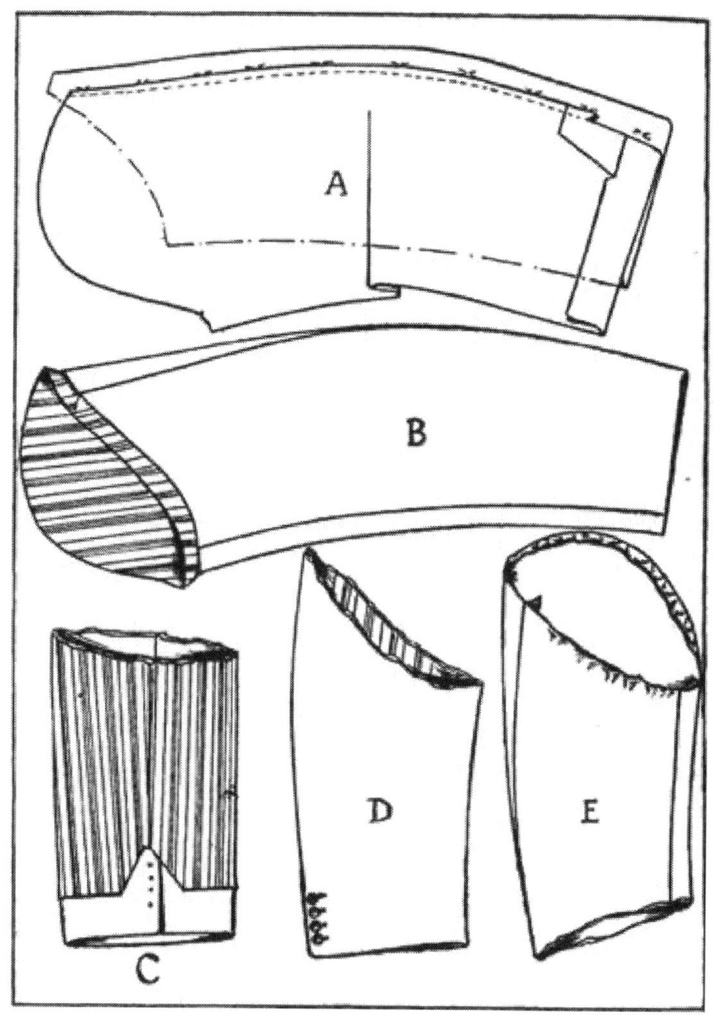

DIAGRAM 56.

After the sleeve has been basted in, the coat should be held up on the palm of the hand to ascertain if the hang is right. The front of sleeve should hang in line with the centre of flap, as illustrated by Diagram 54.

If the sleeve is not right, it must be taken out and the pitch altered according to requirements. For instance, if the sleeve is too backward-hanging the front pitch must be raised, and if it is hanging too far forward, the pitch must be lowered accordingly.

Before seaming in the sleeves the fulness must be pressed away; this is done from the inside with a fairly warm iron.

The sleeve seams must be pressed open before the armholes are basted round and then a small piece of wadding basted as near as possible to the seam. This will give a good shape to the crown of sleeve when the jacket is finished.

The sleeve lining must be felled in with a fair amount of fulness, in harmony with the sleeve itself, and special care taken that the linings are long enough.

Finally the garment must be pressed off; any "gloss" removed which may have been made; the buttons put on and then hung up to dry, as there is always a certain amount of damp ness in any garment immediately after it has been pressed.

HOW TO MAKE A WAISTCOAT

By PHILIP DELLAFERA

THE making of a waistcoat is not a difficult task, as there is not the amount of manipulation in the shoulders and fronts that is required for a jacket.

First of all, the stitch-marks must be put in, indicating position of pockets, etc., after which the pockets, usually of the "welt" variety, must be put in.

DIAGRAM 57, SECTION A

This shows the back with stitch-marks down side seams and across the back neck.

SECTION B

This illustrates the right forepart with the top welt stitched on and the silesia pocket included, this being seamed on before the welt is sewn to forepart.

The details of the seam are clearly shown and have been fully dealt with in the article on Jacket-making; therefore, it is not necessary to go over the same ground again, as all welts are made in the same way.

SECTION C

This shows the right forepart with the top welt seamed in ready for the ends to be turned in and tacked, whilst the bottom welt is complete with both ends tacked.

After the pockets have been put in, the foreparts should be basted on to the canvas or interlining, which should be cut the same shape as forepart, but need not extend right over to the side seam.

The pockets may be tacked through this interlining, and if the back tack is not covered with canvas, a strip of linen should be put on and carried to the side seam.

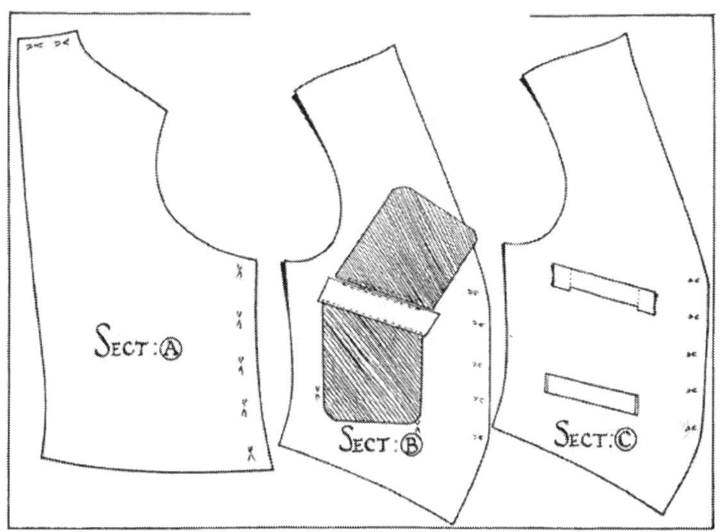

DIAGRAM 57.

DIAGRAM 58, SECTION A

This illustrates the back view of right forepart; the welt tacks are plainly marked; the strip of linen is carried from the back tack of bottom welt up to side seam; the shoulder is stretched slightly, so as to give it a little shape, and in addition to this, linen is basted on the edges and drawn in.

This "drawing-in" must be started about half-way down the opening; the linen must be held very firmly in the region of the top button and then just kept steady down the fronts and bottom.

The excess of material produced by this operation must now be pressed away by using a damp rag and fairly warm iron in the first place, and then finishing off with the iron only.

The foreparts are now ready for the facings; these may be cut in one piece, but in the majority of cases there is at least one join and this is usually at the bottom.

SECTION B

This portrays the facing basted on and seamed round from the neck point down opening and front edge, and also along the bottom.

If side vents or slits are required, it will be necessary to continue this stitching from the bottom edge up the side seam for a distance of about 2⊠ or according to the amount of facing that may be available; in any case sufficient facing must be left so that the forepart lining may be felled on.

After the facing has been seamed on, the edges should be trimmed, taking care not to cut too near the seam; then it must be turned out and basted along the edge.

The inner edge of facing should be fastened to the interlining as shown by SECTION C, which gives the inside view of right forepart with the facing in and ready to be lined with striped silesia or sleeve lining.

When cutting the lining for the foreparts, it is usual to provide for a pleat; sometimes this extends to the full length of forepart, but in most cases it is made from the shoulder seam down to the breast.

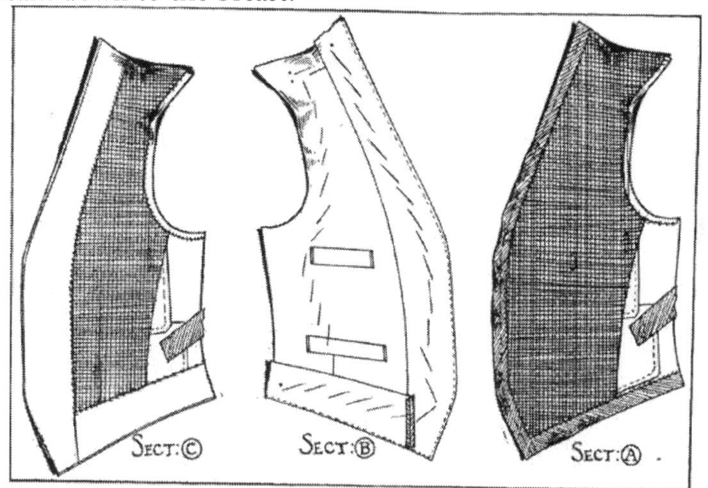

DIAGRAM 58.

DIAGRAM 59, SECTION A

This diagram shows the right forepart completely lined, the pleat is plainly indicated and the stretching of shoulder is also illustrated.

Having finished both foreparts, the back must be prepared, and this is shown by SECTION B.

The centre back seam is sewn up and pressed open; then the back straps are made up and stitched on as illustrated by this diagram; the buckle being fastened on the left strap.

The making up of back straps is a matter of taste; sometimes they are just turned in and stitched along the top edge, and in other cases they are seamed up and turned out, the seam being arranged to come down the centre of strap, thus forming a thin edge both at top and bottom.

The back lining is cut out in harmony with the back, making it slightly smaller at bottom and armholes; this is necessary so that when it is made up the lining will not show itself on the outside.

The back and back lining must be joined across the bottom as indicated by Diagram 60; and the foreparts basted on to the back.

The usual and probably the best method is to baste each forepart separately to the back both at side seams and shoulder seams, as shown by this diagram; and then to bring the lining up so that it is face to face with the forepart lining. The seams must then be basted again, care being taken to get them as near as possible to each other. They may then be seamed round, starting either from neck or bottom as desired, and including the armhole portion, one seam being made from bottom of side seam, around the armhole and across the shoulder seam to neck, whilst the other is done in the reverse direction.

It will thus be seen that the waistcoat is enclosed in a sort of "bag," with an opening at the back neck; and it is through this opening that the forepart will have to be pulled, each forepart being carefully pulled out separately.

The bottom of side seams must be pulled out to their full extent and the same thing must be done at the armhole; this latter may be basted round so that the lining does not show on the outside; or, if desired, it may be pressed right away without basting.

The back neck must then be turned in with the lining brought up to it and felled across, a strip of linen being sewn in so that it will take any strain at this part.

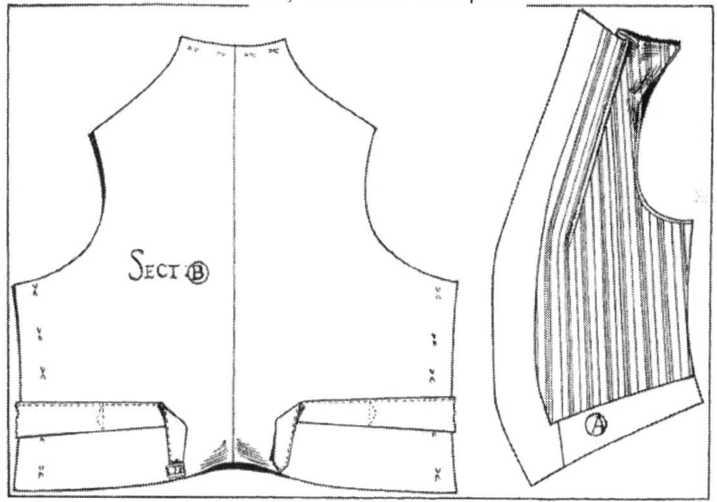

DIAGRAM 59.

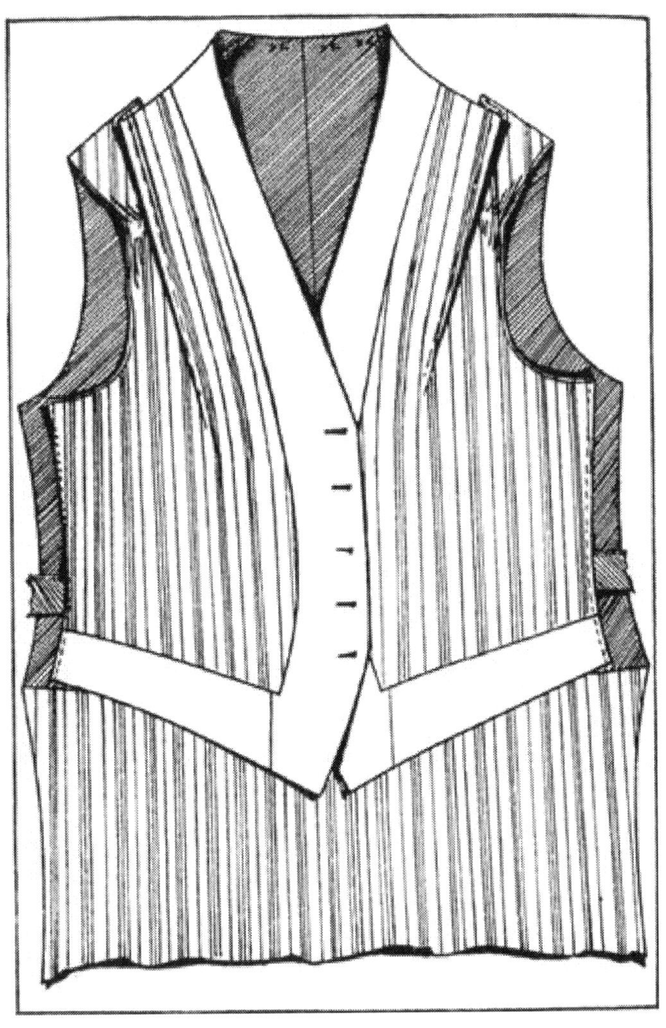

DIAGRAM 60.

DIAGRAM 61.

DIAGRAM 61

This diagram illustrates the finished garment; the holes are worked in the left forepart; the chain hole has been omitted, as this is a matter of taste; the shoulders are slightly stretched and the back lining is carried right up to the top of back.

Sometimes the back neck is made from the same material as the vest, in which case a small strip of material must be sewn on before the facings are put in and thus the two foreparts are joined together at the neck before they are basted to the back.

This method is certainly much stronger than the other, but is liable to be thick and clumsy round the neck, especially if a thick material is being used; whilst if the lining is brought right up to the top it will produce a much thinner edge round the back neck.

GARMENTS FOR MEN AND BOYS

ADVANTAGES OF HOME-MADE APPAREL

1. Although such garments as shirts, blouses, night shirts, pajamas, undergarments, smoking jackets, house coats, lounging robes, or bath-robes, and similar garments for men and simple coats and suits for boys are not generally included in dressmaking, they offer an excellent opportunity for the woman in the home to do a service that will mean a step toward economy and much satisfaction to the male members of the family. Men are more interested in such wearing apparel than the average woman thinks, and there is real economy in making these garments at home. As a rule, material better than that used in ready-made garments can be purchased for much less money than the made-up garments themselves, and it is always possible to keep enough of the material on hand for patching and making new collars and cuffs, so that the life of such garments can be lengthened.

The making of garments for men and boys also offers excellent possibilities to the woman who wishes to specialize. For example, a good business may be built up by making well-fitting shirts of unusual materials, or coats for barbers, surgeons, etc., or suits for small boys.

2. Many women hesitate when it comes to making garments for men and boys because they imagine that the work is difficult. In this, however, they are in error, for when such garments are understood they are simple to construct and the work is easily accomplished. Just as in making garments for women, the chief essentials are suitable materials, exactness of measurements, accuracy in planning and cutting, care in basting, neatness and skill in sewing, correctness in the joining of all the parts, and care in pressing and finishing.

MEN'S SHIRTS

TYPES OF SHIRTS

3. Shirts for men are really of four types—the *dress shirt*, the *negligée shirt*, the *outing shirt*, and the *work shirt*. The distinguishing feature of the dress shirt is its bosom, which may be plain, plaited, or tucked and which must always be starched in laundering to have it give the proper appearance when worn with a dress suit. The other three shirts—the negligée, the outing, and the work shirt—are made without bosoms, although, for semidress occasions, negligée shirts are sometimes made with plaited fronts. These three types differ from one another chiefly in material, because the purpose for which the shirt is intended determines the material of which it is constructed.

4. Front Closings.—Any of the types of shirts mentioned may be made with a front-plait closing when the shirt must be slipped over the head in putting it on. Shirts may be made in the more general style of what is called a *coat shirt;* that is, a shirt that opens all the way down the front and may be slipped on in the same way as a coat.

5. Yokes.—Shirts are made with a shallow yoke in the back and some fulness below it, so as to allow for perfect freedom and thus overcome any danger of splitting because of the expanding of the shoulder muscles. Flannel shirts are sometimes made without gathers in the back, however, such shirts being often worn without a coat as part of a uniform.

6. Neck Finishes.—The neck of a *dress shirt* and a *negligée shirt* is usually finished off with a neck band, to which separate stiff or soft collars may be attached, although in some cases, a permanent collar of the same material as the shirt is put on.

The neck of an *outing shirt* may be finished with a band to which stiff or soft collars may be attached, but generally a permanent turn-over collar is attached.

A *work shirt* is always made with an attached, soft, turn-down collar of the same material as the shirt.

7. Sleeve Finishes.—The sleeves of *dress shirts* are finished with bands that are 1 inch wide when finished. Straight, stiff cuffs are attached to the bands when the dress shirts are worn.

There are three distinct ways of finishing the sleeves of *negligée* and *outing shirts;* namely, with regular cuffs, with French, or double, cuffs, or with wristbands to which separate cuffs may be attached. Separate cuffs are not so much in evidence as attached cuffs, but, as is the case with other articles of wear, styles control the width and particular cut of the cuffs and collars of these two types of shirts.

The sleeves of an *outing shirt* are usually made full length; however, they may be made short or the lower part of the sleeve may be made detachable, generally at a point above the elbow, thus making the shirt an ideal garment for outdoor sports.

The sleeves of a *work shirt* are always made full length and are practically always finished with wristbands.

SHIRT MATERIALS

8. Varieties of Materials.—The materials suitable for shirt making are numerous. Chief among the plain materials are radium silk, crêpe de Chine, tub silk, silk broadcloth, silk lajerz, pongee, habutaye, soisette, linen, oxford cloth, poplin, percale, chambray, sateen, galatea, duck, denim, khaki, and flannel.

Equally as popular as the plain materials are some of the novelty cotton shirtings, which come in great variety, with striped, figured, and basket-weave effects. Of these materials, madras is probably the most popular because of its attractive designs and excellent wearing qualities. There are also numerous striped flannels, silks, and linens, which make attractive shirts. Hickory shirting, a coarse, cotton, striped material, is extensively used for work shirts.

9. Suitability of Materials.—Although the use to which a shirt is to be put governs the material of which it is to be made, taste and judgment must be exercised in selecting materials.

For *negligée*, any of the light-weight fabrics mentioned may be chosen, depending on the use that is to be made of the shirts, the season of the year in which they are to be worn, and the outlay that it is desired to make.

For *outing*, or *sports, shirts* that are to be used for hunting, camping, and similar outdoor sports in which they will be subject to hard wear, materials possessing good-wearing qualities, such as chambray, flannel, sateen, galatea, denim, khaki, and the like, are the ones from which to choose. The weight of the fabric for such shirts will depend on the taste of the person who is to wear them, as well as on the season of the year and the climate in which they are to be worn, and the coloring and the texture will depend on personal taste. As a rule, if such shirts are built on good lines and of shrunken material, they are sure to give satisfaction.

If sports shirts are to be used for town wear, as in playing golf, tennis, and similar outdoor games, such fabrics as fine linen and silk should be considered. Such shirts offer excellent opportunity for the expression of good taste so far as color schemes and textures are concerned.

For *work shirts*, materials that will give service should always be selected, such materials as those mentioned for outing shirts intended for hunting and camping being particularly good, as is also hickory shirting.

10. Findings for Shirts.—Attention should be given also to the thread and buttons to be used in shirt making. The thread to be used for stitching will be governed by the material that is employed. Cotton and linen fabrics are generally stitched with cotton thread, and silk and woolen fabrics, with silk thread. The size of cotton thread to use will depend on the texture of the material, although, as a rule, the thread should be reasonably coarse so that the stitching line will be clearly defined. Of course, good thread is absolutely necessary for men's shirts, because the stitching should be even and smooth and should hold fast until the garment is worn out.

Small, flat, untrimmed buttons should be employed for men's shirts, the better grade of pearl buttons for shirts made of the finer fabrics and the cheaper grade for heavy outing and work shirts. Three, five, or seven buttons are required for each shirt, depending on the front closing.

11. For the bosoms of dress shirts and for the front plait, collar band, and wristbands or cuffs of negligee shirts, it is necessary to provide material to be used as interlining. Generally, such material as butchers' linen or medium-weight muslin is suitable for this purpose, the linen being used for expensive materials and the muslin for the cheaper grades.

Instead of making collar bands for shirts, it is advisable to purchase them ready made, especially if time is an item in shirt construction. Collar bands complete even to the buttonholes and ready to attach can be bought for a small sum in nearly all drygoods stores. If such a band is to be used, purchase it according to the neck measure. These bands have an allowance for shrinkage, so it is not necessary to shrink them before attaching them to shirts, as both will shrink together.

12. Quantity of Material Required for Shirts.—The quantity of material required for a man's shirt depends on the width of the fabric of which the shirt is to be made, the size of the person for whom it is to be made, and, to some extent, the type of the shirt.

As a rule, a person with a 14 1/2-inch neck and a 34-inch chest will require about 3 1/4 yards of 32- to 40-inch material; a person with a 15- or 15 1/2-inch neck and a 36-inch chest, about 3 1/2 yards; a person with a 16-inch neck and a 40-inch chest, about 3 3/4 yards; and so on. Generally, the 36-inch material cuts to better advantage than the narrower widths. For interlining, more than 1/2 yard of 36-inch material is seldom required.

13. In order to determine the exact quantity of material required for a shirt, a good plan is to arrange the complete shirt pattern on paper that is as wide as the material that is to be used and then measure the length of the paper covered by the pattern. For a work shirt, it is always advisable to procure enough material for replacing the collar and wristbands as they wear out, as well as for an extra thickness that will be needed in making the collar. It is well to bear in mind, also, that if two shirts are cut out at one time, the cutting can be done to better advantage and time will be saved in both cutting and making. Of course, for negligée and sports shirts, some men may object to having two garments of the same pattern or design, but for work shirts such a plan is entirely practical.

After the amount of material required for a shirt has been accurately determined, it is an excellent plan, whether a woman makes shirts for members of her own family or is engaged in the business of shirt making for regular customers, to keep a memorandum of it for future use.

14. Shrinking Material and Setting the Color.—If colored material is to be used for making shirts, it is often considered advisable to set the color and to shrink the material before making it up. As shirts are very easy-fitting, however, it is not necessary to do this work if the material is not likely to shrink very much. Of course, not all colors will fade, but when there is any likelihood of such an occurrence, it is always advisable to set the colors.

NEGLIGÉE SHIRT

15. The making of a negligee shirt is considered first, as this is the style of shirt used most. Two styles of negligée shirts are shown in Figs. 1 and 2. The shirt shown in Fig. 1 has a 1 1/2-inch plait and French, or soft, cuffs, and the one shown in Fig. 2 has simply a hem at the front closing and cuffs or wide wristbands that are to be starched. Otherwise, these shirts are identical, each having a yoke across the back and an opening that extends the full length of the front, thus making them coat shirts.

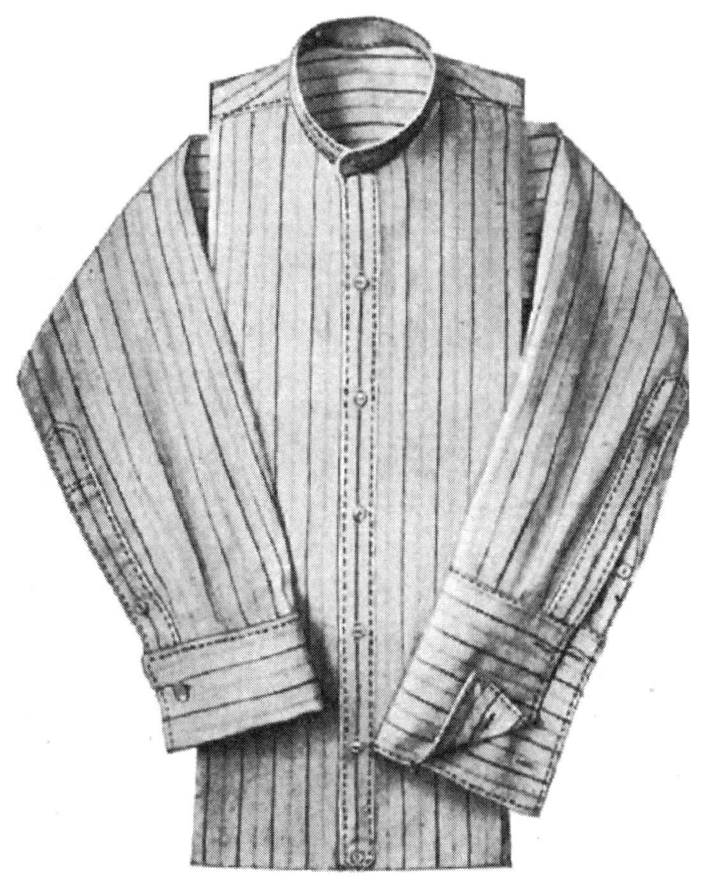

FIG. 1

16. Shirt Pattern. In purchasing a pattern for a shirt, three measurements must be considered; the neck, the chest, and the length-of-sleeve. The neck measurement, however, is the one that governs the size of pattern to be purchased. If this is correct, the other measurements may be altered satisfactorily.

In making a shirt, it is a good plan to use as a guide a shirt that has proved satisfactory. From this garment, the pattern pieces may be altered.

For example, the length of the sleeve may be measured from the tip of the shoulder to a point where the cuff joins. Then this measurement may be used to adjust the tissue-paper sleeve pattern. If it is too short, slash the pattern through the center at the elbow point and separate the pieces. If it is too long, fold the pattern in the form of a tuck to shorten it. In either case, before cutting out the material, make the outer lines of the pattern even where it was altered.

FIG. 2

17. Placing Pattern Pieces on the Material. After the pattern pieces have been measured and altered, if necessary, place them on the material in such a way as to permit the material to be cut to the best advantage. As shown in Fig. 3, lay the material out on a flat surface and place on it first the front-pattern piece, keeping it 1 1/2 inches from the edge of the material. Take care, if striped material is used, to have the center front of the pattern come exactly on a stripe or in the stripe, so that when the plait is turned in position it will lap evenly with the stripe of the material.

In this case, the front plait is cut separately and applied. This is a decided advantage in striped material in order to have the stripes appear well in the plait. However, in most cases, the hem or plait may be cut in one with the center front and then turned and basted before cutting out the fronts so that the stripes will come in the desired location.

Next, place the center back on a fold and place the yoke and the cuff-pattern pieces so that the lengthwise threads run crosswise when the garment is worn. Place the plait section on a single thickness of material.

The collar band is shown in Fig. 3, but this may be made of a lighter-weight fabric than the shirt, or, as previously explained, may be purchased ready-made.

The remaining pattern pieces are shown in position in Fig. 3.

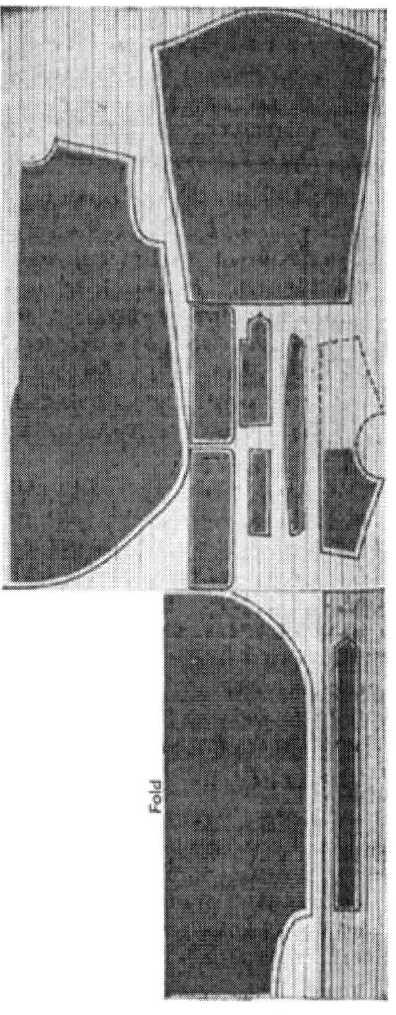

FIG. 3.

18. Allowances for Seam and Edge Finishing. In cutting out the shirt, if no seam allowance is provided in the pattern, make an allowance of 1/4 inch for the seams or finish on the neck edge of the fronts, the neck and the lower edges of the yoke, the upper edge of the back, the lower edge of the sleeves, all edges of the sleeve facings, cuffs, or wristbands, the collar or neck band, and the plait. For the other edges of the front section of the shirt, the yoke, the back of the shirt, and the sleeve, make a 3/8-inch allowance. Whether a plait is used, as in Fig. 1, or simply a hem, as in Fig. 2, there should be an allowance on the upper center front of the shirt for over-lapping. It is always advisable to place a mark on the neck curve exactly at the front line of the pattern to represent the center of the shirt front, so that this point will not be overlooked in making the garment.

In cutting shirts for men that are very large, it is sometimes necessary to provide four shirt lengths of material instead of three, and to piece the sleeve in the back with a lengthwise piece of material about one-third of its width. If this piecing is done neatly with a flat-fell seam, the joining will not be noticeable. By observing custom-made shirts, it will be seen that the sleeves are pieced in many instances, the piecing being done to save material in cutting a number of shirts at a time.

19. Making the Front Plait.—After cutting all the parts required for the shirt, the first step in its construction is to finish the front closing. For a coat closing, that is, an opening that extends the entire length of the shirt, the plait is finished in a manner similar to that shown in Fig. 1.

The length of this plait is a little less than the length of the opening, extending from the neck to the skirt section of the shirt.

Cut an interlining of lawn or cambric to be used under the plait and baste this interlining to the wrong side of the plait section to hold it in place.

In applying the plait, place the right side of the plait to the wrong side of the shirt on the left-hand side, and then baste and stitch. Press the seam open and turn the plait over on the right side, creasing it so that the seam is back from the edge about 1/4 inch on the inside of the shirt. Next, turn in the seam allowance on the other edge of the plait and baste and stitch the plait flat to the shirt, placing the stitching about 1/8 inch from the edge. Then add stitching to the outside edge of the plait to correspond with the stitching on the inside edge. The lower edge may be finished straight across or pointed as in Fig. 1.

20. Making the Front Facing.—The next step is to cut a strip of plain white, light-weight material for facing the right front of the shirt. Cut it 2 inches wide and as long as the strip cut for the plait. Fold this facing lengthwise through the center and place it to the right side of the material on the right-hand side of the shirt, having the raw edges of the facing to the outer edge of the shirt. Baste and stitch. Next turn the facing to the wrong side and crease the seam edges back away from the facing, having the joining back about

1/4 inch from the edge. Baste to the shirt. Then apply a row of stitching from the outside about 1/4 inch from the edge of the shirt. The folded edge of the facing is left free.

On some patterns, an allowance is made for the finish at the front. In this case, the usual method is to turn both sides in a hem.

If a hem is to be turned for the front closing, as in Fig. 2, it is necessary simply to insert a strip of interlining in the hem and to stitch it in place.

21. Making the Yoke.—The yoke in a shirt is made double and extends above the back portion. Therefore, gather the back section on each side and place it so that the top will come between the two thicknesses of the yoke. Arrange the gathers so that they will come over the shoulder blades when the shirt is worn, or 3 or 4 inches each side of the center back. Place the inside-yoke section with its right side to the wrong side of the back. Pin the yoke and back portions together and baste. Then pin and baste the other yoke portion in position, having the right sides of the back and yoke together. Next, bring the right side of each yoke portion up so that the armhole and neck edges come together and baste about 1 inch from the outer edge, taking care to have the yoke portion very smooth. Stitch across the yoke directly on the lower edge where the yoke and back portions join, and then stitch 1/4 inch above so that the stitching will harmonize with the flat-fell seams that are to be used in the side and sleeve seams.

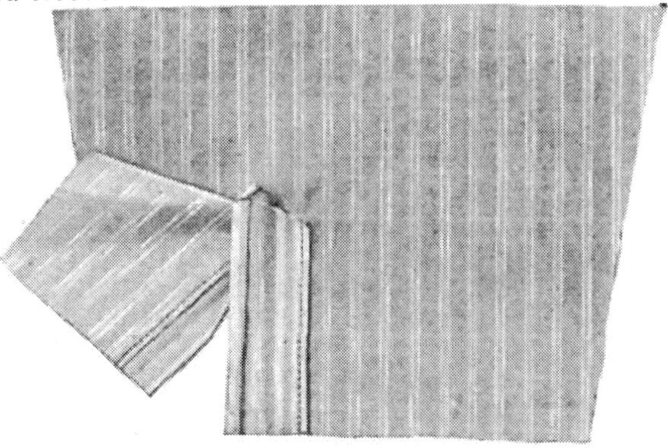

(A)

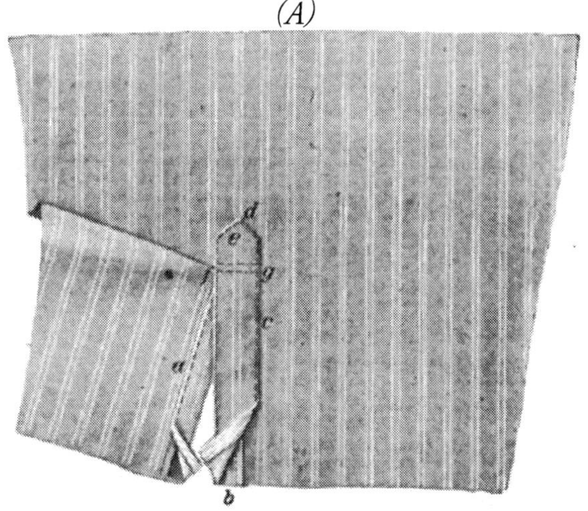

(B)

FIG. 4

22. Making the Shoulder Seams.—After the yoke is applied, join the front portions to it, concealing the shoulder seam between the two thicknesses of the yoke.

23. Finishing the Sleeve Openings.—Prepare the sleeves next by finishing the cuff openings. To do this, lay the sleeve right side down and place the two strips that are cut for the openings so that their wrong sides are up, the larger strip on the front of the sleeve, its shorter side toward the opening, and the smaller one toward the back of the sleeve; baste the strips in position, and then stitch with a 1/8-inch seam, as shown in Fig. 4 (*a*).

With this done, turn the free edge of the smaller piece over 1/8 inch on the side and the upper end and crease the edge. Bring it over to the right side and stitch it down, as at *a*, Fig. 4 (*b*). Then pull the longer strip to the right side of the opening and turn the sleeve right side up, creasing the free edges, as shown in Fig. 4 (*a*).

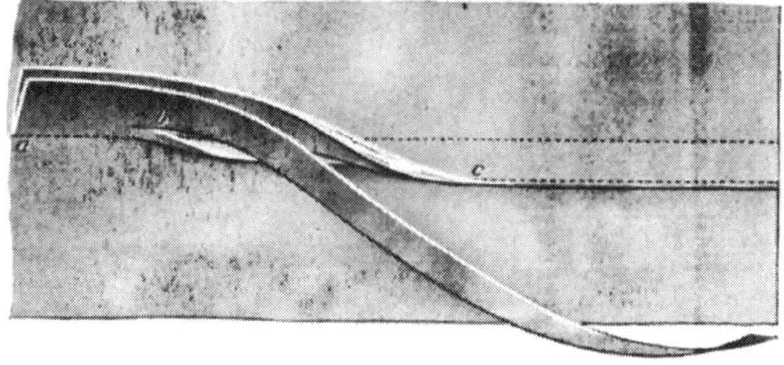

FIG. 5

Next, press open the seam that joins the larger piece to the sleeve and crease it down smoothly, as at *b*, Fig. 4 (*b*). Bring the edge over to the right side and baste it down, as at *c*, taking care that it overlaps the seam edge of the under piece so that this piece will not show when the cuff is fastened. Also, if striped material is used, be careful that the stripes match, as at *d*. When the pointed end *e* is turned under, clip away any surplus material and baste this part down very carefully.

When this is done, proceed to stitch, beginning at *f*, which is close to the end of the shorter strip, stitching across to *g*, and then back again 1/8 to 1/4 inch above the first cross-row, being careful to stitch through the shorter strip underneath with both rows of stitching. Stitch around the point and down on the inside edge, and then from *f* on the outer edge to the bottom of the opening.

24. Inserting the Sleeves.—The next step is to join the sleeves to the armholes. To do this, baste them in position and finish with a flat fell, as shown in Fig. 5, first stitching in a plain seam, as at *a*, trimming away one edge, as at *b*, and then turning the other edge under and stitching, as at *c*. Remember that it is best to have the two stitchings visible on the right side in making this seam.

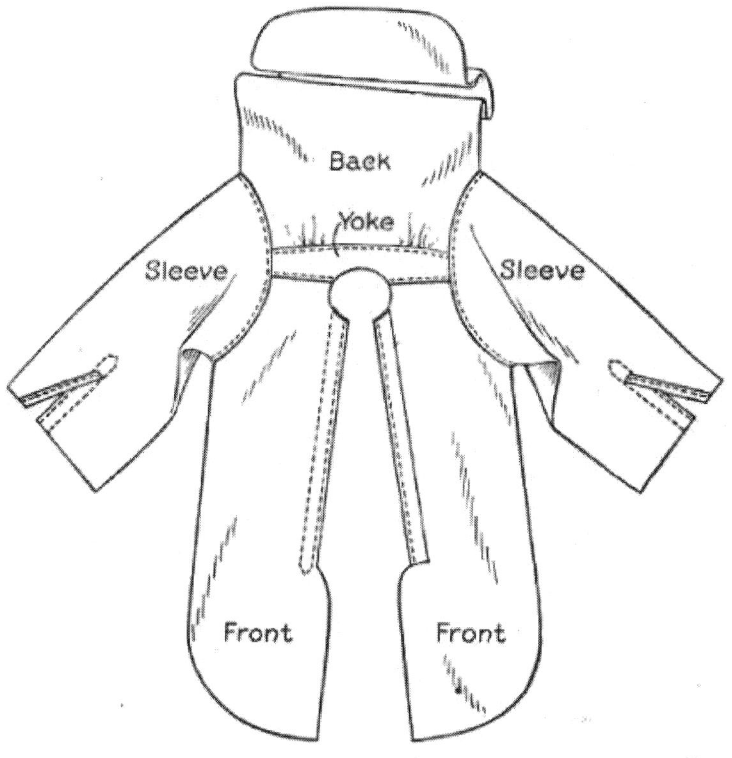

FIG. 6

25. Making the Under-Arm and Lower Finish.—The shirt is now ready to have the under-arm seams stitched. Finish these, also, with a flat fell and stitch them from the ends of the sleeves to a point about 8 inches from the bottom of the shirt, or to the point indicated on the pattern. Fig. 6 shows how the inside of the shirt appears before these seams are stitched.

After stitching the under-arm seams, finish the front, bottom, and side edges of the shirt with narrow hems.

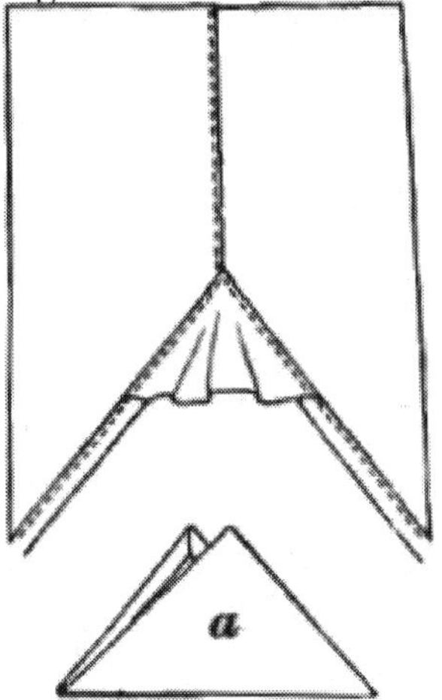

FIG. 7

26. Making the Gussets.—Gussets are placed at the bottom of the side seams to reinforce them. For each seam, cut a square of material that measures 1 3/4 inches on all sides, fold each square diagonally through the center, as at *a*, Fig. 7, turn the raw edges to the inside, making a very narrow turn, and then baste the turned edges together.

After the under-arm seams are stitched and the hems at the bottom of the shirt are in place, place the gusset with the folded, or diagonal, edge down, the point joining the under-arm seam of the shirt, at its termination, and the straight edges lying along the hems of the lower portion. Stitch the gusset securely in place, as shown in Fig. 7. This prevents the shirt from tearing or ripping at the under-arm seams, thus affording considerable protection.

27. Neck Bands.—As stated, neck bands may generally be purchased ready-made. This is a decided advantage, as they are accurate and inexpensive, too. Furthermore, it requires considerable work to make a neck band. If, however, it is not possible to purchase a neck band, one may be made in the following manner.

28. Material for Neck Bands.—It is not always desirable to make the neck band of the same material as the shirt, as this is often heavy or has cords running through it that will not permit of a smooth finish. Firm, even-weave cambric or long-cloth is especially suitable for neck bands of cotton shirts. Also, an interlining is required so that the band will fit up close and not sag. This may be of lawn or the same material as the band.

FIG. 8

29. Making a Neck Band.—Put the right sides of the two pieces of the neck-band material together and over them place the interlining, which has been cut the same size as the neck-band pieces. Then stitch around the band, beginning at the lower edge of the center-front at one end, continuing around the curved end, across the top, and around to the lower edge on the opposite end, leaving the bottom free. After stitching, trim the edge close to the stitching, say to within about 1/8 inch, then turn the band right side out, and smooth the curved edge carefully, pressing the rounding corners back with a hot iron, if necessary, so that they will lie perfectly flat.

With the band thus prepared, draw the two thicknesses apart, leaving the interlining with the under piece of the band, as at *a*, Fig. 8. Then cut a piece of material about 3 inches long and as wide as the collar band, as at *b*, and place it on the outside against the upper part, or single thickness of the band, directly over the center back, with the right sides of the two together. This piece serves as a protection across the back of the collar.

Next, stitch it 1/8 inch from the edge, turn it over on the inside of the neck band, and stitch across the piece, as at *c*. Turn the band right side out and stitch across the upper edge, as at *d*. This stitching will catch the raw edge of the protection piece and hold it in place across the upper edge of the band.

Remember that when the band is lapped for the front closing, it should measure exactly 1/2 inch larger than the neck measurement to allow for shrinkage. If it should happen that the band is too large or too small, the alteration should be made equal on both ends of the band, so that the shape of the band and the position of its center-front and its center back will not be changed.

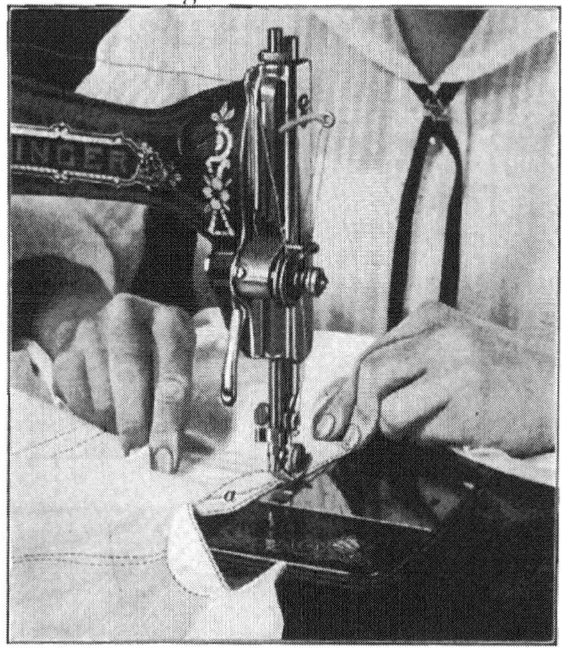

FIG. 9

30. Applying the Neck Band.—The neck band is now ready to be applied to the shirt. To do this, draw the lower part of the band and the interlining apart and crease the free edge of each of these toward the other. Then place the neck of the shirt between the lower part of the band and the interlining, having the interlining over the right side of the shirt. Baste this in place and then machine stitch, beginning at a point 2 inches from the center back and continuing across the center back to a point 2 inches beyond it on the opposite side. Then bring the upper layer of the band down and baste it in place across the bottom, leaving the center back free for a space of 3 inches. Next, stitch across the bottom of the band and up around the center-back opening, as shown at a, Fig. 9, thus leaving a section at the center free, so that the buttonhole may be made through two thicknesses of material only.

If the band, while being stitched on, should appear a trifle large, after it has been tested and found to measure exactly correct, stretch the neck of the shirt enough to permit the outside edge of the front plait and the hem to come exactly even with the ends of the neck band. Or, if it should seem to be a little small for the neck of the shirt after its correct size has been determined, hold the neck of the shirt a little full, but without a wrinkle, so as to adjust it in the band. The safest way to do this is to run a fine gathering thread around the neck edge so that the fulness will be evenly adjusted.

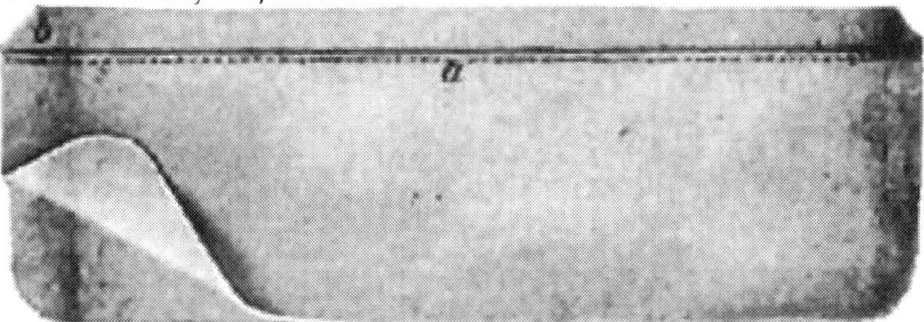

(A)

(B)

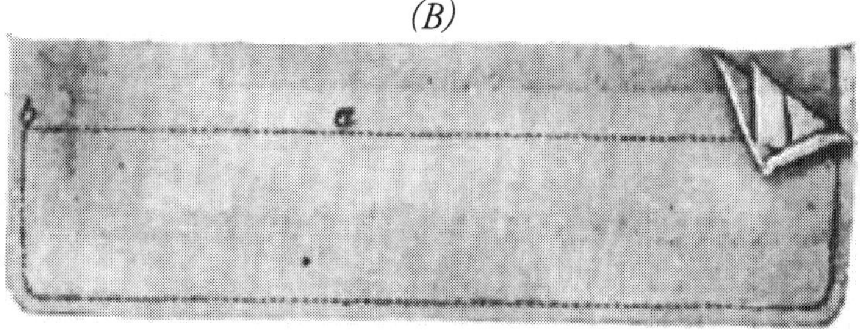

(C)

FIG. 10

31. Preparing Cuff Inter-linings.—Cuffs for a shirt, whether they are to be soft or stiff, require an interlining to give body and enable them to shape well.

For interlining *soft cuffs*, if the material is fairly heavy, one thickness of the material of which the garment is being made will answer; but if the garment material is light in weight, an interlining consisting of two thicknesses of firmly woven material, such as lawn or cambric, should be used.

To prepare an interlining for soft cuffs, if one thickness is to be used, cut the interlining the same size as the cuff, but when two thicknesses are used, make one the same in size as the outside-cuff portion and the other 1/2 inch narrower, as shown at a, Fig. 10 (*a*).

For *stiff cuffs*, use butcher's linen or heavy muslin, using two thicknesses, and cut as directed for soft cuffs.

32. Making Stiff Cuffs.—As shown in Fig. 10 (*a*), put the lower edges of two thicknesses of interlining together, baste and stitch along the upper edge of the narrow one, as at a, and then clip off the corners of the other thickness, as at *b*. With the interlining thus prepared, lay the two pieces for each cuff so that their right sides are together, and on them place the prepared interlining, as shown in (*b*). Next, baste and stitch along the sides and the lower edge in the pattern lines, beginning the stitching at a point about 3/8 to 1/2 inch below the top of the cuff, as at a, and extending it around to the same distance from the top on the other side. Stitching in this manner will permit the cuff to be sewed to the sleeve with ease.

FIG. 11

Next, trim the interlining up to within 1/8 inch of the stitching, as at *b*, and clip the ends, as at *a*, Fig. 11; then, with a small hammer, proceed to hammer the rounding corners, as shown at *b* and *c*. Hammering the edges down in this way insures a good, flat finish, doing away with all bulky edges, which not only are troublesome to iron over, but give the finished cuff a poor appearance. A hot iron may be used to press down the edges.

When the cuffs are stitched and trimmed and have their edges pressed down, turn each right side out and crease it very carefully all around the outer edges. If this work is well done, so that the edges are perfectly even, and each is then carefully pressed, it will not be necessary to baste them before another stitching, because the interlining will aid in keeping the outer portion of the cuff smooth. To insure a true, even edge, it is sometimes well to work the edge out with the point of a pair of scissors or a stiletto.

Before laying the cuffs aside, stitch them at the ends and the lower side and also 5/8 inch from the upper edge, as shown at *a*, Fig. 10 (*c*), so as to make them ready to join to the sleeve. Stitching their outer edges before joining them insures against the twisting of either the upper or the lower section or the interlining. Such stitching serves to hold the cuff sections together, so that, in laundering, the iron will not push them unevenly.

33. Joining the Cuffs to the Sleeves.—With the sleeve wrong side out, as in Fig. 12, gather the lower edge of the sleeve by hand, beginning just beyond the finished edge of the cuff opening on the upper side and gathering to a point about 4 inches from the seam of the sleeve, as shown at *a*; also, from the opening on the under side, gather about 2 1/2 inches toward the seam, as at *b*. Turn the underneath edge of the opening back to the wrong side and pin it in place, or turn its edges in and finish off neatly and let it protrude as at *c*. Then pin and baste the cuff to the sleeve, as shown, joining the interlining and one thickness of the cuff to the wrong side of the sleeve, so that the cuff may be turned in and stitched from the right side, and also so that there will be only one thickness of material to turn, thus insuring a neat finish. The seam of the sleeve should come at a point about one-third the length of the cuff from one end of the cuff, as shown between *a* and *b*.

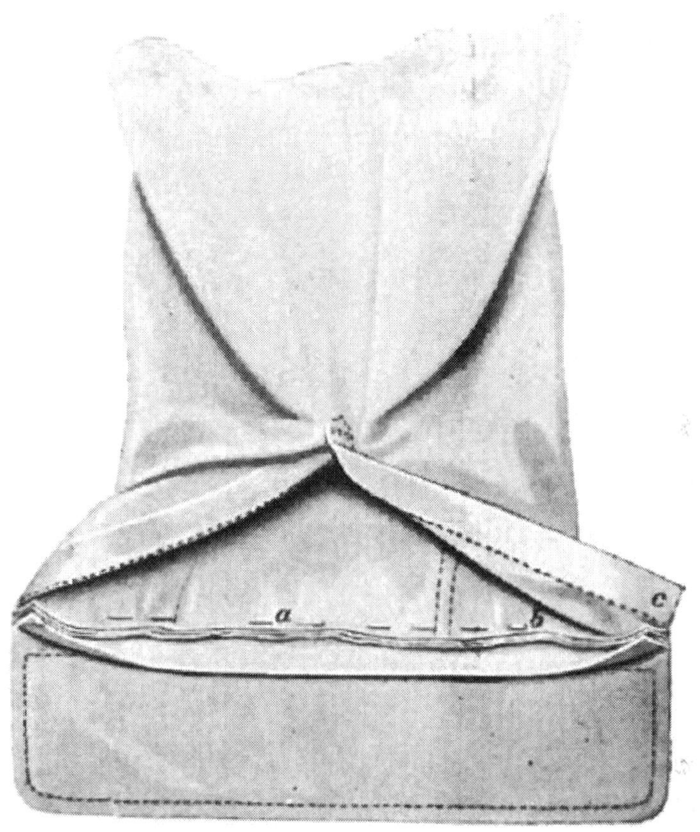

FIG. 12

When the cuff is basted on, stitch in the pattern lines. Then trim the seam edge close and turn the upper edge of the cuff over neatly, after which proceed to turn the seam ends in and to stitch them in position. In this way, a neat finish will result and a bulky seam will be avoided. Begin to stitch at the termination of the first stitching, as at *b*, Fig. 10 (*c*); then turn and stitch across the upper edge. As in every case of stitching in the shirt, remember to keep a good stitch, to stitch straight, and to secure all machine threads.

If the ends of the cuffs are not so neat as they should be, overhand the edges together so that a perfectly smooth line will be obtained.

34. Making Separate Shirt Collar.—If a turnover collar is to be worn with the shirt, one made in the following manner will be satisfactory.

Place the two right sides of the collar material together as in making the cuffs, and over this place an interlining of smooth, lightweight material. If the material of which the collar is to be made is very heavy, an interlining will not be required in the turn-over portion; in such a case, just a firm, very lightweight interlining of one thickness in the standing part of the collar will be sufficient. When the collar is made ready, stitch around the edges as for the cuffs, leaving free the edge that is to be joined to the stand. Trim the seam edge close, as shown in Fig. 13, press the rounding corners, turn the collar right side out, and crease and stitch around its outer edge.

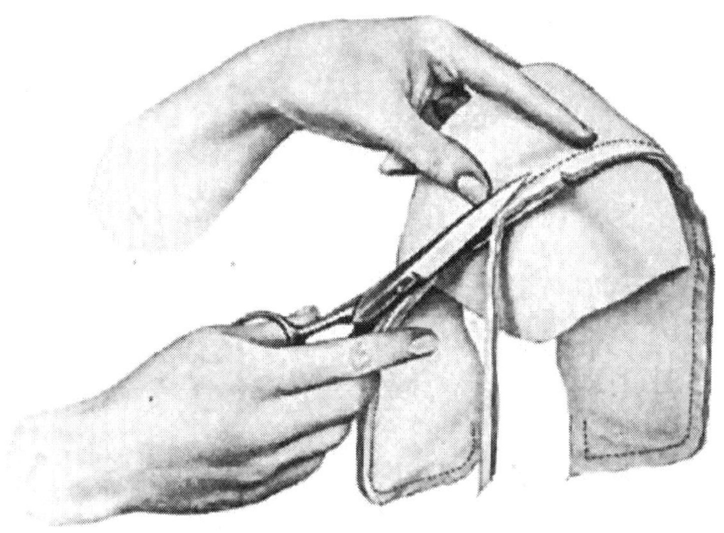

FIG. 13.

Next, prepare the stand section in the same way. To allow for lapping, this section is longer than the upper piece; therefore, in stitching this section, be sure to stitch around the points. Then trim the edges, as described for the collar edges. Turn the stand right side out, press the seams carefully, and turn in the free edges at the upper edge. Insert the edges of the collar between the turned edges of the stand, and baste carefully. Then stitch close to the edge all around the stand.

35. Attaching Separate Collar to Shirt.—Sometimes the stand section of a collar is omitted and the collar is attached directly to the shirt. The method of construction is the same as for a soft stand collar that is to be applied to a shirt, except that the lower part of the collar is left free and the neck of the shirt is inserted between the edges of the collar and stitched flat as in stitching the cuff.

36. Buttons and Buttonholes.—The buttons and buttonholes of a shirt are of great importance because of their prominent position down the front. Small, flat, pearl buttons are satisfactory and they should be spaced as in Fig. 1; that is, so that the distance between the neck band and the first button and that between each two buttons will be the same.

The buttonholes should be placed exactly in the center of the plait, and they should be cut vertically and about 1/4 inch longer than the diameter of the button. As the plait of the shirt will in nearly every case be starched, buttonholes that are too small will be difficult to get over the buttons.

The buttonholes in the cuffs should be located a little more than one-third the width of the cuff from the bottom if single cuffs are used. In double cuffs, a second buttonhole should be placed the same distance from the top, or the joining of the cuff and sleeve, as shown in Fig. 1. Also, a buttonhole is worked in the lap finish just above the cuff, as this illustration shows.

The buttonholes in the neck band should be horizontal and placed 1/4 inch above the joining of the shirt and the neck band. The buttonholes in the collar should correspond with those in the neck band, except that they should be a scant 3/8 inch above the lower edge of the collar stand, so that the collar will fit down well and cover the seam joining of the neck band when the shirt is worn.

37. Preparing the Shirt for Wear.—It is always advisable to launder a shirt before wearing it; that is, if it is made of material that requires starch. Such garments of silk material, however, require only a very careful pressing to complete them.

WORK SHIRT

38. The work shirt differs from a negligée shirt chiefly in that it is made of different material and has an attached collar and wristbands instead of cuffs. After the material is selected, the shirt may be cut out with the aid of the same pattern as is used for a negligée shirt, or a special work-shirt pattern may be used. As a rule, a work shirt requires a yoke that is 2 inches deeper than the yoke used for a negligée shirt, so as to give the wearer protection over the shoulders. Therefore, if a negligée-shirt pattern is used in cutting out a work shirt, it is well to remember that the yoke should be made deeper and the back portion shorter to accommodate the increase in size of the yoke. A work shirt should also have a little more allowance for fulness across the back. This allowance—usually 4 inches is enough—may be provided by placing the pattern piece for the back so that its center-back line is 2 inches from the fold of the material.

The collar and wristbands of the work shirt require an interlining, which may be of any of the materials previously mentioned. It is advisable, however, to use an extra thickness of the material for the interlining, because, when these parts become worn, there will then be this extra thickness underneath to which the worn part may be darned. It may be well to note, also, that the collar of a work shirt may be reversed when it becomes worn. This may be done by simply ripping the stitching that serves to hold it to the collar band and then turning it and stitching it back in place.

MEN'S HOUSE COATS AND ROBES

HOUSE COATS

FIG. 14.

39. For comfort in the home, perhaps no garment is more enjoyed by men than the house coat, or smoking jacket, one style of which is shown in front and back view in Fig. 14. For such a garment, the proper selection of material is the chief essential. Double-faced, wool-knit fabrics, closely woven Jersey, soft home spun, corduroy, velvet, and quilted satin are materials from which a selection may be made. Generally, a house coat requires the same amount of material for its construction as does a man's negligée shirt. The coat is, of course, shorter than a shirt, but the material is needed for the seams, which are wider than those of a shirt; also for the shawl collar and the two patch pockets at the lower side fronts.

40. Cutting out the House Coat.—Before cutting such a garment, to have it a satisfactory length and to have the sleeve correct, test the pattern as directed for testing the shirt pattern. Then place the pattern as for a shirt. Provide a lining if the outer material is such as to require one.

41. Constructing the Coat.—In seaming such material as is used for house coats, extra precaution must be taken to baste each seam with small stitches. If this is not done, the thickness of the material will cause the edge nearest the presser-foot of the sewing machine to slip forward and thus produce an uneven seam. If no lining is used, the seams should be so made that the garment will appear as neat on the under side as on the right side. For the closing of a house coat, simple, durable frogs, like those shown in the illustration, are generally satisfactory.

LOUNGING ROBE OR BATH-ROBE

42. Another comfortable and convenient man's garment for home use is the lounging robe, or bath-robe, two styles of which are shown in Fig. 15.

FIG. 15.

As bath-robes are used as house coats and also as beach coats, the material varies and may include brocaded velvet or silk corduroy, silk poplin, faille, Jersey, soft homespun, eiderdown, light-weight flannel, mohair, ratiné, terry cloth, and blanket cloth. Those used only for lounging robes are, as a rule, quite conservative in color and conventional in material. One would not use, for example, a bath-robe of blanket cloth as a lounging robe. One's own sense of fitness must be brought into play in the selection.

43. Construction of Robes.—A robe of this kind is made in much the same manner as a house coat but it is much longer, of course, usually extending to a point half way between the knees and the ankles or to the ankles. For such a garment, a plain notched coat collar or a shawl collar may be used, as desired. The robe is usually double-breasted, in coat fashion, and a cord or a narrow strap sash of the material is placed around the waist. In order to hold the cord or the sash in position, it is necessary to place small strips at the under-arm seams through which the cord or the sash may be inserted.

A bath-robe usually has the pockets below the waist line and is a trifle larger than a robe that is used as a house coat.

TROUSERS

TYPES OF TROUSERS

44. Short, Straight Trousers.—There are three distinct types of trousers, which may be varied to suit the prevailing fashion. The first type is the short, straight trousers for little boys. This type may be finished to wear with separate blouses or to be buttoned to a blouse, making a suit, the trousers being finished straight or bloused at the lower edges, or having a long flare as in the sailor type.

45. Knickerbockers.—The next type is the knickerbocker style, the trousers that blouse at the knee. This type is generally chosen for young boys, but from time to time, as Fashion dictates, it may be varied to suit both men and women for sports wear. The finish at the knee may be varied according to individual taste, the fulness being gathered or plaited into a band that is worn below the knee.

Breeches may be considered a variation of this type of trousers. These are made roomy above the knee, but below are fitted and laced tight to be worn inside leggings or boots.

46. Long, Straight Trousers.—The third type is the long, straight type of trousers, the lower edges of which may be finished with a plain hem or a cuff. The side seam is sometimes finished with silk braid, depending upon fashion and the occasions upon which the trousers are to be worn.

MATERIALS FOR TROUSERS

47. Outside Materials.—The materials suitable for trousers are many and should be selected according to the season of the year, the occasions for which they are to be worn, and the age of the person for whom they are made.

Such materials include galatea, duck, drilling, khaki, mohair, panama cloth, linen, denim, corduroy, serge, Poiret twill, broadcloth, tweeds, homespun, covert cloth, flannel, and gabardine. There are many other fabrics, however, such as pongee and velvet, that may be used for trousers for very small boys.

48. Linings.—Then, too, there is the problem of linings for trousers, since lining of some kind is necessary for all trousers. At times only a belt facing, a crotch reinforcement, and pocket linings are made; again, the trousers may be lined half way or entirely, depending on the material used. Corduroy trousers for men and boys and woolen trousers for boys are generally lined throughout. When this is the case, a light-weight fabric is used for the lining proper and the pockets are made of a more firmly woven material than is used for the trousers.

For linings, such materials as cambric, percaline, silesia, or sateen may be selected. For pockets, sateen, galatea, drilling, or firm unbleached muslin is suitable.

CONSTRUCTING BOYS' TROUSERS

49. The making of trousers is usually looked upon as a very difficult undertaking, but when one is thoroughly familiar with the foundation principles of sewing and exercises unusual care in the tailoring of such garments, very satisfactory results should be obtained.

There is real economy in making trousers for boys because they can so often be cut down from larger garments. Also, trousers for summer wear can be made of good quality material at considerable saving.

50. Cutting Out the Trousers.—In cutting out the trousers shown in Fig. 16, the point of main importance is to place the pattern so that the center of both the front and the back sections will be on a lengthwise thread of the material.

51. Stitching the Back and Side Seams.—After the material is cut out, join the leg portions at the center back, using a plain seam. Then join the outside edges of the front and the back leg portions with the cord seam, stitching to within 5 inches of the waist line.

52. Stitching the Front Seam and Providing the Fly.—The center-front seam should then receive attention. As a rule, an inside flap, as at *e*, Fig. 16, is provided to cover an opening in the center-front seam of trousers for little boys. This opening is generally 1 1/2 inches to 2 1/2 inches long and comes to about 1 inch above the inside leg seam.

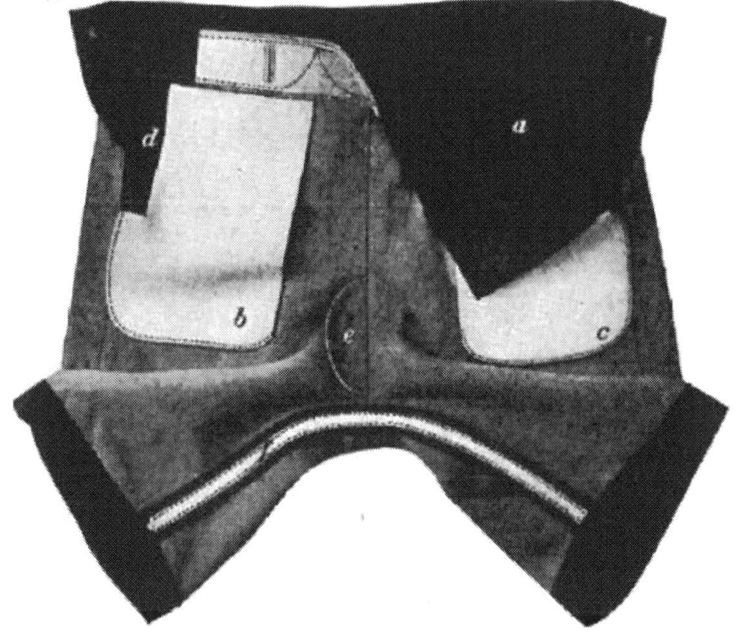

FIG. 16

To make the flap or fly, proceed as follows: Cut a half circle from a piece of the material of which the trousers are made, having it a seam's width longer than the opening on either side; then cut a similar piece from lining material. Place the two together and stitch around the curved edge, leaving the straight side open. Turn the flap right side out and press.

Next, place the flap on the right front of the trousers at the place indicated for the opening, having the right side of the flap to the right side of the trousers, stitch it a seam's width from the edge, and fasten the threads securely.

Now place the right and the left fronts of the trousers together and stitch the center-front seam on each side of the fly, fastening the stitching above and below the opening with several back-stitches to prevent the seam from ripping. The seam edges of the opening are finished when the lining is placed in the trousers.

FIG. 17

In making wash trousers, it must be remembered that there is no lining and the seam edges at the opening in the center front are simply whipped back.

53. Preparing a Blind-Fly Closing.—For trousers of a larger size, the finish of the center-front seam is somewhat different. A closing with a fly-piece, such as the one shown in Fig. 17, is made. In cutting out trousers with this opening, the only difference is to supply the fly-pieces.

The pattern for the fly is laid on a double thickness of the material, either on a lengthwise or a crosswise thread. After cutting this portion, place the same pattern piece on three thicknesses of lining material and cut the facings for the fly-pieces.

With one of the pieces of lining, face one portion of the fly for the left side of the opening and press the facing back 1/8 inch from the edge, as shown at *a*, Fig. 18.

Horizontal buttonholes may now be worked through the two thicknesses, as indicated by the chalk marks in Fig. 18, or if not convenient, they may be worked after the garment is finished.

The next step is to turn back the inside curved edge of a second lining piece about 1/4 inch and crease along this line. Then open this fold, place the prepared fly-piece on it so that its finished edge is about 1/8 inch beyond the creased line, and baste securely. Stitch between the buttonholes, as at *b*,

Fig. 18, sewing through the three thicknesses of material to secure the fly-piece to the facing of the trousers.

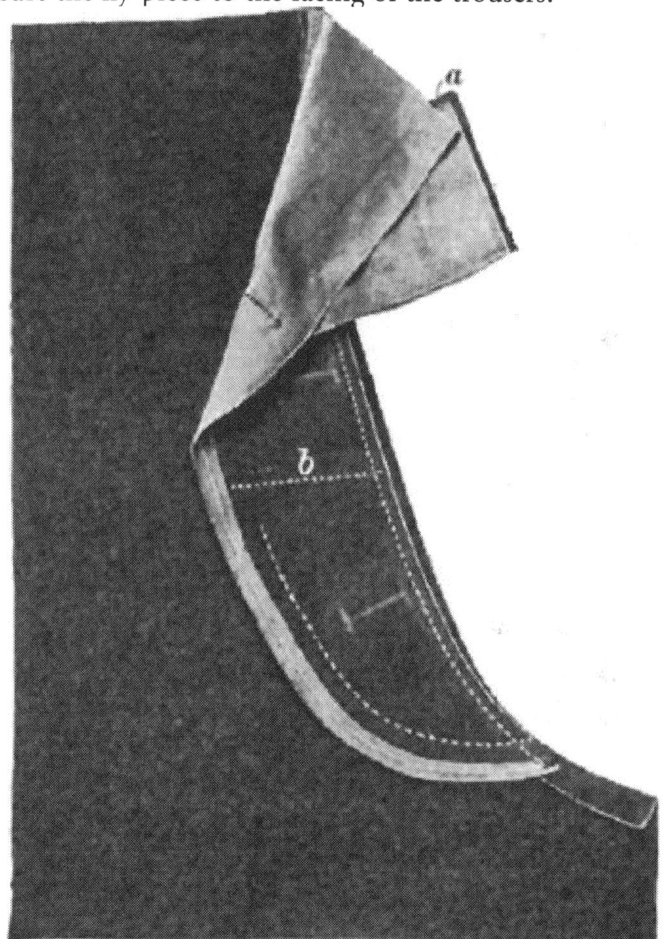

FIG. 18.

54. Applying the Fly.—The fly-piece is now ready to be placed on the left front of the trousers. To do this, first crease the left front of the trouser section 3/8 inch from the edge, as at *a*, Fig. 17, and press. Now place the prepared fiy-piece so that the side with the buttonholes is next to the right side of the trousers, and baste and stitch the underfacing to the trousers about 1/4 inch from the outside edge. This will bring the fly-piece in from the edge of the trousers, thus preventing it from showing from the right side. Turn the fly portion to the wrong side, as shown in Fig. 18. Then baste and stitch the free edge of the fly portion to the trousers as shown at *b*, Fig. 17.

Next, finish the right front. To do this, face the remaining fly portion and place it on the right front of the trousers, as shown at *c*, Fig. 17. Then stitch around the outer edge of this portion to make it firm. The buttons are applied to this piece.

Finally finish the seam below the fly with a double stitching, turning both seam edges to one side.

55. Lining Boys' Trousers.—The lining for little boys' trousers is cut and joined the same as the outside portion, but it is not basted in until the hip welt pocket is made. Place the lining in the trousers with the seam lines in the same general position and having the raw edges of the seams next to the trousers. Pin or baste the lining to the trousers along the seams to hold it in place until the trousers are finished. The seam edges of the opening at the center front should be whipped to the seam edges of the outer portion of the trousers to make a neat finish for the opening.

56. Placing the Hip Welt Pocket.—Place this pocket on the right side of the trousers, midway between the back and the side seams, as shown at *a*, Fig. 16, and apply according to the directions given in Arts. **32** to **39,** inclusive, Chapter III, only using a simple curve, as shown in the skirt at the lower right of the illustration in Fig. 35.

57. Making the Side Pockets.—Next, proceed to make the side pockets. Sew a lengthwise strip of material along the placket edges, turning the front edge over so that the cord seam of the lower side can be extended up to the waist line and arranging both sides alike.

In some patterns, allowance is made for these pieces; therefore, separate pieces will not have to be applied. Then, for the pockets, cut two pieces of lining material 8 inches long by 10 inches wide, or smaller, depending, of course, on the size of the trousers. Fold each of these pieces lengthwise through the center, so that the doubled piece measures 8 inches by 5 inches. Round the corners at the lower edges, as shown at *b* and *c*, Fig. 16, and stitch the folded portions together along their lower edges and sides to within 4 1/2 inches of the top. Bind one of the free edges of the sides of each pocket with a lengthwise strip of material that is 1 1/2 or 2 inches wide.

With the pockets made ready, sew them to the placket strips, as at *d*, so that the material of the pockets will be covered up at the side opening and will not show when the hands are put in the pockets. The pocket must be caught across the top when the band is sewed in position, so that it will not pull down and cause the trousers to get out of shape.

58. Joining the Inside Leg Portions.—After the pockets are in place, join the inside leg portions, making a plain Seam to be pressed open.

If desired, additional strength may be given to the seams of the trousers by securing tape over them, as shown at *f*, Fig. 16. To do this, place the tape so that its center is directly over the seam line and stitch through to the right side on both sides of the pressed-open seam.

59. Making the Back Inside Belt.—The inside belt is the next portion to be considered. Such a belt may be purchased ready made, but if it is not convenient to procure one, a belt may be made, as shown in Fig. 19.

First, for the back waist line of the trousers, cut a facing 2 inches wide and as long as the measurement of the back waist of the trousers, plus 1 inch. Make a 3/8-inch turn on one edge of this piece, and press the creased edge back.

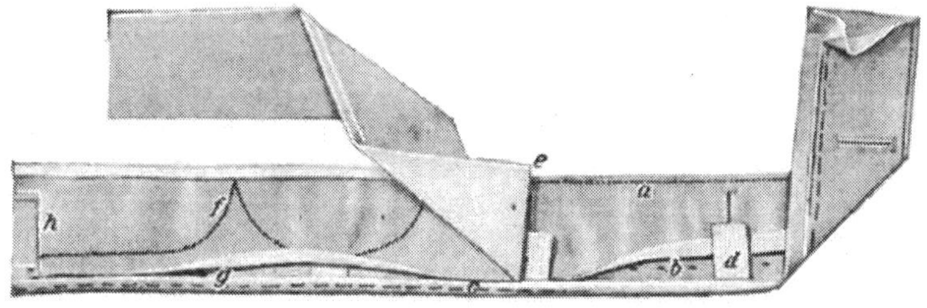

FIG. 19

For the inside-belt portion, which is shown in Fig. 19, cut a lengthwise strip of material 4 inches wide and the same length as the facing. Turn one lengthwise edge of this over 1 1/2 inches and baste and stitch this 1/8 inch from the fold, as at *a*. Then, in the wider, or under, portion of this strip of material, baste a tuck 1/4 inch deep, as at *b*, having the bottom of the tuck 1 1/2 inches from the top of the belt and even with the lower edge of the part that was turned back 1 1/2 inches, as shown. In basting this tuck, do not catch the stitches through the facing strip.

60. When the belt is thus prepared, work the buttonholes. As shown in Fig. 20, there are five vertical buttonholes in the back belt, one in the center back and the others spaced approximately 3 inches apart. Next, turn under the lower edge of the belt 1/4 inch, or just to meet the other edge, as at *c*, Fig. 19. Over the fold, or tuck, *b*, and just opposite each of the three center buttonholes, place a piece of elastic about 1/2 inch wide and 1 inch long, as shown at *d*, and pin in position at the lower edge. This elastic serves to prevent any strain on the back of the trousers when the child is in motion and also to make it easier to button the belt.

Next, baste the belt portion to the facing strip, having the top of the strip about 1/8 inch above the folded edge of the belt, as shown at *e*. The lower edge of the facing strip and the turned edge of the belt should be even, as at *c*. With the basting done, stitch the belt to the facing strip, as at *f*, having the curved part of the stitching come just below the buttonholes and through the elastic, but taking care not to catch the top of the tuck in this stitching. Then stitch the lower edge of the tuck in from each end and about 1 inch beyond the first buttonhole, as at *g*. The rest of the tuck is left free.

FIG. 20

61. Making the Front Inside Belt.—The front belt is made and stitched to the facing in the same manner as the back belt, but, as elastic is used only in the back belt, no allowance is made for a tuck in the front. Therefore, cut the belt portion only 3 1/2 inches wide. At each end of the front belt, stitch a piece of dark material about 2 inches long, as shown at *a* and *b*, Fig. 20, and cut the inside belt away under this piece. This should be done so that the white lining will not show at the sides when the front is buttoned over the back. A buttonhole must be worked through the material and the lining, and this can be done more easily if the inside lining is cut away.

If it is desired to have the trousers fit snug around the waist, a dart about 2 1/2 to 3 1/2 inches long may be placed midway between the center back and the side. A dart so located will reduce the fulness at the waist and give freedom through the hips.

62. Applying the Belt.—In applying a belt to any pair of trousers, place the belt section against the right side of the trousers, having the facing strip toward you and its upper edge 1/4 inch above the waist line. Open out the folded edge of the facing strip and baste and stitch along the creased line. Turn the belt over to the wrong side and baste through the two thicknesses of material at the waist line. Then cut away about 1/2 inch of the inside part of the belt at each end, as at *h*, Fig. 19, and stitch through the belt and the trousers at the sides and the lower edge with two rows of stitching.

FIG. 21

63. Finishing the Trousers.—When the band is on, fit the trousers so as to determine what the length should be. Turn a hem at the lower edge, making it 1 1/4 to 1 5/8 inches wide. As a finish for straight pants, three buttons are usually sewed near the lower edge, just in front of the cord seams.

64. Other Waist-Line Finishes for Trousers.—Besides the belt described in Arts. **59** to **61,** inclusive, there are other ways in which the waist line of trousers may be finished. If the trousers button on the outside of a blouse, as in the Oliver Twist type of suit, the waist line is faced back, as in Fig. 21, and buttonholes are worked through the two thicknesses of material.

FIG. 22

Another way is to apply a facing with an interlining, as at *a*, Fig. 22. Turn the lower edge of the facing *b* in a hem and stitch. Then catch this free edge to the seam with overhanding-stitches, as at *c*. You may catch it also to the pocket portion, if desired. On the outside of the trousers, place straps of the material through which a belt may be drawn or place buttons on the inside of the belt for suspenders.

65. Finishing Crotch Portion of Unlined Trousers.— The crotch portion of trousers, except those for small boys, is usually reinforced by means of four pieces of lining material, as shown in Fig. 23. Cut these pieces so that they fit smoothly and make the two pieces for the front section of the trousers smaller than those for the back. In applying these pieces, stitch them in with the seams of the trousers, as shown.

FIG. 23

The illustration shows these lining pieces notched, as this is the customary edge finish. If, however, the lining material is likely to fray, the edges will have to be turned under once and stitched.

In the case of breeches, as for example, riding breeches, where not only the seams but the material must be reinforced, the lining pieces are stitched to the trousers.

KNICKERBOCKERS

66. Knickerbockers are made in practically the same way as the straight trousers. The only difference is in the length and the finish at the lower edge of the leg portions. Knickerbockers are longer and the fulness is either gathered or plaited in to form a blouse at the knee.

There are two methods of finishing the leg portions; namely, by an elastic or a band of the material.

67. Finishing With an Elastic.—The simplest method of finishing the leg portions of knickerbockers is with elastic and a casing, and this is especially suitable for very small boys.

Turn a hem or casing at the lower edge wide enough to accommodate the elastic. Cut the elastic about 1 inch smaller than the leg measurement and insert in the casing. This will hold the fulness in and form the blouse for the trousers.

68. Finishing with a Band.—For knickerbockers with a band, examples of which are shown in Fig. 24, arrange an opening 2 inches deep at the side of the leg portion above the lower edge and finish the opening by facing or simply hemming it back. Then gather or plait the lower edge of each.

Next, prepare the band for each leg, by cutting a band of material 5/8 to 1 inch wide and long enough to fit around the leg above the knee, plus 1 1/2 inches for finishing. Interline it with canvas or percaline, and then line it with a lining material of a color to match that of the knickerbockers. Place the bands so that the edges of the trousers are between the outer material and the lining of the band and so that the front section of the trousers laps over the back, having the end of the band extending 1 1/2 inches beyond the front section of the trousers. Baste the band and stitch in position.

69. Fastening the Band. There are several methods of fastening the band. Perhaps the most popular way is to place a buttonhole in the band at the end that extends beyond the opening and to sew two buttons on the under portion of the band, spacing these so that one will permit the band to fit around the leg above the knee and the other below the knee.

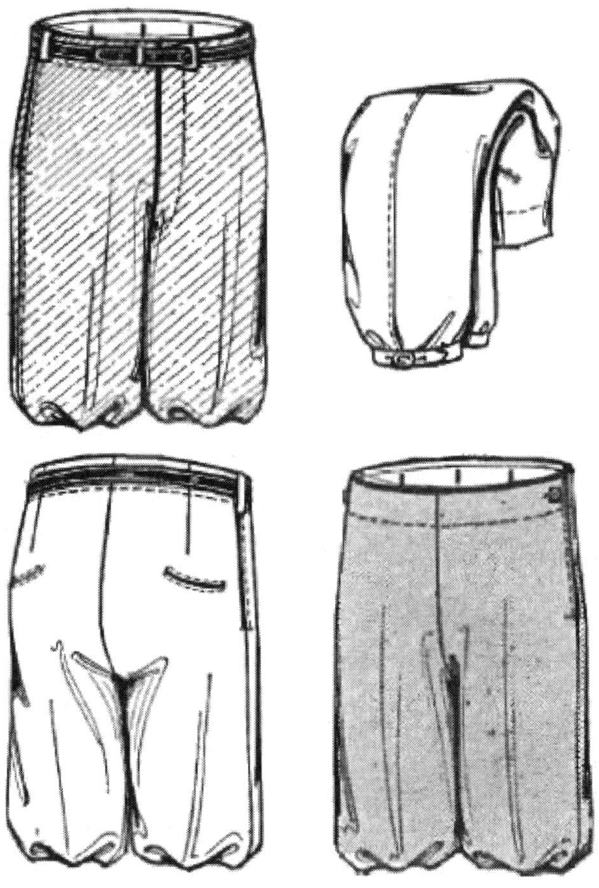

FIG. 24

Another method is to buckle the band. To do this, apply a small gun-metal or nickel buckle, putting it on the same way that a buckle would be applied to a belt, and work eyelets in the strap for the prongs of the buckles. Such buckles may be purchased or they may be taken from a worn pair of knickerbockers. If the buckles are for ornamentation only, they may be sewed to the straps directly below the side seam, and a large hook and eye placed underneath, so as to hold the strap in place.

MEN'S PAJAMAS

70. Men's pajamas, as shown in Fig. 25, consist of a short loose-fitting coat shirt and a pair of loose-fitting trousers. Such garments, which are frequently made in the home, are simple in the extreme; but, in order to be satisfactory, they must be accurately cut and neatly made.

71. Materials.—As to materials, wash silk and soisette seem to be the most desirable for pajamas, but such materials as soft muslins and flannelettes, as well as soft madras, pongee, sateen, long cloth, and firm dimities in attractive stripes or crossbar effects, are frequently employed. Usually, 5 1/2 or 6 yards of 36-inch material or 6 1/2 or 7 yards of the 32-inch material is ample for pajamas to be worn by men of average size, especially if care is exercised in placing the pattern pieces on the material.

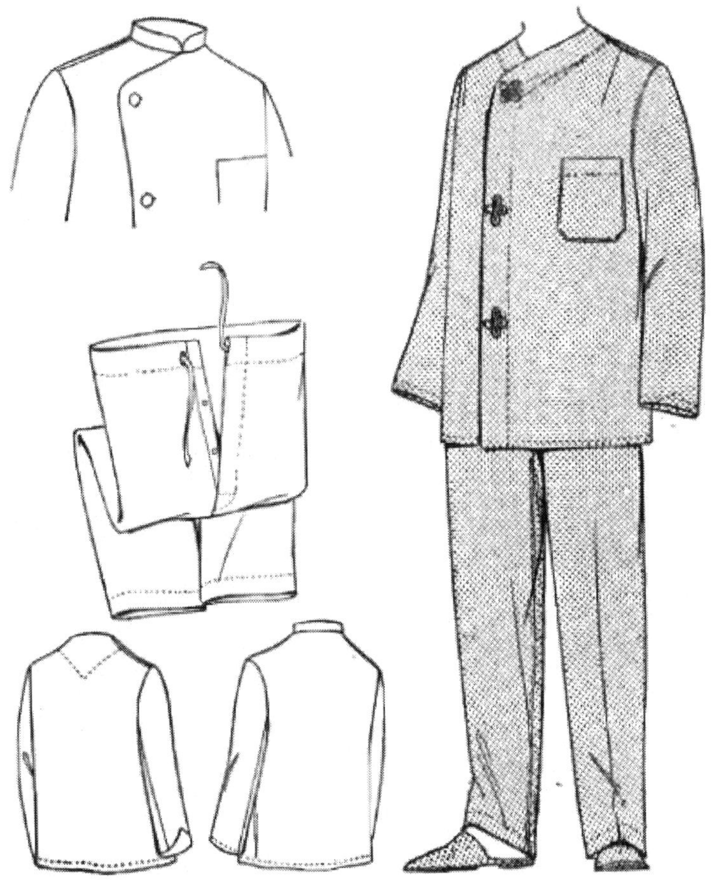

FIG. 25

72. Constructing the Coat.—In constructing pajamas, the coat is seamed up in a way similar to a negligée shirt, but it is finished with a plain hem at the bottom of the sleeves and the coat. Or, as shown at the lower left in Fig. 25, pointed turned-back cuffs may be used.

As to the neck line, there are several appropriate finishes, perhaps the most popular being the fitted facing. This facing should be cut to form a yoke at the back and to extend all the way down the center front. The corners at the center front of the neck of the coat may be rounded, as shown in the illustration; or, if desired, they may be pointed.

Another way in which to finish the neck is to face the left-front section back to the center-front line and attach a military collar to the neck of the coat, as shown at the upper left.

73. Constructing the Trousers.—The opening at the front of the trousers is finished in somewhat the same manner as the opening of a boy's trousers explained in Art. **54,** but with the lining omitted.

The waist line of the trousers is finished with a casing 1 1/4 inches wide, and through this casing is run a 1-inch tape, the ends of the tape extending sufficiently to tie at the center front, as shown. If it is not convenient to use tape for this purpose, a cord that is durable enough to bear considerable wear may be made by seaming up a lengthwise strip of the material and then turning it right side out. Such a cord may be neatly finished by sewing a tiny tassel on each end.

Often an elastic is preferred to a tape or a cord. This should be about 2 inches shorter than the waist measurement.

UNDERGARMENTS

TYPES AND MATERIALS

74. Styles of undergarments for men and boys vary considerably, but as the details of construction are all similar and as the construction of such garments is simple, they may be very easily made at home.

Types of such garments are shown in Figs. 26, 27, and 28. Figs. 26 and 27 show the one-piece garment with different styles of back closings, and Fig. 28 shows the two-piece suit. Any one of these types may have sleeves if desired. Also, they may have narrow facings around the neck or a reinforced back yoke, as in Fig. 26.

75. For such garments one may choose soisette, madras, or the soft cotton cross-bar generally referred to as pajama check. The one-piece type, of course, requires the least material and is the type usually preferred. From 2 1/2 to 4 yards of material is required for such garments, depending on the style of garment and the size of the person.

CONSTRUCTING ONE-PIECE UNDERGARMENTS

76. Cutting the Material.—In cutting these undergarments, the two points of greatest importance are: First, to place the pattern so that it is on a correct grain of the material, and second, to mark the joining points carefully.

77. Seam and Edge Finishes.—In making such undergarments, the same general construction details as given for shirts and trousers may be followed. The flat fell-seam is used throughout to give strength, and for the finish of the neck and armholes, bias facings are necessary, but for the legs and sleeves, if there are sleeves, narrow hems may be turned, as shown.

FIG. 26

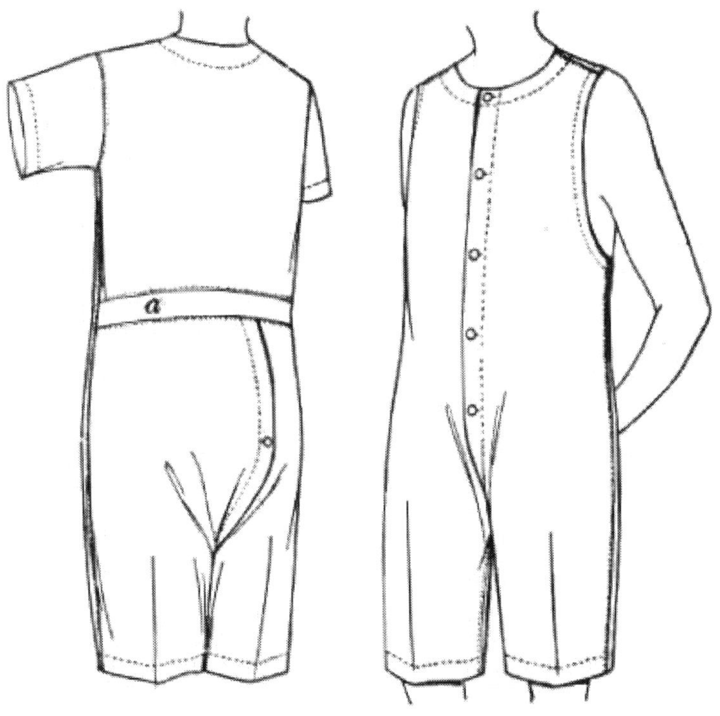

FIG. 27

78. Front and Back Closings.—The *front closing* may be finished in the form of a plain hem, or a bias facing may be applied.

In the case of the *back closing*, the method depends on the style. For Fig. 26, simply seam the back and face the rounded section, providing, of course, the button-and-buttonhole joining as shown.

For the closing illustrated in Fig. 27, join the upper part of the drawers to the lower part of the shirt by means of a plain fell-seam. Or, if strength and ease in this part of the garment are desired, a bias piece of material 3 inches wide may be inserted, as at a, Fig. 27. Another method of preparing such a section is to place a 3/4-inch tuck in the strip and baste but not stitch. The tuck is then secured only at the ends. When the basting is removed, the tuck is free to open, and this gives ease.

If a number of garments are being made, it will be advisable to purchase an inexpensive knitted shirt as such material is preferable for this inserted section. The upper back section is then brought down over this piece and basted and finished with a flat fell.

CONSTRUCTING TWO-PIECE UNDERGARMENTS

79. In constructing the two-piece undergarment, Fig. 28, the front, seams, arm-holes, and neck of the shirt are finished the same as in the one-piece suit, and a hem is turned at the lower edge.

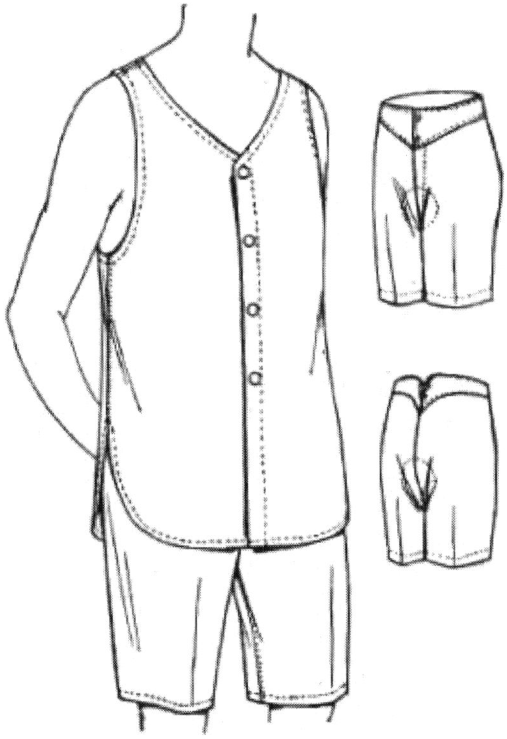

FIG. 28

80. The waist line of the drawers may be fitted slightly by taking a dart at each side. Then the waistband is applied and the yoke adjusted so that its upper edge is along the upper edge of the waistband. The yoke should be on the right side when finished. Such a yoke may be cut double and the drawers section placed between the two thicknesses of the yoke, if desired.

FIG. 29

81. In Fig. 28 stay pieces are shown stitched in the crotch section. Such facings may be applied to any undergarment to give strength.

OVERALLS

TYPES AND MATERIALS

82. Under the term *overalls* are included the straight-pants style, the attached bib overall, the apron overall, which consists of the trousers and bib cut in one, and the one-piece combination overall suit consisting of an overall with a roomy work-shirt top. This last type is generally worn by dairymen and mechanics.

83. For overalls, heavy, coarse materials that are not too firmly woven should be used, as such garments are subject to hard wear and require frequent laundering. Denim, khaki, drilling, and galatea meet these requirements and are very satisfactory.

CONSTRUCTING OVERALLS

84. Trousers and Bib.—The same method of procedure is followed for making overalls as for pajama trousers except that there is no fulness at the waist line.

First, finish the trousers with a placket facing at each side and turn a hem at the top across the back of the trousers. Next, finish the bib section by turning a hem at the upper edge and using a seam at the center front, if necessary.

Then finish the front by joining the trousers and the bib. To do this, place the outside-belt section with its right side to the right side of the trouser portion and baste. Then place the bib with its right side to the right side of the upper edge of the belt and baste. Next, turn all raw edges of the facing, or under section, to the wrong side of the material and place this on the belt section with their wrong sides together, covering the seams, and allowing the facing to extend slightly beyond the edges of the belt piece. Baste it flat and then stitch from the right side, catching all edges.

85. Straps.—To attach the straps, stitch them securely to the waist line at the back, cross them slightly above the waist line, and then stitch in position. To finish the straps in front, you may shape them in a pointed or a rounded end to draw through buckles fastened at the top of the bib, or you may provide them with buttonholes and button them in place.

86. Pockets.—The kind of pockets used in overalls depends upon the use of the garment. For boys' overalls, two medium-size patch pockets each side of the front will prove sufficient.

For work overalls, however, pockets should be both larger and more numerous. Patch pockets may be placed on the front- and back-trouser sections and even on the bib, some being made definite sizes for the purpose of carrying special tools. Straps stitched securely on the back of the trousers also prove convenient for tools. At the side near the placket openings, it is possible to insert long, narrow, inside pockets.

WORK COAT

TYPES AND MATERIALS

87. The work coat covers many uses and embraces many variations in style, including slightly fitted office coats, surgeons' coats, barbers' and mechanics' jackets, and the long type usually worn as dusters.

88. Materials for such garments cover a wide range because of the various uses of the coats. For office coats, light-weight homespun, mohair, and pongee are appropriate. For white coats, butcher's linen and duck or linen-finished suiting are generally preferred. For the typical work jacket, firm coarse fabrics in dark colors, such as denim, khaki, drilling, and galatea, should be chosen. All of these materials, you will notice, will stand frequent laundering, a most important requirement in coats of this kind.

CONSTRUCTING THE JACKET

89. The construction of a jacket like the one shown in Fig. 30 is similar to that of the pajama jacket in that seams are usually made in the form of a flat fell, and the pockets are patch pockets. There are several different features, however, such as the opening at the center front, the neck finish, and the cuff, and in some patterns the placing of the seams. Most patterns have just the seams under the arms, but in addition to these seams some provide a seam down the center back and others have a seam only in the back.

FIG. 30

Proceed as for making the pajama coat and finish the neck and sleeves according to the type of coat desired. If a notch collar is made, remember to place a soft interlining across the back to hold the collar in shape, as directed in Art. **34.**

BOYS' BLOUSES

MATERIALS AND TYPES

90. The same kinds of materials are used for boys' blouses as are employed for men's shirts, with possibly the exception that the quality is usually softer and lighter in weight. About 1 1/2to 2 1/2 yards of material is generally sufficient for a boy's blouse.

As will be seen on referring to the two styles shown in Fig. 31, a blouse is finished in similar fashion to a man's shirt. The collar may be attached, as shown, or a Buster Brown or a stiff upright collar may be worn. The sleeves may be finished with cuffs, or they may be of a length that comes just to the elbow, when they should be finished with a plain 1-inch hem. Such a sleeve finish is very practical for blouses intended for summer wear.

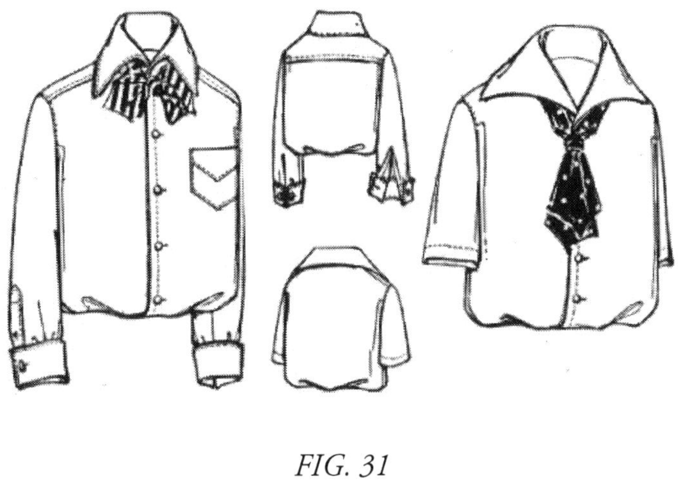

FIG. 31

METHODS OF CONSTRUCTION

91. To develop a boy's blouse, proceed just the same as in making a man's shirt. The pattern will contain practically the same lines as a shirt, and the method of finishing the seams, namely, with a flat fell, is the same.

Making the shirt into a blouse is the one feature that differentiates the blouse from the shirt, this requiring a casing for an elastic. Therefore, to provide for the blouse and a 5/8- or 3/4-inch casing through which elastic is run, allow 3 1/2 inches below the waist line.

BOYS' NORFOLK SUITS

NATURE OF SUITS

92. Although Fashion varies the style of boys' suits as in the case of other garments, the changes are less noticeable. In suits for boys, in fact, there is one type that may be considered almost as a standard, namely, the Norfolk, as shown in Fig. 32. This type of suit consists of knickerbockers and an easy-fitting, straight, plaited jacket, used not only for boys but for girls, women, and men as well. The general lines of such suits vary slightly from time to time, but their construction details remain practically the same.

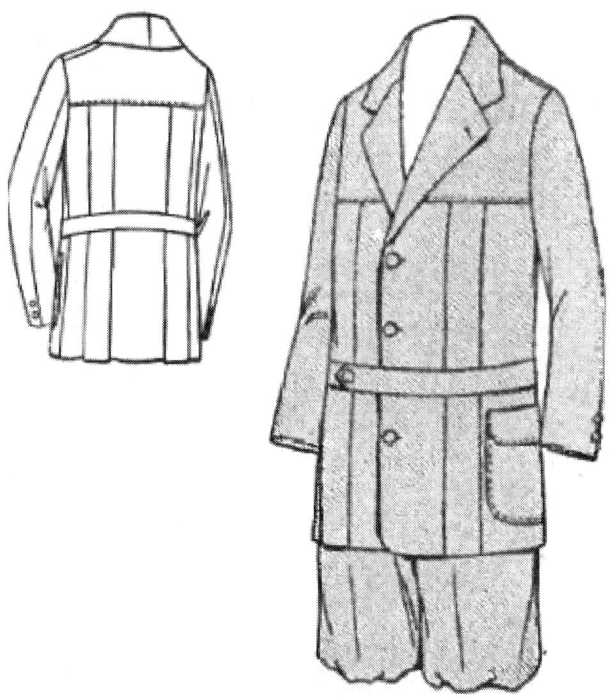

FIG. 32

93. Trousers.—Since the trousers for a Norfolk suit do not differ from separate trousers, the details of trouser making, already covered in this chapter, should be applied to the knickerbockers for a Norfolk suit. A point to be noted is that the trousers of even an unlined suit should have some lining, the inside band and fly facings always being lined.

94. Jacket.—It is the jacket that has special features, differentiating it from other short coats. Chief among these are the yoke, both back and front, and the box plaits at each side, both back and front. A belt, also, is a necessity in a Norfolk suit.

Jackets may be either lined or unlined, as desired, the unlined being generally the jackets of wash suits

MATERIALS

95. The material for a boy's Norfolk suit depends on the season of the year and the purpose for which the suit is required, a typical sports suit, such as this, requiring coarser fabric and reinforcements at points that will be subjected to hard wear.

In determining materials for suits, the same list suggested in Art. **47** as suitable for trousers may be followed. The lining and pocket materials also are the same as for trousers. In addition, for a hėavy, lined suit that requires interlining, tailors' canvas is needed to give body and hold the suit in shape.

CONSTRUCTING AN UNLINED JACKET

96. Cutting Out the Material.—After adjusting the pattern pieces to make them correct in length and width to suit the measurements of the boy, place the pattern pieces on the material with especial care to have each piece on the proper grain of the cloth in order to insure its appearing well in the finished garment.

The pocket pieces for the jacket of an unlined suit are generally cut from the same material as the suit, at least in the case of the side of the pouch that shows inside the coat.

Occasionally, even in unlined suits, a slight firmness is required in the collar and lapels and sometimes in the fronts. Such firmness may be provided by using an interlining of cambric or unbleached muslin. The pieces for the interlining may be cut from the coat pattern and joined in the seams with the outer material.

97. Adjusting the Plaits.—The first step in making a Norfolk jacket is to form the plaits. Lay them in position and then baste, press, and stitch them.

98. Making Shoulder and Under-Arm Seams.—Lay out flat the fronts and the back, and place the yoke sections in position; then join by basting as directed in Art. **21** for the yoke in a man's shirt. Next, baste the shoulder and under-arm lines.

99. Sleeves.—The sleeves should now receive attention. Baste the seams, easing in, at the elbow, the slight fulness that is provided to give an easy fit. If the seam lines are straight, stitch the bottom, but if there are extensions on the pattern seams, leave these free and turn under the extension on the upper-sleeve piece and allow the other to extend under the lap. Baste these in position before stitching.

100. First Fitting.—The suit is now ready for the first fitting. Slip it on, adjusting it carefully, and note the fit of the neck line, the shoulders, the front, and the back, making any necessary alterations in the seams. Mark the position of the pockets. Next, draw on one sleeve to determine its length and width.

After removing the coat, baste the new lines, if changes were made, and then stitch the seams, the kind of seam used depending on the material and the purpose of the suit. Usually, the plain or the welt seam provides a satisfactory finish, but a machine fell may be used for a heavy cotton suit.

101. Taping and Facing.—It is now necessary to tape the edges to make them firm and true. Tape is used whether the coat is lined or unlined, except in the case of a suit of firm wash fabric for a small boy, when taping may be omitted. Apply the tape as explained in Art. 69, Chapter VII, referring to Fig. 28 when doing so.

If the coat is not to have outside stitching, whip the other edge of the tape to the interlining, as shown, using stitches that will hold well in place but that are not tight.

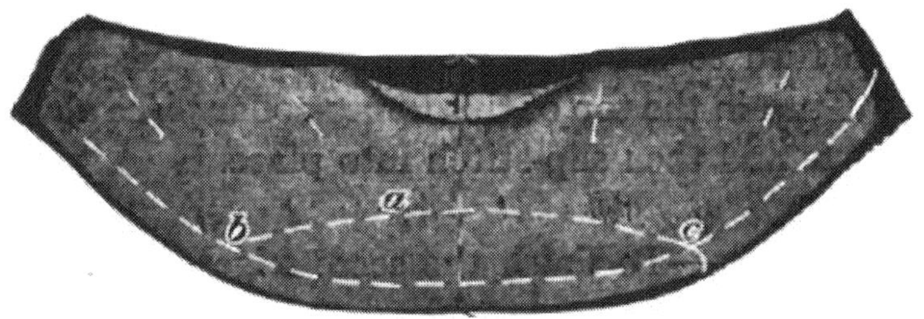

FIG. 33

If outside stitching is to be used, it is not necessary to secure the inner edge of the tape, as the outside stitching serves this purpose.

102. Collar.—In preparation for the collar, first close the center-back seam. Since, even in a suit of wash frabic, it is well to have a firm collar, place over the collar a piece of canvas or firm unbleached muslin cut a trifle smaller than the collar piece. Baste this very flat and then, in the lower section indicated by the basting or break line at *a*, Fig. 33, stitch through the two thicknesses of material from *b* to *c* and then again below this several times to give firmness to this section. Next, press the collar, drawing the stitched piece around to shape it slightly.

Now, turn the neck edge of this prepared piece over the edge of the interlining and stitch into place. Then apply the collar to the coat and slip-stitch it along the neck edge.

103. Pockets.—The pockets may be simple patch pockets or flap pockets. For an unlined suit, patch pockets are advisable because they may be completed without cutting into the coat and are finished on the outside of the jacket.

104. Inserting the Sleeves.—After making the pockets, baste the sleeves into the armholes, turn a hem at the bottom, and whip it into position.

105. Second Fitting.—During the second fitting, adjust the closing properly and see that the collar and break line appear to the best advantage. If alterations are required, fit from the seams.

After fitting, make any necessary corrections and then stitch the sleeves in the coat.

The next step is to place a straight, seamless piece, cut the same as the collar, over the collar on the coat, placing the right side of the piece to the under side of the collar and stitching along the outer edge. Then turn to the right side and baste and press to give a true edge. Turn in the top of this upper-collar piece along the neck edge and baste and then slip-stitch into place.

106. Finishing.—To finish the seam edges in such a suit, the most satisfactory method is to bring the two edges together on each seam and cover them with seam binding. Next, work buttonholes and sew the buttons on the suit.

MAKING A LINED NORFOLK JACKET

107. The procedure in making a coat that requires a foundation, padding, and lining is similar to that in making a wash suit, but more care is required in handling woolen fabric and in cutting the suit.

108. Cutting the Sections.—When cutting out the coat, cut out the lining also. The same pattern may be used for the lining as for the suit, but the plaits should be laid in the pattern pieces and pinned before they are placed on the lining material, and the fronts should be cut to extend only 1 or 1 1/2 inches beyond the front facings. Also, the lining should be cut without a yoke.

In cutting the back lining, place a 3/4-inch lengthwise plait in the center of the material. This plait, when in the garment, is secured only at the top and the bottom and provides an easy-fitting lining.

If the coat is made of firm woolen material, in addition to the lining it is necessary to cut extra strips to be used as an interlining for the fronts of the coat and across the back of the neck. These may be cut from the coat pattern, if pattern pieces for them are not provided.

To do this, pin the yoke section to the lower-front section of the coat pattern. Place this front section on a piece of paper, and trace around the outer edge from the shoulder seam down the front and across the lower edge to a point that will make the section 1/2 inch narrower than the width of the coat facings. From this point, trace a curved line to a point on the armhole near the under-arm seam. This will give a pattern piece similar in shape to section a, Fig. 5 (*a*), Chapter VII. Then place the back of the yoke pattern on a piece of paper, having the center-back line on a fold, and trace the neck curve and along the shoulder line for about 2 1/2 inches. Now measure down on the center-back line 2 1/2 inches and join these two points by a curved line, following the neck line as a guide.

Interlinings of muslin or canvas must also be provided for the yoke, or, if there is no yoke pattern, a section may be traced from the coat pattern, as at a and *b*, Fig. 5 (*b*), Chapter VII. Such sections provide firmness. Pocket pieces also should be cut from firm lining.

109. Assembling the Sections.—In putting the interlinings in the coat, place them flat on the coat material under which they are used and baste thoroughly to prevent any possibility of drawing them out of place in working. More pressing is required in making a suit of woolen material than is necessary in the case of one of a washable fabric, but the general procedure in construction is the same.

Baste the seams of the coat and sleeves, fit the coat, and then stitch the seams that have been fitted. Join the facings by basting and stitching, and make the pockets. Next, make the collar and baste it to the coat; also, baste the sleeve into the armhole.

During the second fitting, it may be found necessary to put in padding at the shoulder and armholes to give a smooth fit. The padding may be joined to the armhole seam, as shown in Fig. 34, Chapter VII. Cut the padding crescent shape of several thicknesses of sheet wadding, having each layer slightly smaller than the preceding one; arrange them so that the smallest is on top; and then fasten them together with diagonal basting. After the second fitting, proceed to finish the coat as far as putting in the lining.

110. Putting in the Lining.—Sew up the under-arm seams of the lining, but leave the shoulder seams free. Next, slip the lining into the coat, turning the inside seams of the lining to the inside seams of the coat. Smooth the lining and baste it carefully in place, bringing the back edge of the lining over the front at the shoulder and joining this seam with slip-stitching. Turn under the outer raw edges of the lining, except at the bottom, bringing the lining over the edge of the facings and covering the joining line of the collar. Baste the lining in place and finish it with slip-stitching.

Finally, turn up the bottom about 1/2 inch from the edge and join to the lining by slip-stitching.

The sleeve lining should now be stitched and put into the sleeve. First, turn the lining up about 1/2 inch from the lower edge and slip-stitch this edge in place. Then turn in the top edge over the coat lining at the armholes and whip the joining.

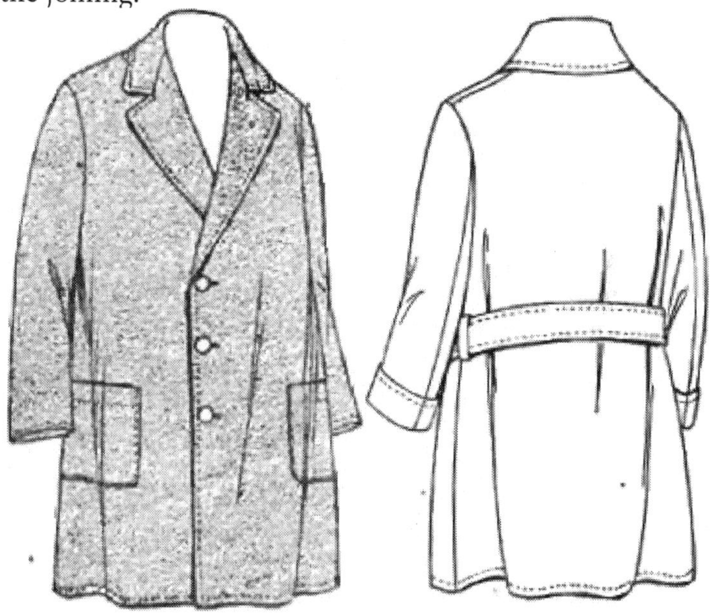

FIG. 34

BOYS' OVERCOATS

TYPES AND MATERIALS

111. There is a place in every boy's wardrobe for at least one overcoat. Such a coat should be made to give warmth, permit freedom of motion, and yet follow the lines of the prevailing fashion.

Boys' overcoats, like others, vary as to fashion features, but they may be divided into two distinct classes; single-breasted and double-breasted. The double-breasted overcoats include the types referred to as reefers and mackinaws and are probably the more popular, especially for the older boys. But for very small boys, the single-breasted overcoat proves very satisfactory. The one illustrated in Fig. 34 is the simplest style to make. This may be worn with or without a belt.

Coats for boys may be lined or unlined, as desired.

112. The materials used for boys' overcoats depend upon the season of the year, the age of the child, and the occasions on which the coat is to be worn. The following materials are all well adapted to such coats: serge, chinchilla, tricotine, Poiret twill, tweed, covert cloth, cheviot, Jersey cloth, kersey, homespun, camel's hair, polo cloth, Bolivia cloth, poplin, gabardine, velveteen, and broadcloth.

The materials used for lining purposes are the same as for the Norfolk suit.

CONSTRUCTING A BOY'S SINGLE-BREASTED OVERCOAT

113. Cutting Out the Coat.—Before placing the pattern pieces on the material, test them to make sure that they correspond to the measurements of the child for whom the coat is intended. Then place the pattern on the material, following the instructions that accompany the pattern in order to have each piece on the proper grain of the material.

114. Cutting Out the Lining.—If the coat is to be lined, cut a lining over the coat pattern. Make the front sections just wide enough to extend a seam's width beyond the inner edge of the facing. This point is usually indicated by perforations on the pattern piece. In cutting the lining for the back of the coat, allow 2 inches at the center back for a plait. This gives ease to the lining and prevents the drawing of the coat across the back between the shoulders.

115. Actual Construction.—The first step in constructing a coat of this type is to baste the shoulder and under-arm seams. Next, baste the seams in the sleeves, easing in the slight fulness at the elbow. Now, try the coat on to see whether any alteration is necessary; then stitch the seams and apply the facings and tape. Next apply the collar and pockets as directed in making the Norfolk coat.

The method of finishing such a coat is the same as for the Norfolk jacket, except that in a coat for a small boy no padding is required.

CONSTRUCTING A BOY'S DOUBLE-BREASTED OVERCOAT

116. Practically the only point of difference between the single-and the double-breasted overcoats is that the front sections of the latter are wider, so that they overlap farther. The instruction for the cutting and constructing of this type of coat, therefore, is the same as that given for the single-breasted overcoat.

The double-breasted coat is sometimes varied by adding a yoke, as in the case of a mackinaw. In that case, the instruction given in regard to the yoke of the Norfolk coat is applicable.

Printed in Great Britain
by Amazon

38609147R00196